# Unravelling the Rag Trade

## Immigrant Entrepreneurship in Seven World Cities

### Edited by
### Jan Rath

**BERG**

*Oxford • New York*

First published in 2002 by
**Berg**
Editorial offices:
150 Cowley Road, Oxford, OX4 1JJ, UK
838 Broadway, Third Floor, New York, NY 10003-4812, USA


© Jan Rath 2002

Berg is an imprint of Oxford International Publishers Ltd.


**Library of Congress Cataloguing-in-Publication Data**
Unravelling the rag trade : immigrant entrepreneurship in seven world cities / edited by
Jan Rath.
      p. cm.
Includes bibliographical references and index.
    ISBN 1-85973-418-9 -- ISBN 1-85973-423-5 (pbk.)
   1.  Used clothing industry--Case studies.   2.  Immigrant--Economic condition--Case
studies.   3.  Entrepreneurship--Case studies.   I. Rath, Jan, 1956-
    HD9940.A2 U57 2001
    381'.4568--dc21                                                    2001004927


**British Library Cataloguing-in-Publication Data**
A catalogue record for this book is available from the British Library.


ISBN  1 85973 418 9 (Cloth)
       1 85973 423 5 (Paper)


Typeset by JS Typesetting, Wellingborough, Northants.
Printed in the United Kingdom by Antony Rowe Ltd, Chippenham, Wiltshire.

# Unravelling the Rag Trade

REGENT'S
UNIVERSITY LONDON

Park Campus
Library

Acknowledgement of outside financial support:

The British Council, Amsterdam
The Canadian Heritage, Ottawa-Hull
Committee for Social Oriented Research (CMO), University of Amsterdam
Institute for Migration and Ethnic Studies (IMES), University of Amsterdam
Netherlands Organization for Scientific Research (NWO), Fund for
    Internationalizing the Social Sciences, The Hague
Transnational Knowledge and Communications Centre of Ethnic
    Entrepreneurship EMPORIUM, Amsterdam
The Wenner-Gren Foundation for Anthropological Research, New York

**For my parents**
**Hans Rath and Riet Rath-Pegels**

# Contents

# List of Figures

# List of Tables

# Preface

This book is about immigrant entrepreneurship in advanced economies. In particular, it is about immigrant contractors in major international centres of garment production such as Paris, London, Birmingham, Amsterdam, New York, Miami and Los Angeles. It is not the first book on immigrant entrepreneurship or ethnic entrepreneurship, as some authors prefer to call it, in this sector of the economy. But all the previous books, save a handful, focus on one specific national or local case. International comparisons are obviously thin on the ground, which is one of the weaker features of the study of immigrant entrepreneurship in general and even more so in sectors as global as the manufacture of garments. This is precisely why this book should fill a gap.

The book evolved from a project initiated by the Institute for Migration and Ethnic Studies (IMES) at the University of Amsterdam. The project was launched as an interdisciplinary case study of Turkish entrepreneurship in the Amsterdam garment industry, but allowed for international comparison from the onset. The first practical step in that direction was to organize an international workshop in 1995 attended by leading experts from Europe and the United States. The workshop was intended to break new theoretical ground and resulted in the publication of an edited volume (Rath 2000b). The next step was to focus on the garment industry. We invited distinguished researchers from France, Great Britain and the United States who were well versed and experienced in the field to play a role and they did so on the basis of our comprehensive research plan. We held a preliminary meeting of all the contributors in Amsterdam in January 1998. We discussed each paper carefully, and formulated the overall structure of issues that each contributor was to address as well as the large themes for the whole book. We held a second meeting in January 1999, at which we commented on the individual chapters and refined the integration of each contribution around the central themes of the book. These international meetings reinforced our ability to integrate the chapters around the central themes. This book is the ultimate result.

A number of organizations helped fund this endeavour. First of all, the support from the IMES and the Committee for Social Oriented Research (CMO) at the University of Amsterdam allowed us to develop an ambitious interdisciplinary and international comparative research programme on immigrant entrepreneurship, which is still in full swing. The Fund for Internationalizing the Social Sciences of the Netherlands Organization for Scientific Research (NWO), the Amsterdam office of the British Council, and the Wenner-Gren Foundation for Anthropological Research in New York granted subsidies for the expert meetings. Furthermore, the Transnational Knowledge and Communications Centre of Ethnic Entrepreneurship EMPORIUM, based in Amsterdam, as well as the City of Amsterdam, made it possible for me to attend the Third International Metropolis Conference in Israel in December 1998, and the Canadian Heritage in Ottawa-Hull enabled me to take part in the Fifth International Metropolis Conference in Vancouver in November 2000. Their support allowed me to discuss the preliminary findings with both researchers and policy-makers. I would like to express my gratitude to Evert Schlebaum, Ravi Pendakur and the delegates at the conferences who made constructive comments.

I am greatly indebted to the faculty members, colleagues and friends who contributed in so many ways to this book. My co-researchers Marja Dreef, Adem Kumcu, Flavia Reil, Aslan Zorlu, and especially Stephan Raes were helpful throughout the project, except when they were distracted by matters as trivial as the completion of their own projects. Rinus Penninx, the director of IMES, put his blind trust in me and gave me all the support I could ask for. Piet Jonker, former Alderman of the City of Amsterdam and responsible for local economic development when he was in office, was kind enough to chair the meetings of an advisory body connected to the project; representatives from a variety of governmental organizations, business support agencies and advocacy groups from the garment industry were in this advisory body. Jeremy Boissevain, one of the first students of immigrant entrepreneurship in Europe, was an enthusiastic participant at the international meetings. His stimulating comments were most welcome. Marja Dreef, Ewald Engelen, Dan Hiebert and Robert Kloosterman read parts of the manuscript. I greatly benefited from their comments. Finally, I thank Sheila Gogol who carefully served as the linguistic editor, and Joost Penninx who processed her comments. Like every other researcher at IMES, I also benefited from the loyal support of our in-house editor Heleen Ronden.

My family endured this project like it did the others in the past and with the same degree of confidence and good spirit (except when I ventured abroad). I express my deep gratitude to Marlein and Wies. Finally, I dedicate this book to my parents who are unable to comprehend the English text and have never visited any of the foreign cities discussed here, but who have unremittingly taught me that learning is the key to social advancement. This book testifies to their vision and loving encouragement.

Jan Rath
Amsterdam/Rotterdam

# –1–

# Needle Games: A Discussion of Mixed Embeddedness
## *Jan Rath*

## General and Specific Processes

Hundreds of Turkish immigrants, legal and illegal alike, who worked in the garment industry gathered on a dark November night in the Moses and Aaron Church in downtown Amsterdam, the Netherlands (Rath 1999). The same church had been in the limelight a few years earlier during a turbulent but successful political campaign resulting in the regularization of a group of illegal immigrants (van Groenendael 1986). Since then, local civil rights activists had attributed a special symbolic meaning to this place of worship, and Turkish entrepreneurs, workers and their organizations did the same when they drew courage from the events of the past. At the rally in 1994, they expressed serious concern about recent develop-ments in the Amsterdam garment industry. In the course of the 1980s and early 1990s, up to a thousand immigrants had set up small garment factories in the city. Together with a predominantly male immigrant workforce they built up what promised to be the revival of the once huge garment industry in the Dutch fashion metropolis. In a medium-sized city like Amsterdam this is quite an achievement. Most of the entrepreneurs operated as contractors or subcontractors in the lower ranks of the industry. Market forces pushed them into cutthroat competition and many resorted to informal practices. Year after year, the government and its law enforcement agencies turned a blind eye when entrepreneurs dodged the rules and regulations, hired illegal immigrants, paid them off the books, evaded taxes, and cut corners in every conceivable way. But in the early 1990s, with the economic position of the contractors already under pressure due to the new production facil-ities nearby and changing logistic procedures, the central government started cracking down on the unlawful practices that had become widespread by then. The City of Amsterdam reluctantly followed suit. While the Dutch economy as a whole reached all time records, the garment industry plunged. One garment factory after another was raided and forced to close down, resulting in a sharp fall in the number of factories (Raes 2000a). The activists at the Moses and Aaron Church demanded that the government stop its repressive campaign and return to its lenient policy.

A few years later, and 4,845 miles to the west,[1] another crowd gathered.

In their final shout from the streets, protesters calling for an end to sweatshops and demanding stronger rights for workers marched . . . from this city's garment district downtown to the Staples Center and then joined a rally there during the last hours of the Democratic convention . . . The Los Angeles fashion district, the site of this afternoon's march, is housed in old office buildings and converted warehouses, where the floors are filled with Asian and Latino immigrants sewing shirts, skirts and pants – including many products for name-brand labels . . . The garment industry in Los Angeles generated billions in revenue and is one of the foundations of the local economy. But unlike Hollywood, it operates largely out of public view. The industry has been controversial, especially in recent years, as it employs mostly immigrant, both legal and illegal, labor toiling for "piecework" wages – earnings based on how fast the workers sew. Many of the employers are contractors and subcontractors who do not pay for health insurance, vacations, sick leave or overtime. Most shops are not unionized and most seamstresses make minimum wage, or less. (*Washington Post*, 18 August 2000)

The aim of this political rally was obviously to improve labour conditions. In the opinion of the activists, the national and local political systems were reluctant to enforce their own laws and regulations. At best, they only paid lip service to the notion of remedying the social abuses in the industry. Political rhetoric notwithstanding, the government had adopted a relatively lenient attitude, allowing for what might well be labelled an outlaw economy. To be sure, the Los Angeles garment industry, including numerous immigrant enterprises, is prospering, ranking fourth in Los Angeles County in 1996 behind engineering and management services, but ahead of the Hollywood film industry (Bonacich and Appelbaum 2000; Light *et al.* 1999).

These two news items refer to two cases with many features in common (for a more detailed account, see the chapters on Amsterdam and Los Angeles in this book). Both these metropolitan areas have a conglomerate garment industry,[2] a proliferation of small enterprises closely connected in chains of dependency, and a strong immigrant presence in the ranks of entrepreneurs and workers. They both exhibit profit making and success, but also exploitation, substandard labour conditions and an abundance of other informal practices that at times provoke public outrage. Any casual observer would rightly conclude that the similarities are telling. What else could be expected in an era when economic, social and political transformations are shaped by the uniformizing forces of globalization?

Despite the similarities the two cases also differ. The rally in Amsterdam mobilized garment workers and *entrepreneurs,* both predominantly male, and was an event in a political movement to protect the contractors and subcontractors in the

Dutch garment sector. The spokesmen blamed the powerful companies in the sector, especially retailers, wholesalers and large manufacturers, for their plight, as their farming-out strategies only served to squeeze out the weaker immigrant contractors. They blamed the government for not targeting the big players in the field, for not taking protectionist measures against cheap imports, and for not making space for small immigrant enterprises. The very fact that informal practices were widespread was either taken for granted or considered something that would automatically disappear in the distant future, and was not a matter for immediate and serious governmental concern.

The rally in Los Angeles was of a different nature, if only because garment *workers* and their advocates, predominantly female, were calling the shots. They explicitly attacked the contractors for exploiting the workforce. Unlike the activists in Amsterdam, who were fighting an uphill battle against authorities who had abandoned their lenient stance and taken action, the Angelino garment workers called upon the government to go beyond political rhetoric, really take responsibility, and target exploitative practices. Any casual observer might rightly conclude that the differences are telling. What else could be expected in an era when general processes are largely contingent on local forces?

At face value, all the observers have a point. This combination of general and specific processes and outcomes is intriguing. For all the similarities in the rag trade, the role of immigrant entrepreneurs varies in terms of historical development, structure, political clout, and so on. This is an important point. Its logical consequence is that once one departs from general theoretical premises, the challenge is to look for explanations that address general trends as well as historically specific conditions. This quest for the interrelationship or dialectic of general and specific factors and processes is not new. In his introduction to the *Grundrisse*, conceived in 1857–1858, Karl Marx (1973: 85) referred to this problematic, though in a somewhat opaque way. But according to exegetes like Miles (1989; see also Bovenkerk *et al.* 1990: 477), Marx argued that the same kind of social relations and processes are found in every mode of production and concomitant social formation, but that they manifest themselves in ever-changing, historically specific shapes. It is this specificity that is really telling.

This book is about immigrant entrepreneurship in the rag trade in Amsterdam and Los Angeles as well as in Paris, London, Birmingham (the West Midlands), New York and Miami.[3] It describes and analyses the development and structure of the immigrant garment industry in seven world cities in four advanced economies.[4] Each of these cities is a major international centre of garment production, and in some of them this has been the case since the early nineteenth century or even earlier. Over the years, immigrants have played an important role in the development of the sector. Without their input the industry would not have been able to establish in these particular spots and would not have stood a chance of surviving over such a long period of time. But how exactly do the immigrant entrepreneurs perform in these metropolitan centres of garment production? What positions do they occupy in the industry? What are the dynamics? What are the reasons why?

This is by no means the first publication on immigrant entrepreneurship or ethnic entrepreneurship, as some authors prefer to label it, in this sector. As I will demonstrate, the immigrant garment industry in Paris, London, New York and Los Angeles has been the subject of previous academic study. There are several other publications on the role of immigrants in the manufacture of garments in cities like Johannesburg (Rogerson 1999 and 2000), Manchester (Werbner 1980 and 1984), Milan and Prato (especially leatherware, see Farina *et al.* 1997; Zincone 2000), San Francisco (B. Wong 1998), and Toronto (Hiebert 1990 and 1993). This book has many predecessors, but all these books, reports, chapters and articles save a handful focus on one specific case (the exceptions are Morokvasic 1988a,b, 1991b and 1993; Morokvasic *et al.* 1986 and 1990).[5]

International comparisons are obviously rare. This may be a weak feature of the study of immigrant entrepreneurship in general, but is quite striking in a sector as global as garment manufacturing.[6] National specificities can only emerge and be identified in a comparative research setting.[7] What is needed is an international comparative approach that appreciates national particularities. Comparing countries alone does not suffice, since immigrant economic incorporation is the product of a multitude of factors at various levels. Besides, as Favell (1999) argues with regard to studies that compare policies of integration across countries, many studies lead to repetitive and moribund research and reproduce national stereotypes and assumptions about the nation-state. Favell suggests that the city is a far better unit of analysis. The city represents a level of research that 'enables both contextual specificity and structural comparisons that allow for the fact that immigrant integration might be influenced simultaneously by local, national and transnational factors' (see also Light and Rosenstein 1995; Persky and Wiewel 1994; Waldinger 1996a). However, city comparisons are sparse too, with only a few exceptions.[8] This is why this book should fill a gap.

For the record, the presence of immigrants in the rag trade has not been confined to the ranks of entrepreneurs. On the contrary, the vast majority joined the workforce as wage labourers, mostly doing unskilled and lower skilled work.[9] The focus of this book, however, is *not* on immigrant workers, notwithstanding their importance. It only examines the workforce in as far as it impacts on entrepreneurial strategies and opportunities. This is the case when we address questions like whether entrepreneurs can tap a pool of cheap and flexible labour, how they cope with the forces of organized labour, and to what extent this pool of labour generates new entrepreneurs. Venturing out of wage labour is an important, gender-specific strategy of mobility. Immigrants who enter the labour market as machinists in a sewing shop and seek self-employment will probably set up shop in the garment industry or an adjacent sector where they can capitalize on the skills and social network acquired in the garment industry. As Hiebert (2000; see also Waldinger 1996b) has shown, there is a high coincidence between the sectoral profile of the labour force and that of the entrepreneurial class broken down by ethnic background.[10]

In the remainder of this introductory chapter, I go into the recent proliferation of immigrant entrepreneurship in general and in the garment industry in particular. I critically examine the literature and argue that solely focusing on social embeddedness, as students of immigrant entrepreneurship nowadays tend to do, does not suffice. For a proper understanding of entrepreneurship, a more structural approach is needed. This is why I introduce a number of leitmotivs or building blocks derived from the concept of *mixed embeddedness* (Kloosterman and Rath forthcoming). This concept acknowledges the significance of immigrants' concrete embeddedness in social networks, and conceives that their relations and transactions are embedded in a more abstract way in wider economic and politico-institutional structures. I explain how these building blocks structure the current study.

## The Proliferation of Immigrant Entrepreneurship

What has the historical development been of small enterprises in general, and in the garment industry in particular? It is important to distinguish between the theory and the reality of this phenomenon. Until a few years ago, leading experts supported the theory that there was no future in small entrepreneurship. Visionaries and scholars such as Marx, Weber, Schumpeter and C. Wright Mills loudly proclaimed that sooner or later modern capitalism, with its inherent tendency towards economies of scale, would absorb or eliminate small enterprise. They focused on the emergence, expansion and internationalization of large corporations and took it for granted that they would contribute to the downfall of small entrepreneurship.

This theory was also thought to pertain to the garment industry, and in part this had to do with the anticipated technological solutions to problems of production. In the late nineteenth century, when the sewing machine and, subsequently, new shop floor arrangements were introduced, there was already the expectation that productivity would skyrocket and that large factories would become the garment production sites. In the post-war period, 'smarter' machines that could work with different garment sizes, materials, styles, and so forth were designed in another attempt to rationalize garment production. Once again, small factories were not expected to be able to adopt such capital-intensive technologies. Indeed, a number of advanced urban economies indeed witnessed a decline in the number of factories. The adoption of advanced technology such as CAD-CAM systems by large factories did not prevent manufacturers from continuing to rely on cheap labour for the assembly of garments. Automated sewing technology hardly took off, and instead manufacturers outsourced this part of the production process offshore. In many world cities, such as Amsterdam, London, New York and Miami, the decline of garment manufacturing was dramatic and the industry began to be viewed as a 'sunset industry'. In sum, well into the twentieth century, the disappearance of small enterprise seemed unavoidable in the garment sector. Under these unfavourable circumstances, only fools would start up new sewing shops.

It remains to be seen, though, whether this pessimistic view of small entrepreneurship had any truth to it. Sabel and Zeitlin (1985: 138) argue that 'throughout modern industrial history observers had been repeatedly struck by the persistence of small firms in the face of ever more confident predictions of their disappearance'. Bögenhold (2000) indeed shows that the share of self-employment among the total labour force (outside agriculture) has only very gradually declined over the years.

More recently, scientists shifted their theoretical attention to small enterprises and started reflecting upon their role in the economy. Besides, the share of the self-employed in the total labour force stopped its gradual decline, and in some cases even began to rise (Bögenhold 2000; Boissevain 1981). This empirically belied the universal claim that small entrepreneurship was dead or dying. Economic restructuring and the role of SMEs became a popular field of study.

Large corporations, of course, are still around and dominate much of the advanced economies, but the SME sector is thriving. Many large corporations feel that cleaning, catering, transportation, security, bookkeeping and, in some cases, even research and development or the actual production of goods are no longer part of the core business and subsequently outsource them (Sassen 1991). This has enhanced the development of a putting-out system where tasks and risks are spread and a myriad of small firms at the higher and lower ends of the market are involved. Whatever the reasons, the twentieth century witnessed a striking continuity of small enterprises, and in some sectors, such as the service and garment industries in advanced economies, even a rise.

It is clear that globalization is not restricted to capital but encompasses people as well (Castles and Miller 1993; Cornelius *et al*. 1994; Sassen 1988). International migration increased in the late twentieth century and has had a tremendous impact on the growth and composition of the business community. Light, and other sociologists, noted its significance in the United States economy as early as 1972, and Boissevain did the same for Europe in 1981. More recently, Light and Gold (2000) and Kloosterman and Rath (forthcoming) collected data from a large number of countries at both sides of the Atlantic showing that immigrants have massively joined the ranks of entrepreneurs (see extensive ImmEnt Bibliography at http://www.emporium.nl). Today, it is hard to imagine cosmopolitan cities like Vancouver or Sydney, London or Paris, Miami or Los Angeles without immigrant enterprises. Their enterprises have changed the urban landscape in many ways and helped contribute to the revitalization of depressed neighbourhoods or backward economic sectors.

The presence of immigrants in the garment industry evidently catches the eye. While emphasizing that the latest developments should be placed in the relevant post-industrial context, it is a fact that immigrants have always been prominent in the garment industry (see Green 1986a and 1997; Hiebert 1990 and 1993; Sowell 1981; Waldinger 1986).

## Mixed Embeddedness of Immigrant Entrepreneurs

An examination of today's theoretical discussions regarding immigrant entrepreneurship shows that many students celebrate the blessings of entrepreneurship and feel that the more entrepreneurs there are, the better. They emphasize the opportunities of small entrepreneurship in a capitalist society and, in doing so, implicitly endorse an economic liberalist ideology (Engelen 2001; see also Bonacich 1993b or Camarota 2000 for critical comments). In the same vein, the *concentration* of ethnic entrepreneurs in particular sectors of the economy is applauded. This is in striking contrast to the lack of appreciation for concentrations of migrant *workers*. The formation of an ethnic underclass, an ethnic sub-proletariat, an ethnic faction of the working class, or whatever other label is given to this phenomenon, has been treated as the hallmark of capitalist exploitation and the ultimate proof of the subordinate position of migrant workers (see Castles and Kosack 1973; Miles 1982; Rex and Tomlinson 1979).

The positive view of entrepreneurship is reflected in the work of authors such as Kotkin (1992), Saxenian (1999), Srinivasan (1995), or Werbner (1984). Werbner applauds the savvy of Pakistani garment entrepreneurs in Manchester, England, who she feels followed the path from rags to riches. Light and Roach (1996) also express a positive view of immigrant entrepreneurship. They ascertain that immigrant entrepreneurs enjoy a 'self-employment bonus', i.e. an income advantage over wage or salary employment net of productivity and irrespective of human capital, age, language proficiency, and other factors that usually affect wages (see also Li 2000). Unfortunately, they fail to explore the extent to which this holds for any sector of the economy in any country. But the point is clear: immigrants as entrepreneurs should be able to achieve sometimes substantial income improvements and secure impressive upward social mobility into the bourgeois class. True enough, a few of them are successful, join the ranks of the rich and famous and become national celebrities. However, the success story certainly does not apply to every immigrant entrepreneur. As will be demonstrated in this book, many start marginal and stay marginal. Their businesses represent no more than 'a sideways shift from Lumpenproletariat to *Lumpenbourgeois*', as Aldrich *et al.* (1984) once described their plight, as the unfortunate entrepreneurs stay on the margins and totter into oblivion.

However, these paths can easily become a bit slippery. 'Success' is a fuzzy concept and is not always clearly defined. Some authors follow an economistic logic and implicitly or explicitly define success in terms of growth and profitability, while others hold that technological excellence and new knowledge and skills prevail. Whitley (1999: 72) distinguishes four major dominant goals and performance standards. 'First, the pursuit of personal and family wealth accumulation. Secondly, high returns to portfolio managers and shareholders. Thirdly, growth in assets, turnover, and markets. Fourthly, increasing technological excellence and reputation. In practice, of course, they are usually combined, but one tends to dominate.' In addition, non-economic parameters such as autonomy and status could come into play. What matters is that we acknowledge that success is a social construction.

The chapter in this book by Grenier and Stepick is a case in point. They examine a conflict about different modes of management in Miami, Florida and look at success from different angles, illustrating that success has different facets, is measurable by different criteria, and is contingent on a multitude of factors. The largest United States garment manufacturer, a Chicago-based corporation, purchased a Miami sewing shop from the manager/owner and reorganized or 'Americanized' the production process and labour management to reach the cutting edge of the industry. The reorganization represented a radical break from the 'familial managerial style' of the previous owner and this caused a rift between the management and the workers, most of whom were older Cuban women. The new management may have been successful in terms of making the production process more cost-efficient, but the workforce remained loyal to the warm paternalism of the previous owner and exhibited indirect resistance, which eventually led to the failure of the firm. The subsidiary of the Chicago manufacturer pursued ambitious goals and implemented an 'Americanized' mode of production, but failed to establish a supportive workplace regime. The previous manager/owner could barely keep his company afloat in the midst of the industry's restructuring, but was successful in securing the support of the workers. Success is evidently not a one-dimensional concept. It has to do with the position of the entrepreneur or the enterprise in relation to other economically relevant actors beyond the direct competitors. This confirms the Polanyian position that entrepreneurship can only be fully understood and explained if a perspective is adopted that is broad enough to capture aspects outside the neo-classical domain of supply and demand (cf. Polanyi 1957).

Since Ivan Light published *Ethnic Enterprise in America* back in 1972, virtually every student of immigrant entrepreneurship – with the notable exception of the economist Bates (1997) – has avoided the direct use of neo-classical economics. Instead they focus on structural triggers such as blocked mobility in the labour market (Saxenian 1999) or racist exclusion (Ram 1994), or they zoom in on immigrants' cultural endowment for entrepreneurship (Metcalf *et al.* 1996; Werbner 2000), their social embeddedness (Lee 1999; Light 2000; Waldinger 1996b; Yoo 1998; Zhou 1992), or combinations of their mobilization of various resources (Light and Gold 2000; Yoon 1997).

In the past, efforts have been made to combine structure and actor-oriented approaches. *Ethnic Entrepreneurs* by Waldinger *et al.* (1990) is probably the best-known example, if only because it is the product of collaboration by prominent international researchers. The authors argue in favour of a more integrative approach that places ethnic entrepreneurial strategies somewhere at the crossroads of group characteristics and the opportunity structure. As such their *interactive model* combines ethno-cultural and socio-cultural factors (agency) with politico-economic factors (structure). According to the authors, the latter entail market conditions (particularly access to ethnic/non-ethnic consumer markets) and access to ownership (in the form of business vacancies, competition for vacancies, and government policies). This interactive model is appreciated as an important step towards a more comprehensive theoretical approach, even though it is more of a classification than an explanatory model. However, it has also been subjected to criticism. Its shortcomings included the methodology (Light and Rosenstein 1995), the lack of attention devoted to gender issues (Morokvasic 1993) and to racialization (Collins *et al.* 1995), the *a priori* categorization of immigrants as ethnic groups and the concomitant assumption that immigrants as ethnic entrepreneurs act differently than mainstream entrepreneurs (Rath and Kloosterman 2000), and the narrow and static way economic and politico-regulatory factors are dealt with (Bonacich 1993b; Rath 2000c). In the light of the model's integrative pretensions, this is particularly striking. The authors conceive market conditions in terms of the ethnicization or de-ethnicization of consumer markets, and confine politico-regulatory factors to a short list of laws and regulations that specifically apply to immigrants.

Theoretical development has continued and, oddly enough, this has led to a convergence of approaches to issues of *social embeddedness*. Many of students of immigrant entrepreneurship, especially in the United States, are indeed fervent adherents to a version of economic sociological thought that focuses on the entrepreneurs' social networks and impact on entrepreneurship. Instead of elaborating on the dynamics of agency and structure, they more or less take the political economic structure for granted and confine themselves to refining agency matters. This narrow focus reveals a tendency towards reductionism and is a *de facto* renouncement of the integrative model. The mixed embeddedness approach is more appropriate, since it relates social relations and transactions to wider political and economic structures.

In spite of its limitations, this version of economic sociology is interesting and relevant. It has explanatory value if it is put in a comprehensive perspective, and enhances our understanding of entrepreneurial processes. This is why the capacity of garment entrepreneurs to mobilize their social networks successfully has been selected as the first leitmotiv in this book. The other leitmotivs are markets and regulation.

## Social Networks

The popularity of social capital theory is not confined to the study of immigrant entrepreneurship, even though Portes and Sensenbrenner (1993: 1325–7; see also Portes 1995) consider it especially applicable to the economic actions of immigrants. They hold that immigrants experience 'a heightened sense of community', and that 'it is the particular circumstance of "foreignness" that often best explains the rise of these types of social capital among immigrants'. Portes and Sensenbrenner posit that 'foreignness' means a group is distinct from the rest of the society or considered to be distinct. It seems plausible that sharing a specific migration history, speaking a language other than the mainstream language in the receiving society, having certain religious beliefs and practices, sharing ethno-cultural features and so on enhance a type of situational in-group solidarity, trust and group-specific social relations. This in turn should impact on the opportunities of entrepreneurs.

There is ample literature showing that entrepreneurs who are embedded in social networks and can mobilize them for economic purposes have an edge. For them, networks are instrumental in acquiring knowledge, distributing information, recruiting capital and labour, and in establishing strong relations with clients and suppliers. Social embeddedness enables these entrepreneurs to reduce their transaction costs by eliminating formal contracts, giving privileged access to economic resources, and providing reliable expectations as to the effects of malfeasance. Particularly in cases where the entrepreneurs' primary input is cheap and flexible labour, as is true of contractors in the rag trade, the reduction of transaction costs by mobilizing social networks for labour recruitment seems key, and this is all the more so in cases where entrepreneurs violate the law. Hiring undocumented immigrants, paying them off the books, dodging taxes, fiddling with health and safety regulations and so forth make entrepreneurial activities informal, and this constitutes a risk. In the formal economy, actors can call upon law enforcement agencies to redress possible infringements of their rights, but in the informal economy they have to use other instruments (Epstein 1994: 2166). They have to rely on their own social arrangements, and on moral codes which put a great deal of emphasis on trust. Particularly in cases where institutional trust is lacking, trust can be generated by personal relations, including relations with other members of the same community (Roberts 1994). This serves to emphasize once again how relevant issues of social embeddedness can be.

Social capital is unequally distributed among multifarious social groups (Light *et al.* 1993). Archetypical contrast groups in American empirical studies are Korean and African-American entrepreneurs, and in British studies Asian and Caribbean entrepreneurs. To put it simply, Korean entrepreneurs are more widespread and perform better because they have larger, stronger and more supportive networks than their African-American peers. But as this example shows, the issue is basically formulated in ethnic terms. Thinking in ethnic categories often implies the assumption that the social networks of immigrant entrepreneurs are confined to their co-ethnics, that they have little or no social contact with people outside their own group, and that ethnic ties are more important, more resilient, and less permeable. However, it is likely that most entrepreneurs have a mixed and gendered network comprising co-ethnics, other immigrants and mainstream people, and that these networks change over time. The number of social relations may, whether or not it is intended, increase or decrease; the network can become thicker or thinner or spread out and assume a different spatial basis; the social relations can become many-stranded or single-stranded or take on a different meaning.

Taking advantage of social embeddedness is a complex and dynamic process, and success is not guaranteed. An entrepreneur might be successful at recruiting workers by mobilizing his social network, but what if the market shrinks following an economic recession, technology changes or new regulations (see Rath 2000a; Schrover 2001)? Likewise, an entrepreneur from a poor community might tap a network of supportive peers, but since they are poor they will not be able to put up much money. This impacts on the entrepreneurial opportunities and can keep the entrepreneur at the lower end of the market (Wolff and Rath 2000). Flap *et al.* (2000) refer to the problem of having too much social capital, so that non-economic influences interfere in the design and implementation of entrepreneurial strategies (see also Marger 2000). Walton-Roberts and Hiebert (1997) cite the imaginary entrepreneur who cannot fire his son-in-law without jeopardizing his relations with the family (see also Valk 1961), for an account of how this pressure can be exerted). Flap *et al.* discuss the problem of one-sided social capital, which is connected to what Granovetter (1983) once called the strength of weak ties. The circulation of new information is limited in tight groups and, subsequently, so are the chances of innovation and business success.

So much is clear: social capital is connected to cultural, human and financial capital (Light and Gold 2000), and is the product of the interaction of structural factors such as migration history and processes of social, economic and political incorporation in the mainstream, as well as their spatial variations. Its impact is contingent on the goals pursued and the political and economic forces at work (Granovetter 1992; Kumcu forthcoming). Specific circumstances foster social capital and make its use feasible and rewarding, but none of this is automatic.

*Markets*

The impact of social capital is contingent on the market and the market position of the entrepreneur, but markets differ and are always in motion. These differences and dynamics exert various influences on the opportunities of entrepreneurs. Not every author is convinced of this truism, though.

According to Waldinger (1996b; see also Waldinger and Bozorgmehr 1996; Waldinger and Lapp 1993; for a more critical view, see Rath 2000c), the economic incorporation of immigrants and the resulting ethnic division of labour is a network-driven process, and economic changes do not really matter. He argues that established groups climb the imaginary social ladder and create vacancies for new immigrant groups below. New immigrants are then funnelled into clustered economic positions by way of the mobilization of network resources, and this fosters ethnic niches. New vacancies are filled by newer immigrants, as older immigrants move up the social ladder, and this is how the 'game of ethnic musical chairs', as Waldinger labels this process of ethnic succession, is played. Waldinger thus envisages this process in a *given* market.

But concrete markets are not given, they are embedded in wider structures. It is hard to believe that recessions or technological advances do not have any effect at all on entrepreneurial opportunities (cf. Rath 2000a). (Take for example the impact of the sewing machine on tailoring.) Although agency obviously matters, the role of the economic opportunity structure still deserves more attention. Thus the role of markets and processes of global restructuring constitute the second leitmotiv in this book.

It does not require much sociological imagination to see that garment sewing shops and small liver pâté factories operate in entirely different markets. Even within the market of garment, there are distinctions between fashionable ladies outerwear, army uniforms, unisex casual clothing, tailor-made suits, and so on. The producers of corsets and sexy lingerie are both in ladies' underwear, but trade in different products, cater for different customers, face different competitors, and deal with different market structures with different and perhaps even contradictory dynamics. In a hypothetical case the corset market can be relatively stable or perhaps shrinking, while the sexy lingerie market might be flourishing. In such a case, dodgy entrepreneurs would probably venture into lingerie and carve out a naughty niche in kinky knickers. Different markets, in short, offer entrepreneurs different opportunities and obstacles, demand different skills, and lead to different outcomes in terms of business success or, at a higher level of agglomeration, an ethnic division of labour. This is why we need to get a clear picture of the market dynamics and the impact on immigrant entrepreneurship.

Engelen (2001), elaborating upon the work by Max Weber (1968; see also Swedberg 1994 and 1998), identifies a number of market dimensions that should help us understand and explain the sorting out of specific groups and individuals. He distinguishes: (1) the objects of trade, (2) the subjects of trade, (3) the structure of the market, (4) its level of institutionalization, (5) the locality of the market, (6) its degree of social embeddedness, and (7) the mode, level and object of regulation. These dimensions can serve as points of departure for further research. The sixth and seventh dimensions refer, in my view, to different social fields. The sixth dimension has been dealt with previously, and the final dimension will be examined later. The remaining dimensions basically address the who, what, how and where of economic transactions. Together they determine negotiations and transactions. To be more specific, they determine the potential competitors within a market and the conditions under which transactions take place.

The *objects of trade* are any goods that can be bought or sold, and thus any legal and illegal objects, goods and services. Entrepreneurial opportunities for markets of technologically or intellectually advanced or less sophisticated goods and services differ, requiring different financial or human capital input. Engelen (2001) suggests that producer markets are less accessible than consumer markets, if only because of the specialized nature of the social and human capital needed to enter the producer market. To what extent this holds true for the garment industry remains to be seen. The production of ready-to-wear garments generally does not require much skill or capital outlay, and this makes the rag trade a low-barrier market. A side issue is whether or not particular goods or services are 'ethnic'. How legitimate in the eyes of the customers is the fair-haired, blue-eyed German businessman who runs a Chinese restaurant in Chinatown in San Francisco, California? In practice, there is no definite answer to this question, as it depends on many local contingencies. It is nevertheless obvious that no social group can claim the inalienable right to authenticity. This is illustrated by the Italian pizza parlours in Amsterdam. Immigrants from Turkey have recently managed to capture this 'Italian' niche (Larsen 1995; see also Gabaccia 1998). The question of 'ethnic goods' seems less relevant to the manufacture of garments, since most mass producers cater to the open market (for a more subtle view, see Bhachu 1997).

The *subjects of trade* are the 'legal entities' that are allowed to enter the market. They can be individuals, households, families, professionals, co-operatives, incorporated firms, NGOs, quangos or public agencies. This dimension is not confined to entrepreneurs – it also pertains to the customers. Which subjects enter the market as entrepreneurs depends on other market characteristics, and on the regulatory regime. It is unlikely that a natural individual will enter the fighting bomber market by establishing a brand new aerospace plant. In some countries, there are very strict rules with regard to who is entitled to work as a garment producer. It is not self-evident who is entitled to become customer. Regulations or social and cultural factors may play a role. In the Netherlands it is prohibited to sell alcohol or cannabis products to youngsters under 16 or to give driving lessons to youngsters under 17 years and 9 months. Children are prohibited by law from entering these markets. In other cases, less formal or even illicit rules, regulations and expectations determine whether or not members of specific racial, ethnic or religious groups are acceptable as customers. The economies in the southern states of the United States under the Jim Crow system or the Netherlands under the supreme reign of consociationalism ('pillarization') are cases in point.

The *structure of the market* refers to the number of actors on the supply and demand sides and the distribution of market power among them. In some markets only a few big players run the show, and in others there are any number of small firms. A typical feature of the garment industry is that production is structured in a series of vertical and horizontal subcontractual relations. In a vertical direction, they include the relations between the jobbers or buyers (who place the orders), the manufacturers (who provide the design and sometimes the cloth, threads and applications) and the contractors (who basically provide the labour) or home workers. In the British case, the contractors are referred to as Cut, Make and Trim (CMT) units. Manufacturers serve as the main vertical link between the few buyers and the many contractors. Contractors may subcontract part of their production to other factories, which then constitute links moving in a horizontal direction. This ideal typical structure is shown in Figure 1.1. As Engelen (2001) emphasizes, 'entering the market does not ensure transactions'. The structure of the market impacts on the opportunities of fledgling entrepreneurs in various ways. Markets

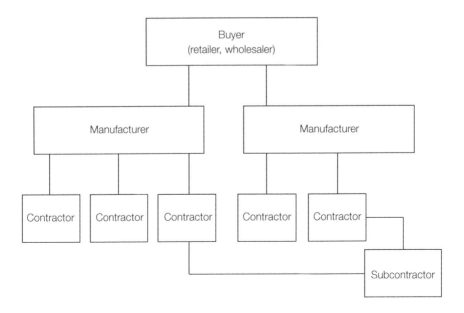

**Figure 1.1** Structure of the Garment Industry

with low access barriers are easier to enter, but are likely to have fiercer competition as there are more competitors. Here, first-mover advantages may be relevant. First movers tend to be better embedded in a particular market and be better able to determine the rules of the game.

*Institutionalization* refers to the more or less standardized patterns of actions and ideas with a normative validity in the context where they are rooted (cf. Buiks and van Tillo 1980: 29). The process of institutionalization is thus conceived in terms of transaction standardization rather than regulation *per se*, and is actually related to the culture of doing business. Long-standing and repetitive business transactions are more likely to become institutionalized than one-shot transactions, simply because they involve social relations that help foster the creation of ties. Market accessibility to outsiders is partly contingent on the prevalence of such institutions. Razin and Scheinberg (2001) show that the informal business practices of Israeli entrepreneurs constitute a barrier for newcomers.

*The locality of the market* denotes aspects of spatiality in two different but connected ways, one being the location as such and the other the spatial market scale. The location involves the factors that shape the business. Why have immigrant contractors in the Dutch rag trade gravitated to Amsterdam rather than Rotterdam? This is related to a variety of factors, perhaps including the presence of other businesses that are important to garment contractors. The agglomeration of garment enterprises can provide various advantages, since it allows for face-to-face contact, the rapid and direct exchange of information, the flexible sharing of resources, and so on. These factors are also important to businesses that are supposedly flexible, such as dot com companies. The expansion of markets is contingent on the goods and services that make up the specific markets, on regulatory opportunities and constraints, and on transaction costs. Some markets are principally local (e.g. tailoring), other markets can be global (e.g. *e*-banking, producing cheap T-shirts). This illustrates how technological advancement makes time–space compression possible, so that the spatial scale of markets can change. In a way, this seems to be the case in the garment industry (Raes 2000a,b).

Drawing distinctions between the market dimensions helps illustrate that markets are not given, but are products of human action and that their emergence involves economic, social and political determinants. These dimensions help solve the problem of distinguishing one market from the other, and are instrumental in assessing how particular groups are divided over markets. Of course, this does not necessarily mean that markets unilaterally determine the opportunities of entrepreneurs. Unlike wage labourers, in principle entrepreneurs can change the nature and extent of the markets where they operate, or even create new markets – for instance by product innovation or the development of new marketing strategies.

The economy as a whole, dynamic as it is, constitutes an ever-changing differential opportunity structure. In the garment industry, these processes vary from changes in fashion and consumer demand (changes in the object of trade), to the rise of international migration and economic decline (the rise of potential subjects of trade, especially entrepreneurs facing blocked mobility), to globalization and the rise of farming out offshore (changes in the structure and locality of the market), or to a changing emphasis on just-in-time delivery (changes in the institutionalization of the market). These processes may be related to the emergence or disappearance, for that matter, of a fashion wear spot market embedded in a local agglomeration of buyers, manufacturers, production units, designers and suppliers of textiles, trimmings and specialized services to the trade.

Some markets have low entry barriers and are quite open to newcomers, while others are less accessible; this helps explain why starting entrepreneurs with only limited resources enter low-barrier markets. The proliferation of immigrant entrepreneurs in the lower tiers of the garment industry has often been approached in this way. However, the sorting out of social groups and individuals is not just the result of the specific way in which starters enter the market, as entrepreneurs may move around, go up-market, or may break into new markets. The odds of this occurring are contingent on the presence or absence of entry barriers of those markets, and also on the growth or shrinkage of the markets in which entrepreneurs operate over time. Kloosterman and Rath (2001) therefore point to the relevance of differentiating between the accessibility of markets and their growth potential.

The manufacture of garments in the city of Norrköping, Sweden, is a gloomy case, illustrating the impact of negative growth. For over two hundred years this manufacturing city was the base of a huge textile and garment conglomerate. Established in the eighteenth century by an immigrant from Belgium, this industry included spinning mills, weaving mills, garment factories, and so on, employing numerous workers, Swedes as well as immigrants. In the 1960s, however, competition from low-wage countries increased. Local workers demanded better working conditions and higher wages, and irrespective of the legitimacy of this demand it exacerbated the situation. One factory after another relocated to Portugal and other low-wage countries until the industry vanished. Today, academics at Norrköping University conduct their work in the comfortably converted factory buildings.[11] The cases discussed in this book obviously show a different picture.

## Politics and Regulation

The dynamics of markets are contingent on processes of regulation. The garment industry in Germany is a case in point. Although it is dominated by economies of scale, there are various small and medium-sized manufacturers and contractors. Immigrant enterprises, however, are virtually absent in the production sector. In the German welfare state the economy is structured around an exclusive view of economic citizenship. Consequently, the small enterprise sector is strictly regulated.

Garment producers are required to be qualified as *Meister* and registered in the *Handwerksrolle*. For most immigrant entrepreneurs, except a few who have qualifications, this is too high a barrier. Immigrants, particularly from Turkey and Greece, are nonetheless highly visible in *Flickschneidereien*, clothing repair shops. Setting up a repair shop is an attractive alternative, because the legal requirements are less strict. Many fledgling entrepreneurs flock to this sub-sector, but as clothing repairmen they are not allowed to perform production tasks.[12]

It is clear that *regulation* or *governance* matters, and this is why it has been selected as the third leitmotiv in this book. Engelen (2001) draws attention to a few aspects. Regulation should not be confused with legislation, as there are two other forms of regulation. There are 'sticks', which Engelen refers to as 'legislation *per se*', and 'carrots' (financial incentives and disincentives) or 'sermons' (persuasion), all different forms in complex packages that define what is 'possible' in a market. Nor should regulation be confused with state regulation. A multitude of agents play a role in regulation processes, such as local, national or international governmental agents, unions, quangos, non-profit organizations, voluntary associations, and individual and their social networks. Regulation can either be imposed or enforced, or be a matter of voluntary action.

These notions are important. They underscore that even in cases where legislation *per se* seems non-existent or is conveniently put aside, as might be the case in the informal economy (see Kloosterman *et al.* 1999; Portes 1994; Rath 1999), economic transactions by individuals are still regulated in one way or another.[13]

They also make it clear that regulation is not just a matter of repression and constraining but also of enabling. Suppressing illicit practices, such as dodging taxes and labour and immigration laws, by prosecuting the perpetrators is an important manifestation of regulation (repression), but so are decisions to tolerate these practices and not prosecute them. The plethora of business support programmes also constitutes forms of regulation (see Dreef forthcoming). Oc and Tiesdell (1999) and Ram (1998) describe how governmentally sponsored Training and Enterprise Councils and Ethnic Minority Business Initiatives target particular social groups and try to support their market position. Light and Pham (1998) describe the success and failure of efforts by the government and private financial institutions to give microcredit to micro-entrepreneurs in the United States. Successful or not, these are efforts to change the market landscape and as such they are forms of regulation.

The notions referred to above make it clear that regulation does not only occur in advanced welfare states. Much of the American literature on immigrant and ethnic entrepreneurship takes regulation for granted (Kloosterman and Rath forthcoming; Rath 2000a,c), assuming that regulation is not relevant in liberal welfare states such as the United States. The United States federal government is admittedly a relatively lean government that supposedly has less means to regulate economic

Jan Rath

life, but this is amply compensated for by the regulation of a more voluntary nature. In the land of the free, economic life (and not only economic life) is severely dogged by litigation. In addition, the federal government has various instruments to regulate markets. Its relatively open immigration programmes for professionals and businessmen have enhanced the proliferation of money-makers in Silicon Valley, where immigrant entrepreneurs own a quarter of the high-tech companies (Saxenian 1999). Next to that, the United States made large and coercive interventions into the labour market through the expansion of the penal system (Western and Beckett 1999).

These notions also emphasize something that can easily be forgotten; namely, that there is a fundamental difference between rules and the enforcement of rules. The Dutch practice of *gedogen*, once referred to as 'a nigh untranslatable term that means looking the other way when you must' (see *The Economist*, 12 October 1996; see also Blankenburg and Bruinsma 1994), is a case in point.

They also indicate that regulation is connected to a variety of spaces. Some forms of regulation govern the global economy. The international garment production and trade are governed by the supranational Multi-Fibre Arrangements and the World Trade Organization (Appelbaum and Gereffi 1994; Mitter 1986; Raes 2000a,b). Other forms of regulation govern the national economy, as in welfare state regulation (Esping-Andersen 1990), or govern particular locations as in cases of redlining particular neighbourhoods or establishing economic enterprise zones (Green 1991; Hall 1996; Kloosterman et al. 1997). Again other forms of regulation target specific sectors (construction, ice-cream parlours, prostitution, the garment industry; see Bovenkerk et al. 1983; Dreef forthcoming; van der Meer 1998; Rath 2000d), or particular social groups (unqualified jobseekers, undocumented immigrants, high-tech professionals; see Engbersen et al. 1999; Saxenian 1999).

The fact remains that all across the world markets are always regulated in one way or another, even if the form and level of regulation might vary. Regulation is not an isolated phenomenon, it is contingent on prevailing models of allocating economic citizenship rights to economic actors. These models, contradictory and incomplete as they might be, stipulate which goods and services and which actors have legitimacy when it comes to market exchange, and under which conditions market exchange and price fixing take place. They shape the welfare state. Kloosterman (2000), following Albert (1991), discusses the kinds of welfare state that produce the best opportunities for small immigrant entrepreneurs. He distinguishes between the neo-American model and the Rhineland model and touches upon such variables as the level of flexibility and job security on the labour market, the level of social welfare (that should guarantee a relatively high minimum level of public purchasing power), the kinds of incentives that generate an income as a wage labourer or entrepreneur in the market economy, the level of the barriers in the form of rules, laws, and measures aimed at protecting existing enterprises, and last but not least, the level of commodification (see also Esping-Andersen 1990). Some welfare states have a higher level of commodification, which means the distribution of goods and services takes place in the market economy at market prices. Others have lower or different levels of commodification, which means the distribution of goods and services takes place outside the market economy, and families, the state, or private organizations that operate at arm's length from the state assume prime responsibility for this. The matter is inconclusive as yet, due to the lack of empirical data, but the point is that different welfare states make for different opportunity structures.

As is noted above, regulation manifests itself in complex packages. It is not feasible to examine each and every instance of regulation and its impact on business opportunities. A convenient alternative is to focus on a limited number of regulatory regimes. These regimes are actually sets of institutions and involve rules, laws, measures and policies governing immigration, the market, and welfare (Freeman and Ögelman 2000; see also Dreef forthcoming).

These regimes are obviously dynamic and subject to political pressure. The news items at the beginning of this chapter serve to illustrate that. Informal and exploitative practices were prevalent at the sewing shops, and this is an indication of how the immigrant contractor segment in the garment industry was regulated. This situation triggered a political response on the part of the people involved. During the process of political mobilization, debates were held about changing the regulation systems. In one case, political activists argued in favour of an abolitionist kind of regulation – *de facto* liberalization of economic practices – and in another case activists called for stricter law enforcement. To what extent these people accomplish their goals depends on a multitude of factors, especially their ability to exercise political clout.

## The Structure of this Book

This book unravels the rag trade in seven cities and assesses the general and specific configurations of social, economic and political structures in effect in each case. The book covers the cases of Paris, London, Birmingham, Amsterdam, New York, Miami and Los Angeles. The following considerations have led to this choice. The cities represent the immigrant garment industry in different historical stages and in different stages of the industry's life cycle. In some cities the industry had a long history, which might mean a strong and well-established conglomerate of garment manufacturers. This is the case in Paris, London, New York and, in a way, Amsterdam, but is less so in Birmingham and Miami. There the industry is relatively new, which may affect the opportunities of today's immigrant entrepreneurs in specific ways. Variations in structure and development in terms of the

# Jan Rath

proximity of an established fashion industry or emerging international competitors indicate variations in the opportunities immigrant entrepreneurs have.

The cities and countries where they are located are part of different economic regions. The United States or France, Great Britain and the Netherlands are geographically linked to particular economic spaces with institutional references to such large supranational entities as NAFTA and the European Union. The implication is that, say, the Mexican *maquiladoras* are important to the United States garment industry, and Eastern Europe or Turkey to Europe's industry. How and to what extent these variations matter can be studied by comparing different cities and *sets* of cities.

The cities are located in various welfare states representing different regulatory contexts. The role of the state in France, Great Britain, the Netherlands and the United States differs dramatically in terms of its provision of welfare, employment trajectories, and attitude to immigration and immigrants. France, Great Britain, the Netherlands and the Unites States represent different types of welfare states, liberal, social-democratic, corporatist or familial welfare states, or hybrids. As Engelen (2001), Freeman and Ögelman (2000), Kloosterman (2000), Kloosterman and Rath (2001, forthcoming), and Rath (2000a) argue, these institutional differences influence small entrepreneurship, even though we do not know exactly how and in what direction. Institutional variations are not always confined to the national level. Within one national framework there may still be local variations, as Bonacich (1993b) and Waldinger (1993) suggest. In their lively debate about the determinants, opportunities and constraints of immigrant enterprises, they mention fundamental institutional differences between the garment sectors in New York and Los Angeles. The chance of these variations occurring is higher in federal states with a low centralization level such as the United States than in centralized states such as France.

Lastly, the development of the garment industry in these cities has been closely connected to the presence of immigrants.

Each garment city has a characteristic history with different groups of immigrants playing different roles in different historical periods. This is important as it puts the current experiences in a historical perspective and, in doing so, sheds an interesting light on the explanations that are *en vogue* today.

In her chapter on Paris, Nancy Green notes that there was an immigrant presence in tailoring back in the 1840s, particularly of Belgian, German, Italian and Swiss women. Eastern European Jews began flocking into the Parisian rag trade in the 1880s, and Armenians and Jews from Turkey arrived in the period following the break-up of the Ottoman Empire. In the 1950s and 1960s, with the decolonization of parts of North Africa, a third wave of Jews moved into the garment industry, especially from Tunisia and Morocco, and a new generation of Armenians arrived from Turkey, Lebanon, and Iran. From the early 1980s on, Turkish entrepreneurs began to appear near the Sentier garment district, as did Serbs from Yugoslavia, Kurds from Turkey, and Chinese immigrants from Cambodia, Vietnam, Thailand, Hong Kong, and mainland China. The most recent arrivals to the garment industry have been Pakistani, Sri-Lankan, Maurician (mostly of Indian origin), and African (Senegalese and Malians).

Prodomos Panayiotopoulos and Marja Dreef trace the role of immigrants in the London garment industry back to the seventeenth century, when Huguenot exiles set up tailor shops. In the late nineteenth century London, like Paris, became the home of numerous Eastern European Jews who opened small garment factories. Later, Greek Cypriots, small pockets of Turkish Cypriots and Bengali immigrants succeeded these Jewish entrepreneurs – the Bengalis particularly in the leatherwear sector. This happened despite the central government's attitude in the 1960s and 1970s that textile and garment manufacturing constituted a 'sunset industry' destined to decline. More recently, ethnic Turks and Kurds from Turkey entered the sector and became associated with Turkish Cypriots.

The situation in the British West Midlands – including Birmingham, Smethwick, Coventry, Wolverhampton, West Bromwich and Walsall – approximately hundred miles north of London, was somewhat different, as Monder Ram, Bob Jerrard and Joy Husband argue. In the 1970s, after the decline of the smokestack industries, the West Midlands went into a deep economic recession. The clothing industry did not amount to much until immigrants started to open small garment workshops (see also Phizacklea 1990; Ram 1994; Werbner 1984). These immigrants, mostly from India and Pakistan, had been made redundant on the labour market, partly due to racist exclusion, and their only option was self-employment. In a way, their enterprises were born under a lucky star, since London garment manufacturers were looking for cheaper and more flexible modes of production at the time. Farming out to local contractors was precisely what they needed.

Stephan Raes *et al.* also describe how Eastern European Jews and Westphalian Catholics gravitated to the Amsterdam textile and garment industries. Continuous immigration from such countries as Russia and Poland procured a steady influx of new immigrants, particularly young Jewish women, who were employed to do the needlework. The sector suffered a near fatal blow in the Second World War, when many Jewish entrepreneurs and workers were deported to concentration camps and did not return. In the post-war period the Jewish niche was only partially re-established, and the local industry declined until immigrants from Turkey revived it. There were ethnic Turks, Kurds, a few pockets of Armenians, and to a lesser degree immigrants from Egypt, India and Pakistan. After the collapse of the immigrant garment industry in the mid-1990s, no other immigrant group has emerged as their successor.

Yu Zhou argues that the dominance of New York over the American garment industry emerged in the nineteenth century, largely due to the role of immigrants. Earlier immigrants, particularly Russian and Eastern European Jews, laid the basis for the organizational structure of today's garment industry in the Big Apple. At the turn of the century, Italians got involved in the sector. Chinese and Dominican groups have succeeded them since the 1960s.

The Miami garment industry has developed, according to Guillermo Grenier and Alex Stepick, as a kind of auxiliary branch of New York. Manufacturers from New York, primarily Jewish, tried to escape the impact of unionization by moving south to Florida; next, female workers from Cuba emigrated to south Florida in the early 1960s and were funnelled to Miami. The emergence of a Miami garment industry also provided opportunities for Cuban entrepreneurs who entered the sector as contractors hiring a predominantly Cuban workforce. Over the years, the workforce changed as Cuban seamstresses left the sector. Entrepreneurs were reluctant to hire Haitians and African-Americans, and by the late 1980s newly arrived Central and South Americans replenished the supply of women.

In their chapter on Los Angeles Ivan Light and Victoria Ojeda describe how Asian and Latin American immigrants have largely replaced ethnic whites, particularly in the wake of the Immigration and Nationality Act of 1965. As a result of its access to immigrant labour, Los Angeles has passed New York City as the garment manufacturing capital of the United States. Today Asian (especially Korean), European and Latin American entrepreneurs hire Mexican and Central American seamstresses.

We took the following steps to address the issues discussed above. All the authors promised to contribute to the book on the basis of a common research plan. We held a preliminary meeting in Amsterdam, where we carefully discussed each chapter. We drew up an overall structure of issues that each contributor was to address, as well as the main themes for the whole book. We held a second meeting a year later, where we continued the critiques of the papers, and further refined the integration of each chapter around the central themes. These international meetings greatly reinforced our ability to integrate the chapters around the central themes.

The authors were not instructed to work within any particular theoretical perspective. What was discussed above is basically no more than a heuristic model, specifying the relevant topics, questions and avenues of research and leaving plenty of room for the authors to develop their own theoretical perspectives. This endeavour is mainly based on the existing data collected by the respective authors rather than entirely new research. The comparison is therefore partly informed by the specific research questions in each case and the cases themselves. In practice, however, there was still sufficient scope for comparison, although not every contributor was able to cover every aspect.

In closing, I would like to say a few words about the terminology. This book deals with entrepreneurship, particularly small entrepreneurship, but small entrepreneurs constitute a heterogeneous category. The authors are fully aware of this. As a matter of fact, one of the reasons for embarking on this comparative work was to explore this heterogeneity. Moreover, we are dealing with various countries where different definitions of entrepreneurship are used, so it would be inappropriate to stipulate any one rigid definition of the entrepreneur.[14] There is a large body of literature on what exactly entrepreneurs are and how they differ from other economically active individuals. Scholars such as Schumpeter (1980) and Kirzner (1997) dedicated much of their work to this topic, and so did their followers (for a discussion of the various views, see Elfring 1999; nDoen 2000). Entrepreneurship, then, has a more specialized meaning: identifying opportunities, building, innovating and risk-taking in pursuit of profit (Boissevain 1981: 3n; see also 1997). Following Boissevain, we emphasize that the extent and psychological conditions under which an entrepreneur can retain control of an enterprise without building, innovating and taking risks are real and relevant, but are not explored here. We view an entrepreneur as a person in effective control of a commercial undertaking for more than one client over a significant period of time. As will be shown in the book, it is not always clear to what extent contractors in the garment industry, dependent as they are on other more powerful economic actors, are able to exert effective control. This, of course, depends on their position in the value-adding chain, a matter indicative of the interaction between the entrepreneur and the social, political, and economic environment. Consequently, the study of entrepreneurship necessitates going beyond investigation in terms of who entrepreneurs are and what they do, but also exploring how opportunities come into existence, what their sources are, and how, when and why some people rather than others discover, exploit and optimize these opportunities, and how, when and why different modes of actions are used to do so (Shane and Venkataraman 2000).

Other concepts that deserve attention include the *immigrant* entrepreneur and the *ethnic* entrepreneur. Many authors use the terms as convenient synonyms, which in my view just confuses the issue.[15] The casual use of these two concepts is problematic for two reasons. Firstly, the entrepreneurs in question are not always immigrants in the true sense in that they were not always born in another country. It might be true in some cases, but not in, say, Great Britain, where many of the 'immigrant' entrepreneurs were actually born. Next to that, the term 'immigrant' has become tainted with all sorts of negative common-sense notions, and is therefore no longer current among British academics (cf. Miles 1993). Instead, people of Asian, Mediterranean or Caribbean descent are now referred to as 'ethnic minorities', and the entrepreneurs among them as 'ethnic entrepreneurs'. The situation in the United States is even more complicated. The Latino category comprises recent arrivals as well as people whose great-great-great-grandparents came from a Latin community. In fact, Latino or Asian are primarily census categories that do not give much information about the history of their arrival, their citizenship status or their cultural features.

Secondly, many authors take it for granted that immigrants of the second as well as the first generation constitute ethnic groups and that their ethnic features inform their business activities. However, the reason for using the adjective 'ethnic' is rarely if ever made theoretically explicit. Does it refer to the origins of the entrepreneurs, their 'ethnic' moral framework, or capacity to mobilize 'ethnic' loyalties and access an 'ethnic' market? Or does it pertain to their management strategies, personnel, clientele, products or a combination of them? Or simply to the availability of empirical data, nicely presented in 'ethnic' categories? Most authors assume, without further reflection, that just because they are dealing with immigrants there are real differences, and that these differences pertain to the entire immigrant population and that they never change (Rath 2000a,c; Rath and Kloosterman 2000).

Acknowledging that the concepts of the ethnic and immigrant entrepreneur merit further theoretical debate, the contributors to this book have 'solved' this matter in a pragmatic way, each using the concepts they find most appropriate. Again, the very fact that large and diverse groups of people engage in entrepreneurship makes it improbable 'that entrepreneurship can be explained *solely* by reference to a characteristic of certain people independent of the situation in which they find themselves' (Shane and Venkataraman 2000: 218). As is discussed in detail in this chapter, we explicitly focus on situational opportunity cues, including the ones that enable and legitimize the mobilization of 'ethnic' resources.

## Notes

1. Information provided by Ms Babke Derks, Martinair flight attendant, on a flight from Vancouver to Amsterdam.
2. In this book, the terms rag trade and garment, apparel and clothing industries are used as synonyms.
3. The West Midlands includes inner Birmingham, Smethwick, Coventry, Wolverhampton, West Bromwich and Walsall.
4. The term commonly used in cases of this kind is actually 'global city', which was coined by Sassen (1991). However, it has a special meaning that does not necessarily apply to cities such as Amsterdam or Birmingham (cf. Shachar 1994). That is why the more general term 'world city' seems more appropriate. I have borrowed it from Ho and Bedford (1998), who loosely apply it to cities

connected to larger international economic systems that experience mass immigration.

5. Green (1997; see also 1986a) wrote an excellent book on the garment industry in Paris and New York, but this book focuses on labour rather than entrepreneurship as such. Bonacich *et al.* (1994) edited an interesting volume on the garment industry in the Pacific Rim. They cover many countries, but their work is not a comprehensive international comparison.

6. Multi-country analyses include Aldrich *et al.* (1985); Barrett *et al.* (1996); Blaschke *et al.* (1990); Jones and McEvoy (1992); Kloosterman and Rath (forthcoming); McEvoy and Jones (1993); Morokvasic (1991a); Razin (1993 and 1999); Razin and Langlois (1992); Waldinger *et al.* (1985); Ward (1987). The chapters by Boissevain and Grotenbreg (1988) and Ward (1988) on Caribbean entrepreneurship in Great Britain and the Netherlands are linked, but do not constitute a total comparison. Light and Isralowitz (1997) have collected a number of essays on entrepreneurship in the United States and Israel, but they too do not constitute a real comparison.

7. The term 'national' is usually linked to nation-states. The assumption is that this is the level where country-specific phenomena can be meaningfully observed and discussed. This view does not appreciate the reality of multi-states.

8. The exceptions in the general study of immigrant entrepreneurship include Aldrich *et al.* (1981 and 1986); Cross and Waldinger (1992); Kloosterman and van der Leun (1998 and 1999); Light and Rosenstein (1995); Morokvasic (1991a); Razin (1988); Razin and Langlois (1996); Razin and Light (1988a,b); Rekers (1993 and 1998).

9. A wide range of structural factors account for that. It is often assumed that immigrants find themselves at the end of the labour queue. Employers prefer local white workers or workers from their own social network, or do not fully recognize the immigrants' educational credentials, or demand education, skills and experiences that immigrants do not have (see for instance Waldinger 1996b). In such cases of mismatch, immigrants flock to sectors of the economy with a high demand for manual or unskilled workers and low entry barriers (Engelen 2001). The garment industry is one of the sectors where immigrants with poor resources constitute a pool of cheap and flexible labour (Reil and Korver 2001; Zhou 1992). It is clear that this certainly does not apply to every immigrant. After all, high-tech industries like the ones in Silicon Valley explicitly recruit highly skilled immigrant workers (Saxenian 1999), and immigration countries such as the United States, Canada, Australia and New Zealand give preference to skilled immigrants under their current immigration systems (see Froschauer 2001; Ho and Bedford 1998). On the bifurcated fortunes of immigrants in the Canadian labour market, see Hiebert (1999); Preston and Giles (1997).

10. But this is no hard and fast rule, as Zhou (1992) demonstrates. She argues that many Chinese immigrants in New York's Chinatown start in the garment industry only to leave it at the first opportunity. Their flight from the garment industry might be an indication of substandard conditions in the lower end of the sector.

11. Information from a personal communication to the author by Carl-Ulrik Schierup, National Institute of Working Life, Centre for Work and Culture, Norrköping, Sweden.

12. Information from a personal communication to the author by Michaela Schier, Department of Geography, Technical University of Munich, Germany. In addition to the regulation of the small enterprise sector, a number of historical idiosyncrasies account for the absence of immigrants among garment manufacturers and contractors. Morokvasic *et al.* (1986) note the vanishing of the Jewish petty bourgeoisie in the Holocaust and the strict immigration regime in recent decades. The former undermined the historical succession process of particularly small enterprises from more established groups to newcomers. (Elsewhere, in France or Britain, the Jewish garment sector remained wholly or partly intact during the Second World War, so that processes of vacancy succession in chain-like configurations did not come to a halt.) The latter prevented the arrival of a large number of new entrepreneurs from abroad.

13. Moral codes, cultural expectations, social institutions and the like can have the power of formal rules and can function as such (Epstein 1994). However, Engelen (2001) subsumes moral codes and expectations under the heading of social embeddedness. As has also been argued by Portes and Sensenbrenner (1993), social networks can only be transformed into social capital if mediated by moral codes and expectations. But moral codes and expectations can also be subsumed under the heading of the institutionalization dimension of the market.

14. Compare the *Report from the Commission to the Council on the Definitions of Small and Medium-sized Enterprises (SMEs) used in the Context of Community Activities. European Communities 1992.* Document Reference: SEC (92) 351. The EU states that: 'Despite their extreme diversity, SMEs are widely agreed to have at least some of the following characteristics: i) Qualitative criteria: Ownership and management in same hands; close link between family and enterprise; independence *vis-à-vis* large enterprises; central position of the head of the enterprise; labor intensive operations; reliance on internally generated funds; small work force and need for external advisers; personalized nature of relations with customers; and dependence on suppliers. ii) Quantitative criteria: Number of persons employed; annual turnover; balance sheet total; fixed assets; value added; combination of a number of criteria.'

Consult the Internet at http://dbs.cordis.lu/cordis-cgi/srchidadb?ACTION=
D&SESSION=165702001-1-22&DOC=2&TBL=EN_COMD&RCN=
EN_RCN:326&CALLER=EN_UNIFIEDSRCH

15. Light and Gold (2000) exemplify the casual use of such anthropological
concepts when they distinguish the 'ethnic economy' from the 'immigrant
economy'. According to them, the ethnic economy consists of co-ethnic self-
employed and employers and their co-ethnic employees, while the concept
of the immigrant economy is applied to cases where more than one ethnic
group is involved. The authors of *Ethnic Economies* do not base this conceptu-
alization on a thorough discussion of the relevant literature and do not even
bother to give a clear definition of ethnicity.

# –2–

# Paris: A Historical View
## *Nancy L. Green*

## Introduction

One of the most striking characteristics of the women's garment industry today is its remarkable similarity – in its basic outline, or silhouette, if you will – with its own early history of a century ago. The other remarkable phenomenon is the lack of historical memory on the part of many industry participants and observers today. Fluctuating styles, widespread subcontracting, homework, and, above all, a largely immigrant and female workforce have been part and parcel of the 'rag trade' since it mechanized and standardized in the late nineteenth century. Yet neither the sewing machine nor set sizing account solely for the particular organization of labour that developed in this trade. Nineteenth-century merchant-tailors and female out-workers set a proto-industrial stage for an industry that would remain 'light' and 'flexible' for well over a century (e.g. Coffin 1996; Johnson 1975; Scott 1984).

As a labour historian, my perspective will be somewhat different than others in this book in two respects. On the one hand, I have taken a *longue durée* approach to the garment industry in Paris (and New York – my work has been explicitly comparative), starting with the growth of the women's ready-to-wear industry at the end of the nineteenth century. On the other hand, I have been particularly interested in the view of entrepreneurship from the bottom up: the ways in which the industry offers employment – often under substandard conditions – to immigrant (and female) workers. The long-term perspective shows how immigrants have been drawn (in)to the industry for over a century in a pattern of successive, yet overlapping waves (Green 1986a and 1997). No one group alone carries with it an intrinsic affinity for sewing, Jewish tailor jokes and women's 'fairy finger' stereotypes notwithstanding.

## Immigrants in the City

In Paris (like New York), the clothing industry has been in the past and remains today one of the major manufacturers still within the city limits and expanding into the nearby suburbs. This is both a result of the economies of concentration peculiar to the industry's need to respond quickly to fashion change and of the availability of female and immigrant labour in the city. Paris-as-fashion-capital has been the subject of an abundant literature which is both descriptive and performative (the enunciation itself helps it take effect; as prolific turn-of-the century French art critic Arsène Alexandre (1902: 54) said, how can you argue with five centuries of good taste?). There is an equally important literature on women seamstresses, particularly with regard to the construction of the image of the higher-skilled *couturières* and lower-skilled *grisettes* and the importance of these images in segmenting women's labour (Coffin 1996; Coons 1987; Perrot 1978).

There is a less extensive but growing literature on France as a historic centre of immigration. Indeed, France was the primary country of *im*migration in Europe for most of the late nineteenth century and the first half of the twentieth (Dignan 1981; Gervereau *et al.* 1998; Green 1985; Lequin 1988; Noiriel 1988). While other countries continued to export labourers, France, given combined demographic woes and labour needs, remained one of the most legally open in the Western world (along with South America) until the 1930s. While Britain passed an Aliens Act as early as 1905, and the United States implemented its quota system in the early 1920s, France was signing bilateral agreements with Poland and Italy to import workers until the Depression and increasing xenophobia closed its door too in the 1930s. If the main focus of those work contracts were the mining and agriculture sectors, the generally open climate benefited immigrants from other countries as well (such as Jews from Eastern Europe and Armenians from the ex-Ottoman Empire) and redounded to light industry as well as its heavy counterpart. The historical formation of the garment working classes in Paris (as in New York and elsewhere) has thus been part of the history of immigration to those cities. Government policy did not target the garment industry in particular, and employers did not need to go abroad to recruit. Rather, ease of immigration provided a mobile labour force ultimately attracted in part to the availability of jobs in the growing clothing industry.

## The Industry

To understand the historic immigrant/garment industry 'fit' it is necessary to understand the structure and growth of the industry itself. In Paris, as in New York, ready-made women's clothing took off in the late nineteenth century, as women, following men, began to accept (certain) more standardized articles of clothing, starting with cloaks and then shirtwaists, eventually spreading to dresses in the interwar period and pants after the Second World War.

While the general functioning of the industry over the last century in Paris is similar to that of New York, three particular things differentiate Paris. The rhythm of development, while globally similar in both cities – i.e., the growth of ready-to-wear to the detriment of made-for-measure clothing – was somewhat slower in Paris. Although *confection* (ordinary ready-made clothes) for women took off, like in New York, at the end of the nineteenth century, the neighbourhood Parisian *couturière* continued to hold favour, and the custom-made dress was still a staple of many French women's wardrobes until after the Second World War. (Ready-made dresses had become standard off-the-rack items in New York by the interwar period.) A second difference has to do with the importance of the export market, as we will see.

The third major difference concerns immigrants, both in quantity and origin. While immigrants became an important source of labour in the industry in both cities from the turn of the twentieth century on, native French women and entre-preneurs continued to be a more important presence in Paris than 'American' workers or bosses in New York. Furthermore, as we will see, the immigrants who did come to Paris were different than those who went to New York. All immigration waves are not alike.

## Growth and Markets

It is difficult to chart the Parisian industry's growth with precision given changing statistical categories over time. However, a study of industrial census figures shows the importance of *travail des étoffes* (garment work) in Paris at the turn of the twentieth century. In 1906, this sector accounted for 290,340 jobs, well over double that of the next manufacturing category (ordinary metalwork); it represented 38.5 per cent of all manufacturing jobs. By 1926, the industry had slipped to 192,853 jobs, with metalwork catching up, and in 1931 the transformation of metals had slightly bypassed that of cloth. By 1946, clothing jobs had plummeted to 85,461, due to the deportation of many Jewish garment workers, increasing standardization in the production process (especially of men's wear), as well as a redefining of statistical categories. In 1962, the garment industry was the third largest industry in the city, employing over 90,000 people, roughly one-quarter of all of the 'mechanized industries'.[1] Yet even as most sectors of the increasingly standardized French garment industry suffered job losses between 1975 and 1987, apparel work in the Paris region (specializing in more specialized women's wear) declined less than elsewhere.[2] With an estimated 40,000 people on some 2,000 payrolls, women's ready-to-wear is still the second largest employer in the Paris area after printing and publishing (*Le Monde*, 2 December 1993).[3]

Paris, of course, was manufacturing for fashion. Indeed, its discourse has always revolved around an image of the artistic nature of the goods produced, even when arguing for greater 'modernization'. Thus, following a long tradition of concern for combining art with industry, Jean Allilaire (1947: 54, 95, 155ff.), in his recommendations for reconstructing the industry after the Second World War, lamented that a 'depressing tendency' of uniformity of manners was emerging. Yet, he also recognized that the production process had to be revamped, so he urged that a 'judicious standardization (*normalisation*) of certain elements of the garment' be undertaken, a rationalization of production which, however, had to be vigilant in order to maintain the cachet of French style.

Threading its way between 'reason and passion',[4] the Parisian and French clothing industry in general has produced for three markets: the export market, department stores, and the myriad of small boutiques in French cities.

The number of small, independent clothing shops is one of the hallmarks of the Parisian cityscape to this day. It feeds the neighbourhood of the Sentier, the wholesale hub, where on Mondays (the day on which boutiques are generally closed) retailers come to fill out their lines. It is at this more individualized retail end (not to mention *haute couture*, another subject altogether) that Paris differs from New York and other garment capitals today.

For a good two-thirds of the twentieth century, however, Paris was unique in another way. Paris produced not just for Parisians and the provinces, but also largely for export well before other garment centres. Two distinct foreign markets, corresponding to the two main segments of the industry, had evolved as early as the end of the nineteenth century. At one end were (are) the international buyers who came to Paris to purchase *haute couture* patterns and the right to reproduce them. At the other end of the spectrum, the expanding colonial market formed an important outlet for ready-made garments from the late nineteenth century until the 1960s.

Largely thanks to the colonial market, the garment trades were the second largest sector of French exports in 1925. Before the First World War, French exports of ready-made garments alone had reached over 252.6 million francs, compared to only 10 million francs worth of clothing imports. At the same time, France had exported 160.6 million francs of custom-made dresses and coats while importing a mere 3.8 million francs worth. In 1926, total garment imports cost France 11.5 million francs, while exports had risen to a value of 1,970.6 million francs; by 1929, imports had reached 18.9 million and exports had declined to 1,434.6 million francs, but clothing still clearly remained an important sector for the French balance of payments (Deschamps 1937: 1–2, 68; Hauser and Hitier 1917: 311–13, 418–21; Simon 1931: 99).[5]

After the Second World War, two phenomena changed the international market for French clothing. First, decolonization in the 1950s and 1960s drastically reduced France's exports to its former overseas territories. Second, international competition began taking its toll. The other industrialized countries expanded their own industries for export, as other chapters in this book describe. But also, well before the end of the twentieth century, cheaper imports from newly industrializing countries were also competing seriously on foreign markets while encroaching on domestic markets as well. Nonetheless, historically, in comparison with other manufacturing centres which produced initially and for a much longer period largely for their own domestic markets, exports have always had a key role to play in the Parisian and French garment industry.

As for domestic distribution through department store (and catalogue) sales, the French situation has, in one respect, not been that different than elsewhere. In Paris, as in New York, department stores helped stimulate demand for ready-made apparel. But in Paris they helped shape supply as well from the very early period. Unlike nineteenth-century New York (where department stores by and large gave up their own workrooms after the 1870s depression), the Parisian department stores innovated and persisted in being manufacturers in their own right. In the early twentieth century, the Bon Marché and Galeries Lafayette had set up some of the largest wholly owned women's wear workshops in town, just as the Belle Jardinière had done for men's wear (Coffin 1985: 60–9; Faraut 1987; Miller 1981: 30–1, 57–8; see also Emile Zola's great classic *Au Bonheur des Dames*, 1901). By the interwar period, however, the large manufacturing units succumbed to the rigidities involved in managing production within a context of fluctuating demand. More flexible production of women's wear would increasingly be relegated to subcontractors, precisely where immigrants could most easily get a foot/treadle in the market.

## *The Organization of Work: Entrepreneurs and Subcontracting*

Adjusting supply to demand has always been particularly key to an industry so dependent on fluctuating styles. By cutting the risk of long-term investment, adjusting the labour force to production needs, and limiting constraints due to union and legislative restrictions that regulate wages, benefits, social welfare payments, and working conditions, manufacturers have slalomed between costly manufacturing units and ever-changing female fashions for over a century. Their response has been subcontracting. Responsibility and costs are shifted elsewhere.

Nineteenth-century outwork was already based around a division of labour: highly skilled male tailors cut and prepared goods which were given out to less-skilled female domestic workers in the countryside. Ultimately, jobbing, both in Paris and New York, would be based around the basic division between cutting and sewing. Manufacturers or jobbers purchase and cut the cloth and send it out to be sewn up. This separation of tasks shifts an important part of the production off-site (to someone else's rent) while limiting fixed costs during the *morte-saison* (literally dead season in French). Subcontracting, based on the division of labour, has become integral to responding to fluctuating demand and organizing the labour force in the most flexible way possible. It has become a pivotal characteristic of the urban garment industry to this day. The contractors' shops have come to represent women's wear, ready-to-wear, the garment industry, and flexible specialization in increasing claims of generality.

Mirjana Morokvasic (1987b: 450) calculated in the mid-1980s that 96 per cent of the Parisian garment shops had fewer than twenty employees. The contractor – *façonnier* or *entrepreneur* in French – needs a minimum of 50,000 francs to set up a SARL (limited liability company), but more likely about 150,000 francs to go into business.[6] The contractors' shops in Paris function much like similar shops elsewhere: small-scale operations, based on low capital start-up, quick turnover of merchandise and often a high rate of firm turnover (failures).

Contemporary entrepreneurial strategies have only exacerbated these long historical trends. Seasons and styles seem to be rotating more quickly than ever. Relatively recent terms such as *le système Sentier* and the *circuit court* (the short cycle, in contrast to the longer production process of more staple items) describe this sense of newness in what is essentially a modern version of the seasonality that has been inherent in the industry from the outset. Garment manufacturers have always complained of style turnover as their *bête noire*. Yet it is a trope of the industry which is also its bread-and-butter.[7] In the last twenty years much has been made of a further speed-up and the fact that there are constant changes now *within* any given season. At the same time, new techniques in inventory control have only encouraged this trend. *Flux tendus,* zero stock control, has become a management ideal, made possible by modern technology and encouraged by retailers wanting to restock as close as possible to actual sales. Computerized inventory controls allow an immediate record of what is selling and what is not, so that manufacturers can respond mid-season to make more blues or more bell-bottoms, as the sales warrant.

Subcontracting, that perennial feature of the business, has thus been perpetuated and extended in order to respond to the need for fast, relatively close-by production. One recent study found up to six levels of subcontracting (Lazzarato *et al.* 1990: 186; see also Dubois 1988: 55–8). This is where immigrants – both entrepreneurs and workers – have their greatest niche and where labour conditions are often at their worst. Seasonal fluctuations and last-minute rushes are the bane of the garment workers' and bosses' lives. Poor conditions, long hours, and low pay have characterized the industry since the nineteenth century. Working to the pressures of the market, the small workshops are often characterized by substandard conditions and, once the downturn in the season comes, precarious employment. The term 'sweating system' has been evoked again and again, an emotional image, implying cramped space, long hours, low wages, child, female, and immigrant labour, exploitative middlemen, and/or germs. And although legislation concerning hours and wages, unemployment insurance and health regulations have eliminated a certain amount of the dirt and dust since 1880, fashion fluctuations and the extremes of overtime and down time have remained.

# The Labour Force: A Century of Immigrant Waves

The Parisian garment industry workforce has been largely female and largely immigrant for over a century. The immigrants have come, in overlapping succession, from Germany and Belgium, from Eastern Europe, from the ex-Ottoman Empire, from North Africa, and more recently from Yugoslavia, Turkey, South-East Asia and mainland China.

In the 1840s, approximately two-fifths of all tailors in Paris were already immigrants, hailing from Germany, Hungary, and Poland. According to one account, almost all of their workers were French women; according to another, two-thirds of the *ouvriers tailleurs* in 1848 were (already) of foreign origin (Chevalier 1950: 182; Johnson 1975: 92).[8] When Käthe Schirmacher investigated immigrant workers in Paris at the turn of the twentieth century (sympathetic to their cause before she became a rabid nationalist), she found German and Belgian tailors rivalling English ones at the top end of the men's garment industry, while Poles, Czechs, Austrians, Romanians and Italians, in addition to the French, brought their expertise to the growing women's wear sector. The ready-made trade, *cette industrie maudite* (that cursed industry), attracted immigrants 'of misery', she wrote; Slavs, Poles, Russians and 'above all the most exploited of all, Israelites, Romanians and Turks' (1908: 71; cf. 67, 92). Yet, curiously, Schirmacher only counted the Belgians, Germans, Italians, and Swiss in her statistics, those border-country migrants who constituted the first major wave of foreign migration to modern France. She thus found (only) 9,410 foreigners in the 277,755-person strong Paris garment industry, a mere 3.4 per cent (but undoubtedly under-represented) portion of the total.

Yet, even from the perspective of these immigrants, garment work constituted the third largest activity for all foreigners in the Paris economy (after domestic service and trade). The industry was the major activity of Belgian immigrants (22 per cent); it gave work to 10 per cent of the Germans in Paris, 12.5 per cent of the Italians, and 9.8 per cent of the Swiss (Schirmacher 1908: 15; cf. Chevalier 1950: 182; Faraut 1987: 28–9; Johnson 1975: 92; Roche 1989: 300–1).

Those whom Schirmacher did not count were the Eastern European Jews, who began arriving in large numbers to Paris (as New York, London, and elsewhere) in the 1880s. According to one source, some 8,860 Jewish immigrants were at work in the Parisian apparel industry in 1910, which represented some 29.3 per cent of their working population in Paris (Speiser 1910: 78–80).[9] Economist Joseph Klatzmann (1957: 81–2) calculated that Jews comprised 60 per cent of the male garment workers in Paris in 1946 and that foreign-born Jews constituted one-half of all the foreign-born workers in the Parisian industry at that time. In the early 1950s, demographer Michel Roblin (1952: 99–100) estimated that 40 per cent of those listed in the Parisian telephone directory under the category 'Confection' were Jews; only the capmakers had an even higher percentage (60 per cent).

In spite of their visible concentration in the field, Eastern European Jews were not the only foreigners sewing in Paris. As immigration remained open to France into the early 1930s, Armenians arrived in the wake of the Armenian genocide and 'Turkish Jews' came following the break-up of the Ottoman Empire (Benveniste 1989: 111, 115, 117; Green *et al*. 1987: chaps. 5 and 6; Hovanessian 1992; Morin 1989). Italians also came to the garment district as Paris became a centre of Italian immigration in the 1920s. Garment work became the second most important line of work for immigrants in Paris in 1926 (after trade and commerce): 4,611 Poles, 3,115 Russians, 2,629 Italians, 2,576 Belgians, 1,328 Romanians, and 870 Armenians/Greeks were in the census that year (Mauco 1932: 300; cf. Couder 1986: 508), although the numbers were undoubtedly higher. In 1933, the Police Department estimated that of 27,978 foreigners in the Seine Department's garment industry, 8,462 were Poles, followed by 5,274 Italians.[10]

While the interwar years added variety to the garment labour force, the Second World War seriously challenged that diversity. The Aryanization of Jewish firms and the deportation of 75,000 Jews from France had an impact down to the garment shops where so many of them worked (Klatzmann 1957: 86; Matteoli *et al*. forthcoming). Yet, ironically, at the same time, the small-scale, informal character of the industry did have one advantage. It allowed some to continue to work clandestinely throughout the war.

With decolonization and the arrival of North African immigrants to France in the 1950s and 1960s, a third wave of Jews moved into the apparel business. Many Tunisian and Moroccan Jews began by plying goods at outdoor markets, as sales representatives or wholesalers before becoming manufacturers. They gave impetus to and profited from the new economic boom of the 1960s and the growing expansion of sportswear in particular. One mid-1980s account estimated that some two-thirds (800 out of 1,200) of the firms in the Sentier garment district were Jewish-owned: 90 per cent by North African Jews (60 per cent from Tunisia; 20 per cent from Morocco; 10 per cent from Algeria), with only 10 per cent still held by Eastern European Jews.[11]

Similarly, a new generation of Armenians made their way to Paris, settling alongside the post-1915 generation in the nearby Parisian suburb of Issy-les Moulineaux. What started out as a residential neighbourhood had, by the 1940s, become an economic fief specializing in knitted goods. The second-generation Armenians who stayed in the business prospered in the mid-1970s with the take-off of sportswear, while a new generation of Armenians arrived from Turkey, Lebanon, and Iran. As the newcomers reinforced community and economic structures, the term 'the Armenians of Issy-les Moulineaux' has come to mean 'knitwear' and vice-versa (Green *et al*. 1987: 172 and chap. 6; Green *et al*. 1988: chap. 5; Hovanessian 1992).

In the last third of the twentieth century, the garment industry initially benefited from France's continued search for labourers. The government signed migration agreements with Turkey and Yugoslavia in 1965 and 1966, and even after the official halting ('suspension') of immigration to France in 1974, special dispensations were made on behalf of Lebanese and Chinese-Cambodian refugees. Mostly Serbs from Yugoslavia, mostly Kurds from Turkey, and Chinese immigrants from both Cambodia and the Wenzhou area of China have all set up business, like the Polish Jews before them, with a few francs and a few machines.[12] From the early 1980s on, a growing concentration of Turkish shops began to appear in the tenth and eleventh *arrondissements* near the Sentier garment district.

Similarly, as large numbers of Chinese refugees (whose parents or grandparents had migrated earlier to South-East Asia) began fleeing the Communist regimes in Vietnam, Cambodia, and Laos in 1975, some 110,000 went to France. The Chinese from Cambodia were the most numerous (40 per cent), followed by refugees from Laos (30 per cent) and Vietnam (27 per cent) (Guillon and Taboada-Leonetti 1986: 133; see also Costa-Lascoux and Live 1995; Green *et al.* 1988: chap. 4; Hassoun and Tan 1986; Ma Mung 1991; Raulin 1988; Tan 1984; White *et al.* 1987: 48). More recently, other Chinese immigrants have come to Paris from Hong Kong, Thailand, and mainland China. The French government's attempt to disperse these newcomers throughout the country failed. Chinese garment shops appeared both in the run-down buildings of an older immigrant neighbourhood (Belleville, eighteenth and nineteenth *arrondissements*) and in the new high-rises of the thirteenth *arrondissement*.[13] By one estimate, in the mid-1980s there were approximately 15,000 needleworkers in the thirteenth *arrondissement* Chinatown, effecting some 70 per cent of the Sentier subcontracting (Delorme 1986: 100, 107).

Finally, the most recent new arrivals to the garment industry have been Pakistani, Sri-Lankan, Maurician (mostly of Indian origin), and African (Senegalese and Malians) men who by and large work the lowest-ranked jobs as helpers, delivery-men, and porters. They sell their labour by the half day, the day, or the hour, at the place du Caire, reconstituting a veritable *chowk* (Urdu for public square, where the daily labour market congregates) in the centre of Paris (Green *et al.* 1987: 108–13, 130–3; *Le Monde*, 22 and 24–25 February 1984, 5–6 August 1984 and 11–12 September 1988; Montagné-Vilette 1990: 118–20).

Due to the dispersed nature of subcontracting, certain illegal labour and accounting practices, as well as the precarious legal status of many undocumented workers, the figures for immigrants working in the Parisian garment industry today are, as elsewhere, difficult to ascertain. Nationwide industrial statistics for 1982 (which count only those firms with more than ten employees) showed only 6.2 per cent foreigners in the combined *textile-habillement* (garment) sector, whereas population census figures for the same period indicated that there were 20 per cent foreigners in that sector countrywide and 43 per cent in Paris. Sociologists Mirjana Morokvasic, Annie Phizacklea and Hedwig Rudolph (1986) estimated that there were perhaps 10,000 immigrants active in the garment industry in the Paris region in that period – double that of the census figures. Yet even their figure still did not take into account the numerous non-salaried homeworkers or undeclared homeworkers or shopworkers (see also Lebon 1977: 79; Morokvasic 1987a: 3, 6, 9, 11 and 1988c).

Why have so many immigrants flocked to this industry? Why the continued streams for over a century? Working conditions are generally bad. Newspaper reports today are not unlike those of the turn of the twentieth century. They write of squalid conditions in deteriorating buildings where illegal immigrants work ten to eleven hours without overtime and for less than the minimum wage. Chinese-Cambodians in Paris have been reportedly working eighty hours a week during the season. Turks complain about how they have to wait for work, often in vain, and then, when the piece goods arrive, they have to work all night to finish assembling the garments for the next day: 'It's like a prison' (*Le Monde*, 20 July 1985; *Libération*, 22 April 1987).

Is it a matter of imported skill? Are all the garment workers of the world uniting in Paris (or New York or Los Angeles)? Clearly not. Although there is some debate as to the importance of prior skill, it is generally recognized that both workers and entrepreneurs can go into the business with little prior experience. Although some of the workers have been tailors at home or, in the case of women, may have had some experience with domestic or even industrial sewing, previous training, for the most part, is not a prerequisite for workers any more than it is for employers. Both sewing and contracting can be learned on the job. The garment workers and contractors in Paris today have been physical therapists, teachers, soccer players, and occasionally tailors in their home countries.

Rather, three factors have accounted for the continuing 'waves' of immigrants to the garment trade in spite of cut-throat competition and difficult working conditions: the low skill and low capital required to get into the business; limited options in the larger labour market; and networks.

*Easy Entry*

'It's as easy as saying hello', commented a Chinese-Cambodian garment worker in Paris, while a Moroccan Jewish[14] entrepreneur remarked: 'It's a job you can start with nothing' (*Actuel*, April 1988; Green *et al*. 1987: 174; Hovanessian 1992: 152–4; Tan 1984: 283). Although the negative corollary of this ease of start-up is that bankruptcies and turnover are high, both entrepreneurs and workers have often learned the business while doing it. In some cases, 'imported' skills may simply have been learned en route: a 'vague apprenticeship' in an Armenian orphanage or learning how to sew in a refugee camp in Thailand, having heard that there were apparel jobs in France (Morokvasic 1993: 86–7; Tan 1984: 282–3; Ter Minassian 1988: 207). But, for the most part, clothing skills – speed and business acumen – have been learned on-site. Expanding opportunity at the turn of the twentieth century, just like specific opportunities in a contracting market at that century's end, has drawn tens of thousands to the sewing machines who had never touched a thimble, treadle or pedal before. While over the twentieth century thousands of tailors and seamstresses from Jews to Turks did indeed bring skills with them from the old country, for many others their fingers had to be retrained.

## Limited Alternatives

At the same time, discrimination and labour market segmentation limit other opportunities in the local labour market. Lack of language and other skills appropriate to available jobs may be compounded by the difficulties in obtaining legal working papers. In contrast, small family or ethnic-run shops can provide an easy entrance into the labour market and a certain sense of security. Furthermore, as one observer commented in the 1980s: 'With 6,000 francs monthly, he [the Turkish cutter] earns ten times more than he would in Turkey, where he would surely be unemployed and have the dictatorship on top of it' (Montagné-Villette 1990: 91).

The variety of immigrants alone seems clearly to argue for the importance of local conditions more than culture or imported skill in determining labour market segmentation. Finally, however, in addition to the push of conditions at home and the economic opportunities in the cities of industrial garment-making, immigrant networks have been the lubricating mechanism, the information conduits and actual micro-labour markets for legal and illegal newcomers alike.

## Immigrant Networks

A brother, a sister, an uncle or an aunt, a former neighbour or his or her cousin have been more important than any job advertisement in the first circle of hiring. Job acquisition, family and inter-community loans can all be found within the immigrant community. Over the last century, Jewish, Armenian, and Chinese entrepreneurs have all hired their own. Families and friends have helped put up initial capital. Chinese immigrants in particular have set up highly structured rotating credit organizations (*tontines*), which have helped finance restaurants and garment shops in Paris. There is no question that, in the first stage, community is key.

Networks have been justifiably hailed for explaining everything from migration routes to parish structure to language continuity to work environments. They have been an important explanatory device for immigration and ethnic history. This is true for Paris as elsewhere. If networks still do not account for how the first emigrant ended up where he or she did, they are a powerful clue as to how others came to follow. They help us understand the dynamic of labour market segmentation and micro-segmentation as well. Workers get information from kith and kin and often prefer the comradeship of a compatriot environment. Interwar images of Polish Jews waiting at the Gare du Nord to hire compatriots fresh off the train parallel those of Serbian contractors who half a century later flew home to recruit garment operators in Yugoslavia for work in Paris.

Immigrant informational and sometimes financial networks help 'nicheing' to occur. There exists a 'dialectique entre les connivences ethniques et économiques', argues Martine Hovanessian (1992: 212) with regard to Armenians in the Paris area. Suzanne Model (1985: e.g. 361–2, 375–6, 407), and Alejandro Portes and Robert Bach (1985) have gone even further in arguing that the immigrant networks mean a positive differentiation within the secondary labour market itself: co-ethnic employment – working for one's own – provides easier access to jobs and greater stability as compared to the higher risks of the non-co-ethnic, less-protected periphery. Roger Waldinger (1986) and Mirjana Morokvasic (1987b) have both stressed, for New York and Paris, how chain migration is crucial not only for understanding economic niches and labour market segmentation in general, but for the garment industry in particular.

## The Limitations of Network Theory

Nonetheless, networks are not the whole story. The economic, political and social environment must be taken into account (Rath 2000c). But even with regard to networks themselves, while ethnic communities have had an important role in the start-up of so many garment firms, their utility is perhaps limited to a one-generation phenomenon at best. If immigrants only hired their own, the industry would be self-perpetuating (which for some groups, to a limited degree, it is) and ethnically homogeneous (which it is not). Yet we observe several phenomena over time: the relative disinterest of the second generation for (and parents who positively discourage their progeniture from) an industry underwritten by stress and poor labour conditions; the arrival of new groups of immigrants; and, indeed, once we look closer, a greater heterogeneity of labour than first imagined by the ethnic business theory.

At each hub of the network there are spokes which lead outward to other groups. Information about jobs is also posted on building doors and in official employment offices. More importantly, simultaneous needs – that of the industry and that of newcomers – encourage freshly arrived immigrants to try their hand at some stage of the process: sewing, sales, *shlepping* (local transportation). In a sector characterized by cut-throat pricing, those in charge of hiring will look beyond their own circle when the next wave of (cheaper) newcomers arrives. As the earlier waves of immigrants both settle in and realize the expense of living in Paris, they may demand higher piece rates, while newer immigrants may still be satisfied with what already looks like a huge raise compared to wages at home. In repetitive cycles of labour market entry, they each do hire their own, but then they also start hiring others.

With regard to network theory, I would thus suggest that three caveats must be taken into account. The long-term historical view highlights its advantages but also its limitations. First, there may be discord and dysfunctioning within the networks. Second, the multi-ethnic nature of many of the shops reminds us that cultural complicity is not the only framework of labour relations. Third, network theory may imply an ipso facto ethnicization of the history of the garment trade.

First of all, internal conflicts within ethnic networks have been minimized by the optimists, if dramatized by the pessimists.[15] While homogeneity implies harmony, and paternalism can be positive, the first can mask discord and the second exploitation. Even Roger Waldinger, in his book explaining the advantages of the ethnic entrepreneur's mobilization of resources within the community network, recognized the limits of ethnic solidarity. He heard contradictory opinions: 'Hiring relatives is good', 'Hiring relatives is not a good thing.' Relatives could take it easy on the job, could interfere with decisions, and if they did something wrong, 'it's very hard to tell them' (1986: 157, 163, and more generally 160–6). As Waldinger writes: '[E]thnic relationships are maintained but transformed under the impact of economic change.' Or, as one of the Dominican owners he interviewed said, 'I'm of the opinion that whoever does the work best, that's it. I don't have to see where he's from' (1986: 165, 161).[16]

Intracultural conflicts are rarely evoked. Yet, as one Maurician in Paris complained, 'You shouldn't count too much on your compatriots. I knew this boss in France, he was a profiteer. He took advantage of me because I didn't have my legal papers' (Vuddamalay 1993: 361). In spite of images of solidarity, Jewish workers and bosses at the turn of the century, like Turkish or Chinese contractors and their employees today, are not exempt from conflict (Green 1986b: chaps. 5–7). Opportunity and complicity within the immigrant milieu do not exclude competition and conflict.

Second, the focus on the co-ethnic workplace has too often overlooked the truly mixed character of the garment districts. As one contractor commented, workers may get their first job through a relative 'but once they get their feet wet, zingo, they'll work anywhere'.[17] I have argued that the phenomenon of ethnic networks is an ever-renewed but ever-temporary phenomenon.[18] While family and friends clearly function as pathways to the shops in the first stage of the life cycle of each immigrant group's 'wave' of arrival, in a second stage the labour force becomes more diversified. Overlapping waves have given a multicultural cast to many of the individual shops and to the industry as a whole at any given time.

Already in the early part of the twentieth century, some thirty Russian, Rumanian, Armenian, Czech, Italian, and Swiss immigrants worked alongside French operators in one of the garment workshops of Printemps (a department store) in Paris.[19] While post-Second World War memory tells the stories of more homogeneous immigrant shops during the interwar years – with Polish Jews by and large hiring Polish Jews and Armenians Armenians – the garment factories today are once again more diverse. In the early 1980s, one-quarter of the Yugoslavs and two-thirds of the Turks in Morokvasic's sample were working in shops of and with other nationalities (1987a: 28).[20] There are Turkish workers with no previous skills working alongside trained French women holding a technical degree in garment making; Turks and Pakistanis sew side by side, not to mention the occasional Serbian or Turkish woman working in a Chinese shop (Groux *et al.* 1989; *Hommes et Migration*, September 1993; *Libération*, 22 April 1987; see also Green *et al.* 1987: 126–9).

Different languages are thus heard on the shop floors, while immigrant contractors do not always hire their own. Some Jews would not hire other Jews in order to avoid conflicts (of practice and of conscience) over working on the Sabbath, or because they assumed non-Jewish machine operators would be more docile. One Armenian contractor said he explicitly avoids working for Armenian wholesalers so as not to create conflicts within the community (Green *et al.* 1987: 188). 'The King of the Sentier' Maxi Librati, son of Moroccan Jews, began with Polish Jewish and Armenian homeworkers; today he works with Turkish, Serbian and Chinese contractors. A Moroccan Jewish firm with a Polish Jewish associate set up a factory on the outskirts of Paris with Pakistani workers. The first major Pakistani manufacturer in the Sentier, Bhatti, works with Chinese subcontractors, while Chinese-Cambodian contractors hire Thai workers, Turks work for Serbian contractors, and everyone hires African and Sri Lankan porters as needed.

This does not mean that mixed shops ignore ethnic favouritism, or that a supervisor will not give the best work to his or her relatives. But the multi-ethnic nature of many shops and work relations, a function of passing time and the renewal of migration streams, challenges an explanation of the garment districts based on 'trust relationships' alone (see Zeitlin 1992a).[21] Common origins clearly help the garment boss hire workers and the immigrants find jobs. But the process seems to be micro-generational, and the ethnic network often soon gives way to the 'cheaper', more 'docile' workforce that has just stepped off the boat, train, or plane.

Third, then, there is a final risk in 'ethnicizing' relations beyond what the historical record can bear. If we look for ethnicity, we can find it. It can be as powerful an organizing principle as class or sex – and just as limiting in its monolithic pretensions (Brettell 1981; Tripier 1987: 362–3).[22] The 'construction' of ethnic networks presumes to a large extent that harmony is internal to the groups and conflict therefore external. Indeed, the garment industry in Paris (as in New York) is not exempt from inter-group conflicts, which consolidate assumptions of internal co-operation (see Green 1997: chaps. 8–9). However, at the same time, intra-ethnic differentiation occurs as well, and the ethnic neighbourhood is not the only source of solidarity or financial aid. Although much has been made of the Chinese community's *tontines* for example, Thierry Pairault (1995), in his recent book on Chinese entrepreneurs in Paris, has shown that they (like other groups), rely less on family and informal loans and increasingly on bank loans.[23]

## Garment Making and the Law

While the Paris garment industry struggles to survive in an increasingly competitive environment, the government has cracked down on its labour and capital practices in recent years.

Illegal labour has been targeted as part of the French government's continued high-profile stance against illegal aliens in general. In 1996, for example, the centre-right government of Prime Minister Alain Juppé sought to reinforce the right of police intervention at the workplace in order to be able to arrest undocumented workers. This encountered two objections, however. First, although foreigners without proper residence permits were clearly those aimed at in Juppé's law, sociologists and labour inspectors responded with report after report showing that most of the off-the-books illegal work (in all fields combined – including home repairs, home help, etc.) is done by French nationals (Brizard and Marie 1993). Second, French labour inspectors have traditionally felt that their mandate is to protect workers, and they protested interference: 'We always have in mind the subordinate relationship of workers to bosses. That is our culture. It is not that of the police' (*Le Monde*, 24 September 1996). As it happened, the measure allowing the police to enter the workplace was thrown out on a technicality, but it would have been reintroduced had Juppé's government survived.

To many of their electors' surprise, the socialist government has subsequently continued a very visible fight against illegal foreigners as a way of appeasing right-wing sentiment against immigrants of all sorts (legal or not). A late 1990s offer to regularize undocumented workers (as in 1981–1983) showed once again that large numbers of them are garment workers – although not all *sans papiers* (paperless or undocumented persons) are garment workers and not all garment workers are undocumented.[24] Ultimately, only a little more than one-half of those who applied have been regularized. The (unlikely) expulsion of all non-legalized workers would have a marked impact on this urban industry.

As for capital, 'creative accounting', as I call it, has been the other industry practice most recently targeted by state enforcement. In what is known as a 'taxi' system, 'taxi' companies issue fake invoices which travel through an elaborate system of false payslips in order to avoid taxes and social charges. Some bank branches have turned a blind eye to suspicious procedures.[25]

In another scenario, a 'cavalry circuit' has been exposed by the banks themselves. In a spectacular enforcement measure, 200 policemen from the financial branch of the judicial police descended on the Sentier garment district at dawn on 18 November 1997. They arrested seventy-three garment entrepreneurs, most of whom were first- and second-generation immigrants; forty-five ended up being incarcerated. A group of ten banks had joined forces to press charges for fraud, fraud conspiracy, bankruptcy, possession of stolen goods and forgery. The 'cavalry circuit' apparently implicated anywhere from 50–700 firms in varying degrees; they had accepted fake orders which they then presented to the banks to obtain credit (*Le Monde*, 19–20 November 1997, 18 March 1998; *Nouvel Observateur*, 1–7 January 1998).

Few draw the distinction between 'creative' bookkeeping and tax fraud, wages and hours abuses, and the employment of individuals without proper residence papers.[26] The garment industry in Paris has indeed become at times the focus of criticism of 'black labour', extending (unfairly) to all immigrants. The widespread fraud among so many 'micro-firms' reflects a deteriorating economic climate amid the usual difficulties of keeping solvent in this razor-edged business. Taxi or cavalry, regardless of the mode of circulation, these practices have implied lost revenue for the state, as well as defaulted bank loans, while revealing the fragility of the economic sector and of the networks that underlie both banking and labour practices.

The terms and images of *travail clandestin* and *les fausses factures* (fake orders), both often synonymous with 'Le Sentier', cover in fact a variety of issues relating to the contemporary Parisian garment industry. Illegal work and illegal capital exist in multiple forms – from fake orders to tax evasion to employers not paying social charges, minimum wages or overtime salaries. Some workers do not have proper resident permits, but even legal immigrants, by nature more vulnerable to the excesses of the secondary labour market, suffer from low wages and long hours. But, as the Pakistani delivery-man said when asked about the mass manufacturers' arrest in November 1997: 'We saw the police cars go by, but this time, it wasn't for us!' (*Le Monde*, 20 November 1997).

Finally, however, public policy with regard to the industry is not always adversarial. When manufacturers argued that they needed special dispensations with regard to labour, fiscal and social charges in order to maintain the very viability of the industry within France, the French government instituted a special programme to subsidize some of the industry's hiring and other practices. However, the European Union subsequently ruled this measure illegal. The manufacturers now have to pay back the sums allocated, although they have been able to negotiate a repayment schedule with the French government. The ultimate political problem for cities, as well as for countries interested in keeping this industry within their borders, has been a constant struggle between maintaining labour and fiscal standards without making the industry too expensive in comparison to less expensive imports. For Paris, there is an added factor: memory, history and prestige. The women's garment industry is part of Paris's fashion window onto the world. This means the maintenance of a viable ready-made sector alongside the more flashy *haute couture* shows. The well-known irony is that so much of the everyday French fashion is indeed sewn up by foreigners.

## Conclusion

It is important to include both the historical long-term and the specific impact of immigrant labour in any discussion of immigrant garment businesses today. On the one hand, the continued prevalence of immigrants in this industry from the late nineteenth century to the late twentieth argues for something beyond regulatory, political, or economically conjunctural explanations. In periods of economic growth of the industry, as in periods of economic squeeze such as today, immigrants have played an important part in the small, subcontracting structure of this urban industry. In this respect the industry is a textbook case of the modalities of manufacturing in response to fluctuating demand. And it is the immigrants who have in large part made French fashion.

On the other hand, it is important to remember that ethnic entrepreneurs function within a community environment in which they rely on their neighbours and relatives to help get started. This is true both with regard to capital loans and with regard to employees. It is the low cost of labour, in addition to the low cost of capital entry, which makes start-ups possible. Immigrant employers provide jobs to their compatriots, albeit most often at substandard conditions. Yet this is but the first stage.

We need to go beyond the ethnic employer/ethnic labour network to examine the second stage of immigrant activity within the garment industry, when bankers more than kin are turned to for help. I have argued that the ethnic entrepreneur model is not sufficient. In a second stage – and this is seen most clearly when the industry is studied over a long period – immigrant entrepreneurs hire non-ethnics, other workers from the next immigrant wave, just as they turn from family loans to local banks. It is this constant process of renewal which has aided and abetted the functioning of this urban industry for over a century.

## Notes

1. See Résultats Statistiques (1925: 1–5 for 1906 in recapitulative table, 1929: 3, 1935: 3, 1951: 38 for 1936 and 1946 in recapitulative table – under the older classification there were 145,971 garment industry jobs in 1936, and 1941: 3); Recensement Général (1966: 43).

2. Increasing their portion of nationwide French garment workers from 20.4 to 23.7 per cent (44,135 people) (Groux *et al.* 1989: 17; cf. the cautious optimism of 'Le Devenir des Industries du Textile et de l'Habillement', *Journal Officiel*, 25 February 1982.

3. Ten years earlier, Mirjana Morokvasic (1987a: 3, 6, 9) counted some 4,301 garment firms in Paris of which 1,180 were listed as specializing in women's ready-to-wear (*confection*). However, as she has well pointed out, the smaller establishments and immigrant shops are undoubtedly vastly underreported. Morokvasic counted 25,700 workers in the Parisian ready-made trade, according to the 1982 census (1986: 11). Other estimates range from 30,000 to 50,000: 30,000 in the Sentier (*Libération*, 16–17 February, cited in Delorme 1986: 106; 30,000–50,000 people working in 10,000 firms in the Sentier and elsewhere in Paris (*Actuel*, April 1988); 45,000 people employed directly or indirectly by the Sentier (*Le Monde*, 6 December 1991).

4. The title of a book written by a contemporary ready-to-wear designer and consultant, Françoise Vincent-Ricard (1983).

5. The latter figures are not broken down for *modèles* and *confection*.

6. By comparison it costs 500,000 francs to start a restaurant (Tan 1984).

7. See Green (1997, especially chap. 1) on fashion change as it relates to manufacturing.

8. See Faraut (1987: 28–9) for the two-thirds figure.

9. For a comparative table of Jewish, Belgian, German, Italian, Swiss, and French occupations circa 1900, see Green (1986b: 122).

10. Reported in *L'Habillement* (Paris), no. 16 (1939).

11. Yet the Institut National de la Statistique et des Études Économiques counted 2,700 firms in the neighbourhood for 1986 (Green *et al.* 1987: 107).

12. On the Yugoslavs, see Friganovic *et al.* (1972: 75, 106); Montagné-Villette (1990: 118); Morokvasic (1987a). On the Turks, see Green *et al.* (1988: chap. 3); Kastoryano (1986); Montagné-Villette (1990: 117–18); Ozturk (1988); Tripier (1990).

13. White *et al.* (1987: 50) estimated in 1987 that there were 10,000–15,000.

14. Actually a French Jew of Moroccan origin.

15. For example the debate between Edna Bonacich and Roger Waldinger in *International Migration Review* 27 (1993): 685–701.

16. This Dominican owner had a mixed Hispanic workforce.

17. Harold Siegel, Greater Blouse, Skirt and Undergarment (Contractors') Association, interview, New York, 22 August 1984.
18. I have set out these points in the conclusion to my book *Ready-to-Wear and Ready-to-Work* (Green 1997).
19. Préfecture de Police Archives, BA1394: Tailleurs, grèves des ouvriers, file 'Grève . . . Printemps, mars 1916'.
20. The sample consisted of undocumented immigrant garment workers whose status was legalized from 1981–1983.
21. Alfred Marshall first developed the idea of industrial districts in 1890, in *Principles of Economics* (1922: 267–90).
22. See also Gans (1981), arguing that ethnicity has been used as a surrogate for class in the United States.
23. Pairault (1995) has mostly restaurant owners but also some garment entrepreneurs in his sample.
24. See the analysis of the 1980 regularizations by Morokvosic and Miller (1998).
25. On the 'taxi' companies, see Delorme (1986: 107–9); Montagné-Villette (1986: 147–63 and 1990: part 2); Morokvasic (1987b: 456–9).
26. But see, e.g., Brizard and Marie (1993).

# −3−

# London: Economic Differentiation and Policy-making

*Prodromos Panayiotopoulos (aka Mike Pany)*
and *Marja Dreef*

## Introduction

The high level of immigrant participation in the London garment industry contains important elements of continuity. Huguenot exiles in the seventeenth century, Eastern European Jewish refugees in the late nineteenth century, and Cypriot and Bengali immigrants in the late twentieth century all found shelter in the trade (see Bermant 1975; Fishman 1976; Kershen 1990; Panayiotopoulos 1990; Schmiechen 1984; Steward and Hunter 1964). Jews fleeing persecution in the 1880s and 1890s worked as pressers and machinists in the garment workshops of London's East End and for many it was an important stepping stone to Ellis Island or their own workshops (Jones 1976). Much of the work was seasonal and casual employment characterized the industry. The Singer Sewing Machine (first retailed in 1853) gave a big push to homeworking and the piece-rate system in late nineteenth-century London, building on centuries-old traditions of sub-contracting in areas such as the Lancashire cotton district and the London tailoring and lace industries (see Panayiotopoulos 2001: 202–4). Concerns about the social conditions of the London poor and the moral panic directed against the Jewish immigrant informed the 'anti-sweating' campaign led by Liberal reformers, resulting in 1905 in the Aliens Act, the first ever anti-immigrant legislation in the United Kingdom.

Minorities continue to play a sizeable role in the garment industry in conditions not too dissimilar from those of the late nineteenth century. Their role increased in the early post-war period as the garment industry was in great need of labour, and the British government (like other governments) decided to facilitate the migration of labour to meet the demand (cf. Bohning 1972; Castles and Kosack 1973; Harris 1995; Jones 1993; Kindleberger 1967; Penninx *et al.* 1993). By 1970, 7 per cent of the United Kindom labour force consisted of immigrant workers, with the single largest concentration in the textile and garment industry where immigrants made up more than 10 per cent of all the workers.[1] In the London garment industry during 1971 nearly a third of all the registered workers were born outside the United Kingdom (UK Department of Employment 1976: 141).

Since then, the garment industry has suffered sizeable job losses due to drastic restructuring. In the 1940s, 1950s and 1960s, London industries were already granted considerable subsidies to relocate to regions facing high unemployment or offering more space for large-scale production sites (Massey 1984). This accounted for the significant spatial and sectoral redistribution of employment to areas such as the West Midlands (see Ram *et al.*, this volume). Furthermore, sectors such as men's and boy's wear and tailored outerwear; both associated with large-scale standardized production, were severely affected by increased import penetration during the 1980s. Garment production nevertheless continues to have a significant presence in the London area (Anderson and Flatley 1997; Graham and Spence 1995). This is largely a result of the increased significance of the women's and girl's light outerwear (dresses, blouses, skirts) and casual wear sectors. In the early 1990s, London accounted for 12 per cent of all the United Kingdom registered employment in the garment industry, and in the women's wear sector it was 20 per cent (Panayiotopoulos 1993: 26). An estimated 30,000 workers – predominantly women – are employed in 2,500 small firms. Most have *dockets* (orders) running to less than 1,000 garments a week and have a yearly turnover of less than £200,000.

The spatial distribution of garment enterprises and employment within the London area is highly uneven, and most employment is concentrated in five of London's thirty-three boroughs (Tower Hamlets, Hackney, Islington, Haringey and Westminster, where many wholesalers are located). In the borough of Hackney, the sector is a major manufacturing employer, and especially in the sub-sectors such as tailored men's and women's wear it remains a major centre for United Kingdom-wide production. The borough of Haringey is a major centre for women's fashion wear production in the United Kingdom (Business Monitor 1992; Panayiotopoulos 1992a,b, 1993: 28–30, 1996a).

The London garment industry is characterised by the prevalence of small firms, low entry barriers, hyper-competition, informality and seasonal troughs. The industry uses relatively simple technology and, importantly for unskilled immigrants, relies on demonstrable ways of learning skills. The tendency in women's wear for greater fashion changes, and even more frequent changes in style requiring even smaller dockets, militates even more against large-scale assembly-line production. This reinforces the role of small firms and enhances hyper-competitive behaviour between contractors, which typically occurs by undercutting the making price (Panayiotopoulos 1990, 1996a). The organization of production is structured in a series of vertical and horizontal subcontractual relationships. In a vertical direction they include the relations between the buyers (who place the orders), the manufacturers (who provide the cloth and design) and the contractors (who provide the labour) and are referred to in the trade as Cut, Make and Trim (CMT) units.

There are specific factors in the continuity of the London garment industry that derive from the historical relationship between buyers, manufacturers and fashion houses in the West End of London (Great Portland Street) and CMT contractors in the East End and North London. The proximity of this relationship facilitates a fashionwear spot market characterized by the small-batch production of rapidly changing styles, placing even greater pressure on delivery times. A necessary precondition for this type of market is the agglomeration of buyers, manufacturers, production units, designers, suppliers of textiles, trimmings and specialized services to the trade in a robust local economy. Minority entrepreneurs have adapted to the London women's wear fashion spot market, typically as contractors, simply because it is there (for comparisons to New York, see Waldinger 1986 and Zhou in this volume). The very fact that the industry as a whole consists of more than just a tier of contractors implies that, in theory, vertical mobility is possible. To what extent immigrant entrepreneurs are capable of taking advantage of this mobility and consequently take part in a process of differentiation is discussed in the following section.

Many studies of immigrant enterprises in the garment industry focus on the mobilization of social capital by fledgling entrepreneurs or their role in a global process of economic restructuring. Although these issues are relevant for our understanding of immigrant enterprises and the dynamics of the sector, they fail to sufficiently take into account the institutional framework and its local variation. As we will show in the subsequent section, much variation has its origin in the local political and regulatory environment. We will discuss and compare how policy-makers at the central level and London and in two particular boroughs, Hackney and Haringey, have responded to developments in the garment industry and how their responses have impacted on the opportunity structure in different ways. We argue that even though most contractors in the London garment industry manage their enterprises under conditions of informalization, some of them have managed to carve out a place in the tiers of manufacturers. This has attracted the attention of policy-makers at the local level. It was this experience, more than any other, that has accounted for changes in the local political arena, leading ultimately to greater sympathy and support for emergent minority-owned garment enterprises on the part of some local authorities.

The chapter presents an overview of immigrant and ethnic minority enterprise in the London garment industry based on empirical research on the women's wear sector. It is a sector dominated by Cypriot entrepreneurs. The primary aim of the chapter is to suggest that minority enterprise is far more differentiated than is sometimes assumed, and that this is an important factor in explaining how the entrepreneurs manage their enterprises and respond to changes in the market and institutional environment. The chapter considers the political dimension of differentiation and the extent to which emergent entrepreneurs who are in a strong economic position are well placed to benefit from local authority support aimed at inner city regeneration. This is indicative of a more complex regulatory and policy environment as informal enterprises are drawn closer to formal organizations.

## The London Garment Industry: Informalization and Differentiation

The most extensive studies of the London garment industry were conducted by the Greater London Council (GLC) during the mid-1980s as part of a larger study of London's economy. The studies not only revealed high levels of participation by ethnic minorities but also a crude ethnic, spatial and sub-sectoral division among them. Greek Cypriots were concentrated in the north London women's lightwear sector (dresses, separates), with the boroughs of Haringey and Islington as the main centres of activity. Turkish Cypriots were more concentrated in the northeast London heavywear sector (coats and tailored garments), with the borough of Hackney as its epicentre. Bengali immigrants were heavily concentrated in east London's leatherwear sector (mainly coats and jackets) within the borough of Tower Hamlets (Greater London Council 1985: 119–39, 195–217). During the late 1980s and 1990s new entrants included increased numbers of mainland Turks and Kurds clustered around the areas and sub-sectors associated with the Turkish Cypriot community.

These entrepreneurs have responded to the opportunities – poor as they may be – provided in the United Kingdom and, *casquo*, in the London economy. The garment industry in the United Kingdom has been able to remain onshore, at any rate to some extent, by minimizing labour costs. This has been done by equipping factories with the best available technology, purchasing fabrics from the lowest cost sources, and making use of local contractors. In doing so, the industry could strengthen quality and minimize delivery times. This process was driven by a highly concentrated garment retail sector. Marks & Spencer (M&S), and its historical commitment to a 'made in the United Kingdom' policy, is its most characteristic example. M&S currently places textile and garment orders to the value of £5.7 billion, about 70 per cent of which are currently produced in the United Kingdom. In the 1980s this was significantly higher at 90 per cent of sales (see Anson 1997; Barnes 1994).

The ability of the retail sector to structure and restructure the garment industry in the United Kingdom is a reflection of its highly concentrated nature and considerable corporate power, with three leading chain stores – M&S being the most significant – accounting for nearly a third of total garment sales. It was very significant when M&S openly asked its suppliers to source more of their production abroad for the first time in May 1998.[2] This put considerable pressure on M&S domestic suppliers. Suppliers put pressure on their manufacturers and they in turn on their contractors to remain price-competitive in the face of global competition, and this impacted ethnic entrepreneurs and workers. The long-term implications of market changes are not certain, but it is clear that many ethnic CMT contractors in the London women's wear sector, who as contractors are the least capable of adapting to the changes in the market for garments, have come under intense pressure. One outcome based on previous experience of coping with market crises is that current trends will further add to the informalization of the industry and growth of subcontracting as a cost-cutting management strategy.

Production relations are conditioned by the institutions of informality routinely implemented by many of the entrepreneurs. By institutions we mean a set of relationships which are structural characteristics of the garment industry and appear in the form of homeworking, 'clear-money' (cash-in-hand), illegal selling activities ('cabbage' sales), 'doing a liquidation' to avoid taxation and 'design pinching' of the latest fashion (Panayiotopoulos 1996a: 450–4). Although these practices should not be seen as the cultural property of any particular ethnic group, they appear as an associated condition (and possibly a necessary one) for minority participation in the London garment industry. The pattern of employment in the industry, the financial management of the enterprises and the organization of production are sensitively linked to these activities. They shape management–worker relations and relations with the outside world. These institutions initially appeared in response to a macro-economic environment characterized by falling or static making prices given by manufacturers to contractors and increases in Value Added duty. Many contractors tried to compensate for depressed prices by increasing volume output in extra-legal ways or resorting to homeworking. The informalization of production can be understood as a response by entrepreneurs to changes in the market and institutional environment which developed into a general survival strategy adopted by many contractors. This brought the entrepreneurs into conflict with various branches of the British state.

In the recruitment of labour, entrepreneurs make use of complementary social networks involving kinship, ethnicity, caste, village or town origins, 'school-boy' friendships, and membership in political and cultural organizations (Anthias 1992; Ladbury 1984; Ram 1993, 1994). Many London Cypriot entrepreneurs make use of the large range of community associations (Church, village organizations, own-language schools, political parties) and informal gatherings such as weddings and baptisms, which serve as places for sharing information including that about work (Josephides 1987, 1988; Rex and Josephides 1987). The pooling of family labour in the form of 'partnerships' is often an important resource amongst new entrants, but it can also be a source of friction related to gossip, rumours, and occasionally malevolence between the families whose labour is a critical part of the pooling of resources. An acrimonious break-up between partners can often result in an acrimonious break-up between families, which may include long periods of non-communication and mutual disrespect (Panayiotopoulos 1993). These internalized labour recruitment practices are relatively common among minority entrepreneurs and are not untypical for the garment industry as a whole. One recent development amongst Cypriot enterprises, however, is that many faced severe problems in recruiting machinists, and this often became a critical issue. The ageing of first-generation women immigrant machinists, the unwillingness on the part of many young second-generation women to enter the garment industry, and tight immigration controls forced the entrepreneurs to change the ethnic composition of the labour force and the role of family labour. The result was a greater degree of representation for non-Cypriot workers and considerably more home-workers (Panayiotopoulos 1996a: 442–5). One illustration is the labour force composition of a not untypical CMT unit in Tottenham, North London (see Table 3.1).

In the London garment industry, management in the wider sense is linked to the institutions of informality routinely implemented by many of the entrepreneurs. The avoidance of institutional costs by employing unregistered labour to reduce wage expenses significantly is standard institutional behaviour. Other types of behaviour include the following:

1. *Cabbage sales* are crucial to the day-to-day financial management and liquidity and represent unregistered sales. *Cabbage* is essentially an official or unofficial 'allowance' that the contractor squeezes out of the cloth (and design) provided by the manufacturer. If the cloth makes 1,000 garments and the firm manages via the skill of its cutter to squeeze another 75–100 garments out of the cloth, this amount is referred to as 'your cabbage' which is then sold privately to shop and stall-owners. Cabbage sales by contractors represent a response to the production weakness reflected in low making prices. To some contractors, selling activities also represent a conscious effort to diversify the source of income by way of pseudo-wholesale activities (Panayiotopoulos 1990, 1993).

2. *Doing a liquidation*, or more commonly carrying out a voluntary liquidation, is a means of avoiding paying creditors and paying Value Added Tax (VAT).[3] This tax is added to the retail price and is recoupable by the entrepreneur, but first it has to be paid. However, as the question of liquidity (often manifested as late payments) assumes a disproportionate weight in this sector, the money is spent, frequently just to retain the machinists during slack periods. The Customs and Excise office does not routinely pursue, since the relatively small amounts owed by small contractor firms do not warrant the high cost of pursuit

**Table 3.1** A Garment Factory in Tottenham, North London: Labour Force Characteristics

| | *No. of workers* | *Type of workers* | *Sex* | *No./Origin* |
|---|---|---|---|---|
| Factory | 1 | Entrepreneur | Male | Greek Cypriot (brother) |
| | 1 | Master Cutter | Male | Greek Cypriot |
| | 1 | Assistant Cutter | Male | Greek Cypriot |
| | 1 | Sample machinist | Female | Greek Cypriot (sister) |
| | 2 | Special machinists | Female | Greek Cypriot (aunt) |
| | 7 | Machinists | Female | 4 Afri-Caribbean<br>3 Greek Cypriot |
| | 1 | Driver | Male | Greek Cypriot (brother) |
| | 3 | Passers | Female | 2 Greek Cypriot<br>1 Irish |
| | 2 | Pressers | Male | Afri-Caribbean |
| Sub-total | 19 | | | |
| Homeworkers | 4 | Machinists | Female | Afri-Caribbean |
| | 6 | Machinists | Female | Greek Cypriot |
| | 10 | Machinists | Female | Indian |
| | 1 | Driver | Male | Indian |
| Sub-total | 21 | | | |
| Total | 40 | 30 machinists | 33 female<br>7 male | 18 Greek Cypriot<br>11 Indian<br>10 Afri-Caribbean<br>1 Irish |

*Source:* Panayiotopoulos (1993: 155)

of mobile enterprises. In a study on companies undergoing liquidations and insolvencies in the London garment industry, the majority of the companies in the women's wear sub-sector were Cypriot-owned (Panayiotopoulos 1996a: 452). The implications of such trends have not been missed by the United Kingdom Customs and Excise Department.

3. *Pinching* the designs of the latest fashion has become widespread among minority entrepreneurs in the London women's wear sector and this can be seen as a perverse reflection of the differentiation of the milieu. As manufacturers, many emergent ethnic contractor enterprises now use design input as a

negotiating lever with buyers. In legal terms, it affects all the cabbage sales, since along with the cloth, it is the manufacturer's designs (samples) which are put to use. 'Design-pinching' represents a considerable and strategic saving for emergent entrepreneurs. This sort of activity is also a source of friction, with undertones of potential and sometimes actual physical violence to persons and property.[4]

To many entrepreneurs, management simply consists of following the advice of the burgeoning ethnic accountants and 'liquidators'. Many rely on them, and their services are highly valued. Estimates of their earnings range between 10 and 20 per cent of the VAT payment that is avoided. Many accountants have become very wealthy and are major proxy beneficiaries of minority participation in the London garment industry. Many workers in the industry use pejorative terms, such as *karharia* (shark), to describe their activities (Panayiotopoulos 1993: 175–87).

Although under these conditions, 'marginalization' may be an accurate description of the precarious condition of many and possibly most minority contractors, one important dimension of the restructuring of the London fashionwear sector has been the *differentiation of minority enterprise* in terms of size, purpose and labour input: some are small family enterprises or firms critically dependent on family labour input, and others are large employers who recruit female labour from a wide range of ethnic groups (Panayiotopoulos 1996a).[5] Differentiation also represents a move away from the weak positions in production and distribution systems in which many minority entrepreneurs operate as contractors or franchisees or are disadvantaged in some way by distortions in the price mechanism by quasi-monopolistic suppliers. Emergent enterprises in the London garment industry have moved away from the contractor's role and taken on functions associated with the manufacturer's role. Some buyers who found it more convenient to deal directly with some of their larger ethnic CMT units have encouraged the repositioning of the entrepreneurs. This has been a strong feature of Cypriot participation in the London garment industry, where some firms broke out of the ranks of small contractors to become significant employers in local areas and have become manufacturers and operate as micro-multinational companies in international outward processing (Panayiotopoulos 1992b, 1996b, 2000).

It is in marketing that one observes the differentiation of ethnic minority enterprise in its most concentrated form. For many of the contractors, the issue of marketing is formally not relevant. Producing to order on specifications set by the manufacturer for a given buyer allows little formal scope for choice in market segment or product style. By and large they produce what they are given, and this tends to be in the quantity market. It is for this reason that contractors appear as the least capable of adapting to changes in the market environment. For many of them it is a struggle to maintain Cut, Make and Trim activities, and they resist, if they can, becoming mere Make and Trim assembly units of pre-cut work, since this way they cannot make any 'cabbage'. At the same time, however, there is considerable scope between being a CMT contractor and producing on one's 'own account'. Some large CMT units also produce independently of manufacturers, often with the cloth and design provided by the manufacturer, and this has been an important entry route into becoming an ethnic manufacturer (Panayiotopoulos 1993).

Emergent enterprises in the London garment industry have responded to changes in the garment market in different ways and the market segment where they operate has influenced this.

1. *Outsourcing*. Enterprises sensitive to price competition (quantity production) have resorted to a more expansive system of subcontracting to lower-cost production centres such as Cyprus, Asian-owned enterprises in the West Midlands and, increasingly, to Eastern Europe and North Africa. One case reputedly involves the employment of 2,000 workers in Morocco by one Greek Cypriot manufacturer. This firm was a major beneficiary of financial support by the London Borough of Haringey.[6]

2. *Developing new products*. Among enterprises in the women's fashionwear sector, where product differentiation is a more important factor in competition, branded style may command a considerable price mark-up. Efforts to engage in more value-adding production and marketing activities typically take the form of increased design and fashion input, and this has been an important factor in the differentiation of minority enterprise. One such enterprise (Ariella Fashions Ltd) is a leading United Kingdom women's fashionwear manufacturer, designer, exporter and producer on its own account of brand name goods. It has an extensive collection of agents and collaborators in most European countries and won the British Apparel Export Award for 1996 and the Queen's Award for Export Achievement in 1998.

3. *Direct sales*. Some CMT firms have circumvented the 'traditional' West End manufacturers who act as middlemen and now maintain direct relations with the buyers.

The differentiation of minority enterprise in the London garment industry, and thus the successful extension of marketing by some Cypriot entrepreneurs, is physically manifested in the Fonthill Road area of North London. It is a major centre for the United Kingdom women's fashionwear spot-market and includes approximately 150 ethnic manufacturers and wholesalers, most of whom are Cypriots. The success is also illustrated by the fact that a number of West End manufacturers, such as Frank Usher, have felt the need to establish a presence in the area. The establishment of the Fonthill Road Traders Association (FRTA) in 1993 brought together the manufacturers and property owners of the Road, and the FRTA acts as their representative in dealings with the local authority (the Borough of Islington), national government and business support agencies. The officers of the FRTA are the wealthiest and most powerful among the Cypriot entrepreneurs. Two of them are listed among the United Kingdom Top 500 wealthiest individuals, substantially as the result of their ownership of most of the property on the Road.[7] The ability of a significant layer of ethnic manufacturers to accumulate great wealth, engage in expansive outward processing, maintain direct relations with buyers and make significant additions to design input suggests a scope for mobility within the sector and illustrates the considerable extent to which emergent enterprises have differentiated themselves from the ranks of co-ethnic CMT contractors.

## Central Government Policies: Support and Repression

The relationship between the central government and its policies and regulations has general and specific implications for minority entrepreneurs in the London garment industry at both regional and the local level. Central government policies encompass industrial policy, support for the small firm and ethnic entrepreneurship, controlling activities in the sphere of working conditions, controlling activities by tax and national insurance officers, and immigration policies and control.[8]

In the 1960s and 1970s, the central government was actively involved in rationalizing the textile and garment industry, resulting in tremendous job losses in the larger textile mills in the Midlands and northern Britain. In the 1980s, the central government saw the textile and garment manufacturing industries as 'sunset industries' and aimed at managing rather than reversing the industrial decline (Taplin and Winterton 1996; Totterdill and Zeitlin 1989). These top-down policy assumptions were, however, challenged by local developments which witnessed a revival in the role and vitality of some garment manufacturers. This revival was caused in part by a demand for higher-value fashion, style, quality and quick response. In the 1990s, regeneration policies did begin to have a trickle-down effect on some of the emergent inner-city garment firms in the boroughs of East and North London. One result was that the Department of Trade and Industry (DTI) has recently devoted more attention to the garment industry, focusing on the promotion of fashion content and greater interaction between producers and suppliers in the context of local networks linking buyers and manufacturers.

Support for the small-firm sector has been a characteristic policy feature in the United Kingdom over the last two decades, and it is an important element of continuity in the current policy. Given that most minority entrepreneurs are in the small-scale sector and in inner-city centres characterized by high levels of deprivation, in theory they became highly relevant to policy-making. Although of variable quality, the support for small firms on the part of the central government has been extensive and has included the Loan Guarantee Scheme, the Enterprise Allowance Scheme, grants provided under Local Enterprise Agency schemes, grants for training under the Training for Enterprise Scheme, funds provided through Regional Enterprise Units, and inner-city employment-related initiatives such as Urban Aid and, subsequently, Urban Challenge.[9] These initiatives might not all have directly stimulated the garment industry, but they clearly indicated a climate where small business initiatives were promoted, or at least treated in a lenient way as far as government regulations were concerned. Other policies favouring small firms have included budgetary measures such as lowering the VAT threshold and exempting small firms (twenty-five workers or less) from certain regulation and reporting responsibilities. For example, firms employing fewer than ten workers were exempted from the requirement to reserve jobs (for up to twenty-nine weeks) for women workers returning after childbirth. Given the role of small firms and the fact that women constitute the bulk of the labour force, these measures are particularly relevant to the garment industry. Another important area of change in the institutional environment has been the active promotion by the central government of small business ownership and self-employment on the part of ethnic and racial minorities in the inner-city areas of the United Kingdom. In fact the advisability of promoting entrepreneurship as an antidote to urban racial deprivation was the main conclusion drawn by the government inquiry chaired by Lord Scarman to investigate the Brixton riots in 1981, which were sparked by intense policing in the Brixton area of South London.

In the past two decades there has been little government enthusiasm for controlling and regulating businesses. In the Thatcher era, it was politically too embarrassing to tamper with health and safety regulations. The government simply left them in place and underfunded the Inspectorate. At one stage only about twenty civil servants were available to control the health and safety of the whole of Britain. According to an informant, on average a firm could expect to be visited by the Factory Inspectorate once ever twenty-one years.

The failure to enforce the rules and the undermining of the regulatory services were widespread and the garment industry was no exception. There were, however, exceptions such as the Inland Revenue and the National Insurance Scheme. They were both having a hard time collecting taxes from the London garment industry, and in the mid-1990s the Inland Revenue set up a Special Compliance Unit targeting the garment industry. It met with little success. In many cases, the workers could not be traced. Most orders are paid in cash. The owner might be a straw man, or he might leave with the money. The properties and machinery are generally rented, which offers the Inland Revenue little redress. According to an official of a London local authority, a firm could only expect a controlling NI officer to come by once every four to five years.

The Customs and Excise Department has created special surveillance units targeting the North and East London garment industry. According to some informants, the Customs and Excise Department is quite actively pursuing VAT money. It seems rather easy, though, for employers to use double-entry bookkeeping – one system for the Customs and Excise Department, and one for the National Insurance Agency and Inland Revenue.

The scale of the conflict was illustrated by a raid by Customs and Excise officers on premises in the Dalston and Stoke Newington areas of Hackney in East London, which resulted in forty-four people being charged with Value Added Tax evasion in the region of £2–3m. All the people charged were Turkish Cypriot entrepreneurs in the garment industry. 'Operation Anchorage' involved 300 officers who raided a total of forty-nine premises. Among those charged were a number of accountants. The charges related to the fraudulent preparation of VAT invoices. The invoices are used to reclaim VAT on purchases, matching payments made on the basis of sales.[10]

Immigration policies and checks have influenced the labour supply and demand and periodically contributed to skill shortages (see Lloyd 1996). British immigration policy is generally typified by intensive checks at the border, but until recently relatively moderate checks throughout the country. In 'fishing' for undocumented aliens there is the risk of focusing on 'foreign' or 'black' people, and that is exactly what is forbidden in Britain by the Race Relations Act (1976). This is why undocumented workers generally run little risk of being caught by the authorities. In the mid-1990s, however, 'illegality' became a more politicized issue in British politics. Rules were applied with greater vigour and checks were intensified. Now and then, garment firms or community houses were raided. Local government officials do not generally support raids by the Immigration Department. However, the raids do not require the consent of the local government. In boroughs with numerous residents of diverse ethnic origin (such as in Hackney and Haringey), raids on undocumented aliens are opposed by the local community, which leads to social and political agitation. Several informants said this opposition discourages the Immigration Department from raiding in Hackney, a borough with a tradition of solidarity among the various ethnic groups. Also, Hackney's Metropolitan Police do not seem eager to co-operate in raids on illegal immigrants, partly because they have to deal with the ethnic communities and the other residents on a daily basis.

Central government policies reflect a supportive climate and lenient treatment of the garment industry, but there has recently been a more repressive approach by tax and immigration officers. Periodic joint raids by the Customs and Excise Department and the Home Office ('fishing' for illegal asylum seekers and refugees) signify an intensified repression (Panayiotopoulos 1993).

## Local Government Economic Support

The relationship between entrepreneurs and the official agencies involves a mutual 'understanding' of the importance of small business activities, but it also involves a conflict over the avoidance of taxation and the illegal status of the workers involved. Relations with the local government have become more supportive. The 1980s and 1990s were characterized by a discernible shift in policy thinking towards ethnic minority firms in the inner-city areas of London. It was strong feature of a number of Labour-controlled London boroughs (Haringey, Hackney) and in the Greater London Council (GLC). Entrepreneurs in the garment industry came to be seen by policy-makers as a useful vehicle for the promotion of desirable social objectives ranging from employment creation to racial equality. This was partly driven by the growing role of garment sector employment in the face of even more severe contraction in other sectors. It was also a reflection of the realignment of local Labour Party politics, with minorities becoming more prominent, resulting in increased political representation.[11] It was in this context that Cypriot and other ethnic minority entrepreneurs began to be seen in a different light by the planning authorities. In certain cases, they were major beneficiaries of local government economic support. The changed institutional relationships between the local government and minority entrepreneurs witnessed important practical changes in the garment industry, which included decriminalizing homeworking and easing planning regulations on 'change of use' of buildings (Panayiotopoulos 1992a). These changes are illustrated in a summary of sympathetic policy-making by the GLC and the London boroughs of Hackney and Haringey.

### The Greater London Council

The Greater London Council was a London-wide unitary local authority that became a centre of opposition to the Thatcher administration under Ken Livingstone's leadership. In a short time span (1981–1986) the GLC, and its industrial arm the Greater London Enterprise Board (GLEB), conducted a number of important studies for research and policy purposes, such as London Industrial Strategy in 1984. The growth of mass unemployment during the 1980s was the primary policy concern and the GLC aimed to create well-paid employment, 'restructuring for labour', as an alternative to low-wage strategies. The garment industry was a key sector where 'restructuring for labour' could be realized. In exchange for financial support, conditions were stipulated for the participating firms. They had to guarantee the employment of women and ethnic minorities, trade unions' right of access, and conformity to certain minimum social standards.

There was a consensus at the GLC on the necessity to fight unemployment, but not about how 'restructuring for labour' was to be realized. There were two points of dispute on strategy. The first concerned whether individual firms should be directly supported or whether support should entail improvements in the collective infrastructure. Jonathan Zeitlin and Michael Best (see Best 1990: 203–26) argued that the London contract garment industry was the place to realize the concept of 'flexible specialization', since they viewed the branch as a conglomerate of small flexible firms, which only lacked supporting facilities related to product development, technology innovation, and marketing. As a result, there was a policy emphasis on the collective provisioning of inputs and the creation of intermediary structures, such as Fashion Centres, to provide common marketing and technological development, such as Computer-Aided Design and Computer-Aided Manufacturing technologies (CAD/CAM). These ideas on flexible specialization won the GLC policy battle.

A second controversy within the GLC concerned the size of the firms to be supported. Initially the GLC advocated support for larger firms since they were more likely to pay higher wages. Others saw this as 'racist', since it excluded participation by ethnic and racial minorities which are concentrated in the small enterprises. The policy officially focused on the larger firms, but in practice small firms turned out to be the beneficiaries. This controversy further legitimized promoting small firms and flexible specialization as anti-racist policy measures and provided a platform for the collective services to the sector as a whole, with special attention for ethnic firms and co-operatives.

Advocates of flexible specialization saw the growing role of small enterprises in the advanced industrial economies as representing an 'epochal' transition[12] in industrial policy and organization, characterized by the growth of 'small batch' production and need for a more 'skilled' or 'flexible' labour force (Piore and Sabel 1984; Sabel and Zeitlin 1985). Hirst and Zeitlin (1989) suggest that as production runs became shorter and style changes more frequent in the London garment industry, even the larger firms were forced to encourage machinists to become more proficient and flexible at a wide range of sewing operations. Mitter (1992: 5–6) draws similar conclusions and argues that flexible specialization leads to 'enhanced use of existing skills of women operatives'. In the model of the 'progressive' industrial district, these analyses see a functional relationship between relatively independent producers and the local government, within which the property rights of small capital are limited by obligations to the workforce and community. This had considerable influence on radical policy-makers in London (see Greater London Council 1985; Mackintosh and Wainwright 1987; Murray 1987: 87–112; Zeitlin 1992b).

For various reasons, actually putting the abundant and enthusiastic ideas of the GLC into effect turned out to be barely plausible. In the first place, there was the informal nature of the garment industry. As the GLC noted, the first barrier encountered by GLEB was frequently 'the unwillingness of most owners of London garment firms to give any role in the firm to the workforce or the local authority, in many cases because the firm was breaking the law' (see Greater London Council 1985: 135).[13] Secondly, the enthusiastic ideas were voluntarist in nature and tended to underestimate the extent to which garment industry dynamics primarily conform to the international division of labour and capital, leaving a limited scope for local government intervention. Thirdly, critics suggest that GLC officials failed to understand the social embeddedness of the industry sufficiently. GLC officials generally had good contact with trade union officials, but not much with the workers in the garment firms. In the fourth place, the GLC was short lived. Once the Livingstone Council took office Thatcher saw it as her personal mission to break its power. In 1984 she announced its abolition, and actually effectuated it in 1986. During the 1984–1986 period, the GLC 'muddled through' as regards the London garment industry; firms were supported, official campaigns were organized to stimulate 'good employers' to pay 'fair wages', stimulate good working conditions, and try and prevent racial and gender discrimination. Significantly, the GLC introduced subsidized transport for Londoners. Industrial policy, however, made little impact on the structural problems in the garment industry. When the GLC was abolished in 1986 London became the only capital in the Western world directly governed by the national government, and this continued to be the case until quite recently.[14]

## Hackney

The GLC did not achieve much as far as the regional London garment industry was concerned, but the policy experience in the boroughs of Hackney and Haringey was more complex. In Hackney, the local government has always been involved in the 'ups' and 'downs' of the garment industry. In the 1960s, Hackney's garment industry employed 30,000 people, but by the mid-1990s only about 3,000–4,000 were employed in the branch. This decrease was a common feature of manufacturing industries in general. In the 1980s and 1990s Hackney's unemployment rate was 20 per cent. Faced with mushrooming unemployment, the local authorities began to look more seriously at ways to protect employment in the local industry. In the 1980s, Hackney's local authorities were frustrated by the central government view of the garment branch as a 'sunset industry' and its failure to support the remainder of the industry. Town Hall officials welcomed the GLC ideas regarding the garment industry, but criticized the fact that the policy initiatives were barely implemented.

The borough of Hackney did take three steps in the mid-1980s. Firstly, a Group Training Association was set up as a joint project of the Boroughs of Haringey, Hackney and Islington to improve the workers' skills. This project continued for three years and was terminated because the trained employees used their skills to move from one employer to another in an effort to earn higher wages. This is not exactly what employers had hoped for. A second step pertained to the Hackney Fashion Centre, a kind of expertise centre that provided showroom facilities with changing collections. Due to administrative shortcomings and financial deficits, the Fashion Centre was closed down in 1987 (Panayiotopoulos 1992a). A third step involved a financial assistance programme in the early 1980s, in which Hackney Council supported twenty-five firms in the garment industry for a four-to five-year period.

During the second half of the 1980s, the steps the Hackney Council took regarding the contract garment industry came to a dead end and the branch retained its sweatshop image. After no local government intervention for almost a decade, in the mid-1990s the garment sector became the focus of more attention in the context of urban regeneration politics. The urban regeneration steps included developing a garment manufacturing zone in Dalston to promote flexible special-ization, reinforcing the links between chain stores such as M&S or Mothercare and the local garment manufacturers, and promoting the local manufacturing activities on the Broadway Market.

Although it is hard to evaluate, the impact of Hackney's support seems to be rather limited. The small number of steps, the limited financial means, serious doubts about the future of the industry, and the organizational problems in the sector add to this. Having said that, it is not inconceivable that the rather lenient approach by the central government's law-enforcing agencies until the mid-1990s was more relevant to facilitating the economic dynamics in the local economy than the limited support by the Labour-led local government.

## Haringey

In the neighbouring borough of Haringey, other steps were taken in the garment industry by the Labour-led Council. One was a campaign to register homeworkers and thus advance their rights and improve their situation. This began as an effort by Cypriot community activists, some of whom went on to become Labour coun-cillors in Haringey. Two major problems were addressed by this campaign. Firstly, as the community activists were drawn closer to the Council they became more distanced from the community. Secondly, as soon as homeworkers began to register the employers began to look for other homeworkers and the Council could do little to stop this. What the Council did achieve, however, was to decriminalize the use of industrial sewing machines during certain times of day and to stop taking legal action being taken against non-compliers.

The Haringey Council also supported a major property development that combined various activities in the sphere of garment manufacturing. The Greek

Cypriot owner of the building closely co-operated with the Haringey Council, which provided considerable grants and was a beneficiary of money from the Urban Regeneration Programme. The building consisted of a supply chain of fourteen units, with joint facilities for information technology, pressing services, catering facilities, and so forth. The London Borough of Haringey Economic Development Unit (EDU) saw the intervention as a 'prime example' of how to use the Urban Aid Fund efficiently. It resulted in the saving of sixty-seven jobs and the creation of another 186 (Panayiotopoulos 1992a: 57). This firm accounted for 57 per cent of the entire EDU allocation for one financial year and made up 27 per cent of all the floor space developed in the borough during a three-year period. The funds amounted to 59 per cent of all the funds allocated for Ethnic Minority Enterprise (EME). They single-handedly accounted for all the EDU grant support given to firms from the Cypriot community (Panayiotopoulos 1992a: 57–8). The support was conditional on the implementation of, or at least a willingness to implement, the Council's 'Good Employers' Charter', which covered a comprehensive range of policies.[15] One of the conditions set by the local government was that the trade unions would get access. However, the involvement of the National Union of Tailors and Garments Workers (NUTGW) was originally accepted and subsequently rejected, leading to the discontinuation of the subsidy (Mavrou 1994). In the meantime, the owner of the firm accumulated considerable assets.

It was the growth and persistence of unemployment that forced Haringey Council to devote serious attention to the existing garment firms. Council officials estimate that within its boundaries, 20 per cent of the manufacturing activities take place in garment firms. In Tottenham, in the eastern part of Haringey, the unemployment rate was one of the highest in Britain and included 20 per cent of the labour force in the late 1990s. Tottenham is one of the areas where garment firms are concentrated. Local officials don't know how many people work in the industry, but they highly value employment in the informal economy because they estimate that many of the people working here would find it difficult to get jobs elsewhere. The policy aim is to preserve jobs, despite criticism of the low pay and the precarious nature of employment in the industry.

The local support in Haringey seemed to have a modest impact; with a relatively large amount of regeneration money, a considerable clothing business had been developed. However, in evaluating the local support, one needs to relate this 'success' to the amount of money spent, to the distribution pattern of the financial support, and to the ideological aspirations of the officials involved (e.g. trade union involvement). In these perspectives, we consider its success rather limited. We think that in the borough of Haringey, as in the borough of Hackney, the economic dynamics in the clothing business as a whole were more facilitated by the reluctant central government enforcement policies until the mid-1990s than the support provided by the local government.

## Preservation of Jobs in the Community

It is interesting how local officials deal nowadays with the informality of the firms. They generally stress the importance of preserving jobs. And their support is not restricted to formal businesses. Haringey Town Hall does not condemn home-working, since it provides 'members of the community' with an income. They don't generally see it as their task to check whether CMT units pay their taxes and social benefit premiums. It is more a matter for the National Insurance, the Inland Revenue and the Customs and Excise Department (controlling agency on Value Added Tax) and other central government agencies. No licence is required for running a manufacturing firm, so it is not of any interest to local officials. Most local officials also argue that British immigration law fails to take sufficiently into account matters of family reunion and family formation, and this results in many immigrants remaining illegal 'aliens', sometimes for decades. Local officials do not denounce undocumented residence; the problem is the exploitation of undocumented workers who are threatened with deportation. For local officials, 'informality' mostly refers to social abuses, low pay and poor working conditions. They criticize recent central government efforts to discourage illegal residence, because such efforts only drive people further underground. They argue that recent asylum legislation in the United Kingdom has made this even worse. Officials suggest that this is exactly what happened to the Kurdish refugees in North and East London. They are concerned that the garment sector is becoming an even more 'cash-in-hand' economy, and central immigration checks have contributed to driving enterprise further underground.

## Concluding Remarks

From the 1950s onwards participation by immigrant and second-generation entrepreneurs in the London garment industry has contained powerful elements of continuity and change. Most of them continue to crowd the small-scale sector, typically as CMT contractors in East and North London. For many, life is precarious and they are constantly subject to changes in the marketplace that many of them are ill-equipped to respond to. For many, 'being chased' by the VAT Department and other creditors is a recurrent experience. At the same time, there are important changes in the minority participation between and within diverse ethnic groups and in how they relate to particular sectors of the garment industry. This chapter notes that ethnic minority enterprise is far more diverse than is generally assumed in terms of scale as well as purpose. One recent report on minority enterprise in the United Kingdom refers to a situation where most entrepreneurs from a variety of ethnic backgrounds have to struggle and work very long hours just to survive. At the same time, a significant proportion are trying to 'break-out' of the ethnic economy and enter the economic mainstream (Ram and Jones 1998; see also Poutziouris 1999). The experience of emergent ethnic enterprises in the London garment industry would give substance to this observation. Typically, 'breaking out' represents a move away from the ranks of the numerous CMT contractors towards the ranks of the fewer manufacturers. A much smaller number have become owners of considerable property. This process is not clear (since it is in formation) but has definitely been experienced by Cypriot entrepreneurs in the London garment industry. There is considerable variation within ethnic minority garment enterprise, and this differentiation suggests that it would be unwise to make any generalizations for research and policy purposes about an 'essential' ethnic enterprise, typically in the form of the 'family firm'. There is a need to consider the implications of differentiation on how diverse entrepreneurs manage their enterprises and how they relate to the market and institutional environment in which they have to operate in.

The regulatory framework is sensitively linked to the process of differentiation. One dimension is the widely held view among contractors that 'they' (the regulatory authorities) 'pick on the little people'. A reverse political dimension of differentiation is that emergent manufacturers who are in a stronger economic position, more integrated in the local host society and embedded in community organizations, are better placed to benefit from local and central government support (see also Ram 1998). A number of entrepreneurs have shown strong capacities for political brokerage. Frequently it is the most successful of the entrepreneurs who act as community representatives and intermediaries with policy-makers. The reasons for this are complex and reflect on the restructuring of the garment industry, the economic power of the entrepreneurs, the nature of local economies and policy-makers themselves.[16] One revealing consequence of the repositioning of a significant section of entrepreneurs from the ranks of contractors in the London garment industry is that a significant group has become an important focus for local government support and is now well placed to benefit from mainstream business support agencies.[17] The experience suggests that differentiation is a critical factor in reshaping institutional relations and informs the selectivity of the institutional response, be it promotion or repression, 'soft' or 'strong' state action. This variation indicates an important element of change in the London garment industry.

It is surprising that most research tends to ignore this variation in the institutional framework, i.e. the role of the politico-regulatory framework. At best it represents the government as unfamiliar with the needs of minority enterprises or as a repressive agent somewhere in the background. In our account, we suggest that there are important differences between the central government support rhetoric and the concrete support provided by local authorities such as the GLC and the boroughs of Hackney and Haringey. In the beginning of the 1980s, these local authorities adopted a combination of pragmatic and ideological attitudes towards the employment potential of local garment enterprises. The decriminalization of homeworking in Haringey and the efforts concerning trade union involvement were important dimensions of the ideological attitude. In both Haringey and Hackney, urban regeneration funds were targeted towards entrepreneurs with the express purpose of generating employment. Among some policy-makers, the promotion of ethnic enterprise was seen as an example of ethnic empowerment. The GLC saw the promotion of minority enterprise as an anti-racist policy measure. This ideological position underpinned and legitimized the more pragmatic approaches. In the second half of the 1990s, local government approaches, in the sense of job preservation, had a chiefly pragmatic orientation. The pragmatic and ideological approaches both found ready-made partners in the upwardly mobile Cypriot and other minority entrepreneurs in higher tiers of the industry. It was this relationship more than any other which explained the local variation.

We observe that after a relatively *laissez-faire* period in the 1980s and early 1990s, in the mid-1990s checks and raids by immigration and tax officers were intensified. Local government officials however still stress the viability and growth potential of the London garment industry, and do not restrict their support to completely formal businesses because strict requirements could lead to unemployment or underground activity.

The potential and limits of local intervention for changing the opportunity structure of minority enterprises in the London garment industry, and by implication empowering the ethnic communities, are debatable. We have argued that a significant number of entrepreneurs have moved up in the industry, some with local support. At the same time, we have argued that employment changes in the garment industry are primarily driven by multinational sourcing policies and global competition. The current changes in Marks & Spencer's sourcing policy are a sobering example. These changes are influenced by, but not subject to, local variation. In fact the ability of any local authority to control key variables to produce the desired policy results is restricted by the mobility of the entrepreneurs. It is not unusual for entrepreneurs to receive support in one borough and then relocate to another borough, or, in the case of the more successful, to other countries. This relationship between the relatively mobile enterprises and the fixed local authorities is indicative of severe local planning limitations. Perhaps the greatest question pertains to the extent to which support for the entrepreneurs amounts to support for the ethnic communities as a whole. This is a matter requiring further research at the enterprise level as well as the local economy level. Increased political representation, within which successful entrepreneurs appear as the public face of the ethnic communities, needs to be informed by the unwritten histories of immigrant women machinists, second-generation youth, and other sections of the ethnic communities.

## Notes

1. There are few studies of the previous occupations of immigrants during the 1950s, but one study of Cypriot immigrants reveals that many were skilled manual workers (tailors, dressmakers, shoemakers, builders, carpenters, blacksmiths, mechanics) and over 40 per cent of all the immigrants who specified a previous occupation had these skills (Panayiotopoulos 1990: 290–1). This contrasted sharply with the decline of manual skills among workers in the advanced capitalist economies of Western Europe during the post-war boom as was reflected in a historical decline in small enterprises and a reduction in the number of people working for their 'own account' (i.e. the classical self-employed) (see Boissevain 1984).

2. Manufacturers estimated that during 1999, 40,000 jobs were lost in the textile and garment industry in the United Kingdom, and it was estimated that another 30,000 jobs were lost in 2000 (see 'Textile sector expected to shed 70,000 staff in two years', *Financial Times*, 18 May 2000). Union sources estimate that more than 20,000 jobs have been lost in the industry as the result of the change in M&S sourcing policy alone (see Peter Booth, National Secretary, Transport and General Workers Union quoted from the *Observer*, 'Final Cut', 13 September 1998).

3. According to research carried out by the Great Universal Stores (GUS) retail group, nearly 4,000 company directors of United Kingdom garment companies (four times more than was previously thought) have been associated with ten or more failed companies. Many deliberately closed down their companies to avoid paying debts and then set up new ones. Nearly half the 'serial' failures (i.e. with two or more failures) lived in London and the south-east region (see '4,000 directors thought to be serial failures', *Financial Times*, 28 October 1998).

4. The United Kingdom Fashion Design Protection Association (FDPA) was established by London Cypriot garment manufacturers and has campaigned successfully for the creation of special legislation to cover copyright infringement (i.e. 'design pinching'). There are now new statutory guidelines for company directors to bar 'repeat' liquidations which were informed by trends in the industry.

5. Much of the research views minority enterprise as a precarious response to discrimination in the segmented labour market and as a collective survival mechanism in the face of ethnic and racial disadvantage (see Anthias 1992; Barret *et al.* 1996; Kabeer 1994; Ladbury 1984; Mitter 1986; Shaikh 1995).

6. Personal communication, Manos Stellakis, London School of Economics, 25 November 1996.

7. Kyriakos Tsoupras, 'Fonthill Road', *Parikiaki Haravghi*, 29 August 1996.

8.  The information in this section on central government policies and in the subsequent sections on local government policies is partly based on the field-work carried out in the autumn of 1997 by Marja Dreef in the context of the preparation of a Ph.D. study about the political and administrative developments in the garment industry in Amsterdam and London over the period 1980–1997.

9.  For a detailed assessment of some of these measures (which characterized the Thatcher years), see UK Department of Employment/Training Commission (1988) (no ethnic breakdown is given).

10. 'Customs V.A.T. raids lead to 44 arrests', *Financial Times*, 1 March 1990.

11. The Cypriot community in the borough of Haringey, where it is most concentrated, makes up about a fifth of the borough electoral register. Bernie Grant was the Leader of Haringey Council before he became the first Member of Parliament of African origin (for Tottenham, North London). The Cypriot community were an important part of a Rainbow Coalition-type of political mobilization which propelled Grant to national prominence and provided a significant challenge to the traditional right-wing leadership of the North London Labour Party during the 1980s. Bernie Grant died in April 2000 and his funeral was attended by many members of the community. It is of note that during the May 1998 local government elections, three Cypriots stood as Labour Party candidates in Haringey and another six in neighbouring Enfield (*Parikiaki Haravghi*, 7 May 1998).

12. Critics of flexible specialization, however, suggest that the analyses indicate an oversimplified dichotomy between forms of production, which fails to recognize diverse and contingent labour processes, how they may change over time, and how they are shaped and reshaped by a continuum of transactions involving local, global and sectoral variables. Research drawing from the experiences of restructuring in the southern European and London garment industry uses 'intermediary labour regimes' as a term to describe a functional relationship between 'fordism' and small units of production. One observation made in these studies is that different forms of production can co-exist within the same profit centre, and this suggests something less than an 'epochal' industrial transition (see Lambrianidis 1995; Panayiotopoulos 1992a,b, 1996b; Simmons and Kalantaridis 1994, 1995; see also Barlow and Winterton 1996; Das and Panayiotopoulos 1996; Rainnie 1991).

13. For a critical review of the policy effort, see Geddes (1988) and Gough (1986).

14. Following the Labour election victory in May 1997, London witnessed a reconstituted authority, i.e. the Greater London Assembly and an elected Mayor (both with limited powers). Ken Livingstone, the old Labour leader of the GLC, was forced to stand as an independent candidate for the Mayorship and won, mainly because of his opposition to the privatization of the London

Underground and because many Londoners feel an affection towards the GLC for standing up (in limited ways) to Margaret Thatcher.

15. These included compliance with legislation relevant to fair wages, trade union representation, training and equal opportunities. In relation to homeworking, the code asked that employers comply with the Council's Homeworking Code of Practice and to 'comply with Section 133 of the Factories Act 1961 which requires lists of homeworkers to be kept and provided to the Factory Inspector and the Council' (Panayiotopoulos 1992a: 89–91).

16. Frequently driven by what Barret *et al*. (1996: 803) refer to as 'the customary uncritical acceptance of entrepreneurship as a prescriptive remedy, a kind of policy Prozac for those disadvantaged by racism'.

17. Support agencies are driven by the need to produce results and meet competitive and self-financing criteria. The targeting of existing minority enterprises trying to break out of the ethnic niche offers a potentially higher-yield and lower-risk area for this kind of investment. This approach of 'wagering on the strong' (or those breaking out – see Ram and Jones 1998) may well conflict with equity objectives aimed to address issues related to gender, racial and other forms of social exclusion that place more emphasis on start-up enterprises among groups under-represented in the small enterprise sector.

# −4−

# West Midlands: Still Managing to Survive
*Monder Ram, Bob Jerrard* and
*Joy Husband*

## Introduction

During the 1980s, the decline of garment manufacturing in Britain was such that it began to be viewed as a 'sunset industry' (Davenport *et al.* 1986). Between the mid-1970s and the early 1980s, employment in the clothing industry fell by a third to less than 200,000, and the previously stable British market with its well-established characteristics of mass production, predictable design and long production runs became increasingly vulnerable to newly industrializing countries such as Hong Kong. Despite the potential threat from other sources, the British clothing industry managed to survive on a significant scale (Phizacklea 1990). Explanations for the industry's apparent resilience have been discussed at length (Piore and Sabel 1984; Taplin and Winterton 1991; Totterdill and Zeitlin 1989). They range from the view of 'flexible specialization' inspired by Piore and Sabel to the more pessimistic picture of labour intensification in sweatshops (Hoel 1982; Mitter 1986). Although these seemingly disparate approaches are not necessarily contradictory and can exist in the same enterprise (Taplin and Winterton 1991), there is little doubt that the presence of ethnic minorities in the clothing industry has played an important role in maintaining the viability of the industry nationwide. Indeed, one commentator goes so far as to say 'the survival of fashionwear production in Britain in the 1980s would not have been possible on such a scale without the presence of ethnic minority entrepreneurs and labour as producers in this sector' (Phizacklea 1990: 11).

This chapter focuses on the dynamics of one of the most significant areas of ethnic minority garment manufacturing in Britain: the West Midlands clothing sector. A number of issues are explored. How and why did Asians from the Indian sub-continent and East Africa (business owners and entrepreneurs) enter the garment trade in such numbers? An assessment of marketing relationships is provided which outlines the particular niche that many local clothing firms occupy and how this shapes their working practices. The nature of the work relations is examined, and the institutional context of the clothing firms in the West Midlands is discussed.

In structuring the discussion of Asian garment manufacturers this way, immigrant entrepreneurship is viewed in its social, economic and institutional context rather than reduced to an 'ethno-cultural' phenomenon (Kloosterman *et al.* 1999).

## History of Developments within the Industry

Before the mid-1970s, clothing manufacturing was not regarded as a significant part of the West Midlands industry. In 1966, only 7,100 people were employed in the sector of a total industrial labour force of 820,000 (Leigh and North 1983). Clothing manufacturing was concentrated in large established firms producing men's outerwear and waterproof garments. These firms fell prey to competition stimulated by high sterling exchange rates, which encouraged cheap imports into Britain. This trend was exacerbated by the increasing capacity of newly indus-trialized countries such as Hong Kong to export into the region, and the established clothing firms in the West Midlands struggled to remain competitive in the face of these pressures (Ram 1994). A spate of closures ensued, resulting in a fall in employment during the first half of the 1970s of 7.3 per cent to less than 6,500 workers (Hayden 1992).

Since the mid-1970s, however, there has been a marked increase in clothing-sector employment due to the emergence of new firms manufacturing untailored garments at the lower end of the market (Hayden 1992). These predominantly small Asian-owned companies have often developed flexible and relatively low-cost production facilities. This in turn has led to a concentration on lower volume and untailored products such as work clothing and jeans, women's light outerwear and weatherproof outerwear. Within the last product area, there seems to be a concentration on padded jackets, sports and leisure clothing and casual wear, rather than tailored raincoats and overcoats. These products typically involve short run lengths and relatively simple production methods.

The area of general untailored outerwear is thought to account for about 500 mainly small firms in the West Midlands area, although the situation is unclear given the existence of many unregistered workshops and the prevalence of home-working. The main concentrations (in decreasing order of importance) are in inner Birmingham, Smethwick, Coventry, Wolverhampton, West Bromwich and Walsall (WMLPU 1991). In comparison, a maximum of fifty older firms throughout the region are producing tailored garments and more formal outerwear. It is estimated that there are 319 clothing firms in Birmingham, and 53 per cent of them are con-centrated in the same district (Jackson 1996). They tend to be small to medium-size operations with fifteen to twenty employees, headed by a single entrepreneur (Grice 1995). Most of these firms have a turnover of less than £250,000 (Jackson 1996).

The total number of workers now employed in the West Midlands clothing industry is difficult to establish with any precision, given the prevalence of 'informal' working practices, but it is estimated to be between 20,000 and 30,000 workers (AEKTA 1995–1996; WMLPU 1991). The situation is further complicated by the lack of accurate records on the incidence of homeworking, which is regarded in the industry to be very significant (Jackson 1996). One estimate suggests that for every registered employee there are two unregistered homeworkers (Handsworth Technical College 1984a).

## The Labour Market Context

Establishing small garment manufacturing businesses as a means of coping with an inauspicious opportunity structure appears to be a recurring pattern and has been noted in many studies of Asian self-employment (Aldrich *et al.* 1981, 1982 and 1984; Jones 1981; Jones *et al.* 1989 and 1992; Mullins 1979; Ram 1992; Robinson and Flintoff 1982). Employers in Ram's (1994) study of Asian clothing manufacturers emphasized the importance of the social and economic climate in explaining their decision to enter the clothing industry. Self-employment was viewed as one of the few means of earning a decent living; they had a choice between menial factory work or setting up a business. Few had any real experience managing or running a business. They tended to be former machinists or factory workers who turned to clothing because it was cheap, the purchase of a few machines being sufficient to get the venture off the ground.

While the majority of Asian entrepreneurs are male, most of the workers at West Midlands clothing firms are women who are employed as machinists and are generally regarded as unskilled or semi-skilled workers. Ram (1994) found that 243 out of a total of 289 workers at the firms he investigated were women. Moreover, 276 of these employees were of Asian ethnic origin and 246 were actually born in India. Explanations for Asian women's participation in the garment industry sometimes stress the role of this type of labour as an important source of 'competitive advantage' (Ward 1991). According to this view, co-ethnic and familial ties are drawn upon to provide the firm with a steady supply of 'reliable' labour (Werbner 1984). Although this is undoubtedly important, Phizacklea (1990) contends that the position of minority women in clothing firms needs to be assessed within the broader context of racism and sexism. Racism and sexism were enshrined in British immigration legislation. The Commonwealth Immigrants Act of 1962, designed to restrict the number of black people entering the United Kingdom, meant that most minority women (particularly Asian women) entered after that date either as 'family' women or on a voucher sponsored by a relative in business. Hence, rather than recognizing women as free workers, 'British immigration law has been framed on the assumption that women are the chattels of men' (Phizacklea 1990: 96). This situation did not change until 1988. Before that date, the British legal system did not recognize female immigrants' rights, and treated them merely as dependants of men. Dependency has therefore been reinforced by laws that have helped perpetuate cultural stereotypes of Asian women as weak and passive, thereby lessening their chances in the general employment market.

Asian women's involvement in the clothing industry was also boosted by the lack of opportunity in the wider labour market. Studies on minority-owned garment firms (Mitter 1986; Phizacklea 1990), and West Midlands clothing manufacturers in particular (Ahmed 1990; Hoel 1982; Leigh and North 1983; Ram 1994) high-light the importance of the adverse opportunity structure in explaining the role of Asian women in these settings. These studies note that workers' employment choices were severely constrained. For many, the only option seemed to be to work at Asian-owned clothing companies. Moreover, clothing employers wanted Asian (i.e. cheap) labour, and workers turning to these companies did not have to go through interviews or other formal recruitment procedures (Jackson 1996; Ram 1994).

From this discussion, it is clear that the Asian domination of the clothing niche in the West Midlands can be explained by the limited opportunities in the wider labour market, the availability of family and co-ethnic labour, and legislation that could be exploited to channel women into poorly paid work. However, other minority groups, notably African-Caribbeans, have also been faced with a lack of economic opportunity, so how can their absence from the clothing sector be explained? This question touches upon the broader issue of the 'African–Caribbean–Asian' divide, which has been addressed at length in the British context (Basu 1991; Ram and Jones 1998; Reeves and Ward 1984) and the United States (Bailey 1987; Sanders and Nee 1987). Without necessarily going into the details of these debates, a number of factors can be advanced to explain the limited involvement of African-Caribbeans in the West Midlands clothing sector. First, many of the African-Caribbeans who migrated to Britain were originally from a working-class background, and were effectively used as a 'replacement workforce' (Basu 1991: 102). Asian migrants to Britain appeared to have a broader socio-economic profile, and therefore greater access to class resources. Second, African-Caribbeans gravi-tated towards public sector employment, while Asians were able to establish a presence in small-scale economic activities; this created social networks and training opportunities that acted as catalysts for self-employment (cf. Bailey 1987). Third, residential settlement patterns influence business development amongst minority groups (Kloosterman *et al.* 1999). Reeves and Ward (1984) argue that the relative dispersal of African-Caribbean settlement compared to the concen-tration of Asians, their numerically smaller population and the apparent lack of culturally specific needs, combine to limit the market potential for small businesses. Finally, African-Caribbeans are constrained by their comparatively low levels of home ownership, which diminishes their capacity to offer collateral for business start-up funding (Basu 1991). These factors, which are grounded in the social, economic and political context of ethnic minorities rather than 'cultural' attributes, largely account for the contrasting fortunes of African-Caribbeans and Asians in clothing and other small business activities.

## The Market for Clothing

Since the 1970s, the British clothing industry has had to face intense international competition and major shifts in the pattern of consumer demand. These pressures have had far-reaching implications for the clothing industry in the areas of pricing, design, quality, manufacturing processes and employment (Phizacklea 1990; Rainnie 1989; Totterdill and Zeitlin 1989). In the 1970s, traditional British manufacturers, particularly High Street retailers with their own manufacturing capacity, found themselves unable to compete with low wage producers in newly industrialized countries. Standard garments such as suits, rainwear and jeans, where seasonal fashion changes tended to be minimal, were particularly susceptible to competition. Despite the negotiation of quotas under the Multi-Fibre Arrangement (MFA), designed to stabilize market-production relationships, by the close of the 1970s imports were approaching 30 per cent of the British clothing market (WMLPU 1991).

Radical changes to retailers' buying patterns added to the force of these changes. The early 1980s witnessed a 'retail revolution', which was occasioned by demands for more frequent style changes and garments with a high fashion content (Davenport 1992). Retailers like the Burton Group, Sears, Storehouse and Next tried to lure consumers away from relatively cheap mass-marketed clothes by promoting a new co-ordinated look combining high fashion with value for money, with an accompanying shift towards 'niche marketing' and 'customer differentiation' (Phizacklea 1990: 15). United Kingdom manufacturers have been profoundly affected by these changes, which have generated considerable pressure to organize production more flexibly. As retailers moved away from long standardized runs with an emphasis on 'economies of scale' associated with Fordist mass production, they insisted that manufacturers provide improvements in design and quality, shorter lead times, smaller batches and frequent style changes (Hendrie 1993: 61).

This is the broad market context that garment manufacturers in the West Midlands are now part of. More specifically, there are three main outlets for local clothing firms: wholesalers who usually sell their merchandise to market traders and individual shopkeepers; agents, often white, who tend to deal directly with the major retailers; and larger firms who use smaller manufacturers to bolster their production at particular times of the year (these smaller manufacturers are commonly referred to as agents and Cut, Make, Trim (CMT) operators).[1] Wholesalers, who are often Asian themselves, are a popular market for manufacturers. This outlet was identified as the most important market by one of the earliest studies on the West Midlands clothing sector (Handsworth Technical College 1984b). Despite the importance of the wholesaling route, this is the market segment most characterized by intense competition, which is exacerbated by the relatively easy access into this market.

Using agents is an important marketing strategy for many West Midlands clothing firms. In Ram's (1994) study, manufacturers supplying chain stores through agents were often ambivalent about their relationship with them. They received fairly regular orders from the agents, which they appeared grateful for. However, there was also a feeling that the agents were using them and that different companies were being paid different rates for the same product. These companies were being used to 'top-up' orders. The chain stores have tended to place the bulk of their orders in countries like Portugal. It is, however, difficult to re-order from foreign concerns because their turn-around period is three months as opposed to two weeks at local companies. A comment by a local manufacturer interviewed in a separate but complementary study summed up this situation: 'The trade revolves around the middlemen. We get the orders because we can turn them around quickly, quicker than the foreign suppliers. But they only come to us after they have exhausted all the other possibilities, and then they grind us down in terms of price' (Ram 1992: 610).

The other main category is composed of CMT operators that are generally used by larger manufacturers to cope during periods of intense demand. An estimated quarter of Birmingham's clothing firms are engaged in CMT to some extent (Jackson 1996). This market segment is characterized by high levels of competition and dependency. The irregular nature of the orders and the fact that the orders tend to be small and involve almost continual style changes pose problems in production since the changes put pressure on machinists. The inability of many of the firms to respond to the requirements of large contracts also makes it necessary for local firms to pool their resources and work together, which is only happening to a limited extent at the moment (*Birmingham Clothing Sector Forum*, 3 June 1998). This market situation seems to lend credence to the following observation:

> The typical West Midlands untailored outwear company . . . finds itself within a complex web of relationships between suppliers, other producers and retailers. In addition, most of these will be much larger than the individual company and with substantial market power. Given that the end product itself is increasingly subject to fashion changes and demanding requirements concerning price, style and quality, the company is constantly subject to a wide range of intense competitive pressures. (Mawson 1988: 6)

Some argue that the more successful manufacturers are the ones that have managed to diversify by introducing new technology, producing their own designs and being flexible enough to respond to the market fluctuations (Hardill and Wynarczyk 1996; Totterdill and Zeitlin 1989). However, there is little evidence to suggest that technological investments could solve the problems of Birmingham's clothiers. The basic requirement for machinists would still exist, yet these workers could be subject to a degree of de-skilling causing their labour to become further devalued and exacerbating the homeworking problem (Hendrie 1993; Mitter 1986; WMLPU 1991). Rather, an increase in subcontracting due to technological advances has been documented in studies on the West Midlands clothing industry, and is largely the outcome of retailers' efforts to minimize the risk and uncertainty they are exposed to by passing the risks and costs of production 'backwards' onto their suppliers (Hendrie 1993: 62). This creates a situation of dependency, whereby retailers are in a position to exert considerable pressure on the margins of manufacturers in a period of recession and uncertainty (Rainnie 1989). In times of heightened competition, it is the manufacturing base that suffers from the dependent nature of a relationship of this kind (Phizacklea 1990).

There are a number of difficulties confronting garment manufacturers who try to expand and develop. For instance, moving into fabric sourcing, design, sales and marketing ultimately involves investing capital in stock with no immediate prospect of profit. Under-funding continues to be one of the most intractable problems facing ethnic minority small business owners, and remains a major constraint upon their development (Ram and Jones 1998). Moreover, local firms tend to deal with numerous buyers placing small orders at short notice, whereas fabric producers often insist on a minimum order and operate tight credit facilities (Hayden 1992). Since a feature of Birmingham clothing firms is their dependence on a minimum initial outlay and subsequent low profit margins, moving into 'make through' can carry more risk of failure than remaining in CMT (Lewis 1996).[2] Consequently, while many firms now engage in aspects such as design (80 per cent), only a quarter of them produce all their own output (Jackson 1996). The majority tend to modify copies of established garments rather than try to be innovative in terms of creativity.

## Managing the Workplace

In this section we explore how manufacturers manage the pressures arising from an increasingly competitive marketplace and a shrinking labour market. The highly informal, ad hoc and rudimentary nature of management practices in typical Birmingham-based clothing firms has been alluded to already. For example, a lack of innovative design, chronic under-funding and a reliance on informal sources of finance often mean a lack of resources for the substantive growth of the enterprise.

Next to that, attracting workers depends upon ethnic ties rather than formal recruitment processes. This modus operandi was equally prevalent at the workplace itself, particularly in relation to the management of production, pay and working conditions.

*Production*

Despite reported innovations in the production methods and work organization in the clothing industry (Taplin and Winterton 1991), the division of labour at typical West Midlands clothing firms is characterized by continuity rather than change. Men often perform 'skilled' jobs, like lay planning and cutting, and tend to be family members. This allows the management a certain degree of control over the production process and often saves on costs (Ram 1994). In sharp contrast, garment manufacturers usually have a number of 'unskilled' employees engaged in more general work. Their activities can include storing merchandise, packing garments, cleaning the work surfaces and similar tasks.

However, the production organization at most firms revolves around the work of the machinists. A sectionalized production process is common at West Midlands clothing firms, where machinists specialize in producing part of a garment rather than the garment as a whole. For example, at one of the firms investigated by Ram (1994) the process was divided into five stages:

1. trimmings (collars and belts);
2. pockets;
3. linings;
4. zips;
5. finishing.

The stages were not equally complex, and required varying degrees of skill. Making linings was the simplest task, being essentially a question of sewing straight seams. The most complex tasks tended to be making pockets and finishing garments, both of which demanded more complicated manoeuvres and stitching. Consequently, the pocket makers and finishers were apt to be the better-paid machinists. For this type of production system to operate 'efficiently', it was not only necessary to have a continuous supply of work but also a constant supply of 'appropriate' work. There had to be enough pockets, linings, zips, trimmings and so on to keep the differently skilled machinists continually occupied. Organizing this work was not entirely done by the management. Making a garment was a sequential process insofar as it entailed a number of distinct stages. Thus pocket makers were unable start working until the trimmings had been attached by the previous machinists, the linings could not be sewn until the pockets had been completed, and so on.

Management were dependent on everyone to work in such a way that all the people down the line kept each other supplied with work. Despite the significant extent to which management were dependent on the workers' skills to address production problems, the logic of the production system was that the machinists would complete their operations as quickly as possible and develop an adeptness at a particular function. Yet the pressure for continual style changes was such that the machinists often had to work on jobs they were not specialized in.

## Pay

Most workers are paid on the basis of the number of garments or parts of a garment produced, i.e. according to a piece-rate system. Piece-rate can be highly variable as money is lost whenever work is slack or an employee is unable to work. Recent figures on the clothing industry show that machinists on piece-work earn between £80.00 and £150.00 a week, with an average gross income of £120.00 or £2.46 an hour for a fifty-hour week (AEKTA 1995–1996). Other factory workers may be paid less than this, including general assistants who work long hours and tend to be paid cash-in-hand and often live under a constant real or perceived threat of dismissal. The National Minimum Wage introduced in April 1999 was set at £3.60 and was designed to address the issue of low pay. However, the 'informal' nature of pay in these settings may discourage its successful implementation.

Low pay is an even more serious problem for clothing homeworkers. In 1990, 70 per cent of the homeworkers in Britain were members of ethnic minorities, and they locally constitute a particularly vulnerable group that earns much less than factory machinists. In 1996 the normal pay for homeworkers in Birmingham was approximately £40.00 to £60.00 for a forty-two-hour week (AEKTA 1995–1996). The costs of electricity and other expenses incurred by working at home are rarely taken into account. The work is done in isolation and entails repetitive tasks, and there is little chance of being promoted or receiving any further training (Pennington and Westover 1989). Homeworkers caught in the grey area of self-employment work under extremely poor employment terms and may miss out on welfare benefits such as holiday pay, sick pay and maternity leave or pay. They have no rights to redundancy money, would have a hard time claiming unfair dismissal and are the group most likely to have health problems, particularly stress-related ailments (Palmer 1990; Pennington and Westover 1989).

Phizacklea (1988) notes that Asian women working in the local clothing industry have been involved in struggles for union representation, and that a number of disputes have taken place within the region. However, even though clothing workers have been incorporated into the United Kingdom's third largest trade union, the specific political and economic situation of clothing workers in Birmingham has left local unionization weak (*Clothing and Textile News*, 21 April 1998; Pennington and Westover 1989). Moreover, employers are able to deal with problems in a number of ways. If there are no Employment Contracts and workers are paid cash-in-hand, it means they can simply be dismissed. The relatives of disgruntled employees can be called in to help the manager settle disputes, and this exerts a powerful and preventative presence that keeps people from complaining or putting up resistance (Hoel 1982; Phizacklea 1988). More drastic measures include closing down companies, which then re-open under a different name after having dismissed the employees who caused the conflict, thus avoiding legal measures. Moreover, it is not always in the interest of the workers to disclose their true employment status, since it could have a negative effect on their ability to claim welfare benefits. This combination of factors has created an unwillingness among Asian women to remain in the sector, and has led to a 'labour shortage' (WMPLU 1993). However, as Hendrie notes: 'It is not a lack of skilled labour per se, but of cheap, immigrant, female labour; women workers who, primarily through their lack of opportunities in mainstream employment, are forced to accept the poor wages and conditions which characterise employment in the clothing industry' (1993: 101).

## *The Institutional Framework*[3]

Despite the whole body of employment, health and safety regulations, illegal practices are still common at some of Britain's small clothing enterprises.[4] Poor working conditions are a feature of many firms in the West Midlands clothing industry, and the West Midlands Low Pay Unit found clothing firms operating from 'disused factories, old warehouses, back street rooms above shops and people's front rooms' (WMPLU 1991). People were working in cramped conditions, with inadequate lighting, ventilation and sanitation facilities. Health and safety aspects were unsatisfactory, there were no emergency fire procedures and the exit doors were blocked.

Various health and safety problems continue to be reported. The most persistent ones are the fire hazards and the injuries from cutting machinery. Other dangers include dichloromethane, which is a component in glue and is used in laminating machinery. It is dangerous if it is inhaled and it presents a problem for workers if they are not provided with masks or are not made fully aware of the need to wear protective equipment. Dust and fluff also cause sneezing and coughing if there are no extractor fans at the domestic or factory workplace. Headaches, eyestrain and repetitive strain injury are other common complaints due to poor lighting, continual noise and operating machinery over long periods (Palmer 1990). Workers also run the risk of needles going through their fingers if they are not fitted with guards, cutting accidents if they are not provided with hand protection, slips and falls if material is left in gangways or uneven floors, and back injuries from lifting heavy goods and equipment (Halliday 1991). Ill health is compounded by unfamiliarity with employment rights, which allows employers to avoid having to give sick pay or proper holiday pay (AEKTA 1995–1996).

Firms operate in a climate of political tolerance, which is in sharp contrast to the situation in the Netherlands, where a recent government crackdown on illegal employment in the industry resulted in the virtual termination of clothing manufacturing in Amsterdam.[5] The inadequate law enforcement in Britain is partly due to the limited number of agencies that police the United Kingdom clothing industry. Businesses often go unnoticed, fail to register for taxes and generally flout the employment laws. Firms also neglect to register with the local authority and frequently liquidate, often re-emerging under a different name. Tax evasion is reputed to be commonplace, and many workers in the local clothing industry receive no payslips or P60s summarizing their annual premiums. Even if National Insurance is paid, it is often not credited, so that employees are not entitled to unemployment or pension benefits (*Financial Times*, 3 October 1996). Moreover, many firms in Birmingham are probably operating illegally in places that require planning permission. Only very few applications for planning permission are submitted for clothing enterprises, even though they are known to operate at residential premises.

Some regulation of the industry does occur as a result of direct intervention or indirect factors. The control and regulation of the industry may have been indirectly aided by the gradual tightening of immigration laws, reducing the migration into the country. Ever since 1994, each immigrant into Britain has had to prove his ability to 'maintain and accommodate himself and any dependants adequately without recourse to public funds'. People entering the country who intend to establish themselves in business have to have £200,000 of their own money and held in their own name even if they are joining an existing business as a partner (Statement of Changes in Immigration Rules (HC395) 1994). Ever since January 1997, any employer using workers with restrictions on their rights to work can be fined. These factors might serve as a deterrent to the casual employment of people who do not have sufficient documentation to allow them to work in the United Kingdom and reduce the ability of other migrant workers to set up SMEs (*Outworkers News*, Summer 1997).

Other forms of indirect intervention include the introduction of a National Minimum Wage (NMW) in April 1999. It was set at £3.60 an hour for everyone above twenty-one years of age (it has recently increased to £3.70 per hour). The Inland Revenue is responsible for ensuring that the NMW is paid, and it has the right to inspect employment records. However, legislation on payslips is vague and although employers have to stipulate the deductions, they do not have to state the number of hours. This makes it impossible to tell from payslips whether or not the NMW is being paid. An employee may work forty hours, and the employer can claim that he is working less, and the Inland Revenue would have to prove the records are incorrect. Some employers in the textile industry ignore the law by dismissing or refusing to employ people who will not work for less than £3.60 an hour, and others are changing to piece-rate and then illegally claiming that some workers are not entitled to the NMW because they do not work hard enough. Inland Revenue Enforcement Agents and the Knitwear, Footwear and Textiles and Apparel Union (KFAT) would like to build up a national model of clothing and textiles establishments to make it easier to target firms, but this plan is still in an early stage (KFAT 1999). Since a number of clothing SMEs continue to flout employment law with impunity, a minimum wage may remain a meaningless concept for many of the workers in Birmingham's clothing industry (AEKTA 1995–1996; KFAT 1999).

There has been direct intervention on a national level by the Health and Safety Executive (HSE). There are various forms of premises inspections, some of them routine or follow-up visits, and other times certain areas are targeted for 'blitzes'. The main way to get firms to upgrade as regards safety, however, is by persuasion, and actual prosecutions are comparatively rare. Local agencies have been set up to monitor and solve the problems of poor pay and poor conditions in the clothing industry. The West Midlands Low Pay Unit (WMLPU) and the Clothing Industry Action Research Project (AEKTA) are the main agencies that police the industry at the level of employment.[6] The AEKTA acts as an advisory group and plays a role in various campaigns – for example, to make sure sick pay is given to employees and National Insurance premiums are handed over to the authorities. It also has links with other organizations that raise public awareness as regards the problems facing workers in the industry. However, its function is limited and recent government rulings have prevented it from representing workers at tribunals.

Homeworkers are a particularly neglected group since there is no national policy in force for them and they have to rely on pressure groups that advocate reform (Pennington and Westover 1989). Legally, they face very specific problems because the 1921 Factory Act merely described them as outworkers, leaving their economic function and standing open to interpretation. Ever since 1961 employers have been required to keep lists of their names and addresses that have to be produced on request and sent twice a year to the District Council. However, only a small number of homeworkers are ever registered with the local authorities, leaving the whereabouts and extent of homeworking largely unknown (Harris 1988). The now illegal practice of failing to issue a Contract of Employment helps employers get away with claiming that homeworkers are self-employed (WERAS 1998).

Parallels can be drawn with the Los Angeles case study where, to a certain extent, the intervention by the authorities appears to have been more or less symbolic.[7] On the surface, action seemed to have been against the people breaking the employment law, but in reality the firms continued to do business and were given little more than a warning. In part, this is because of the reduction in the number of employees policing the industry. The West Midlands clothing industry only has two Health and Safety Inspectors responsible for clothing and textiles to cover the whole area. This makes it even more difficult to trace firms that have failed to register for tax and planning purposes.

Unlike the case in Amsterdam, where many of the employees in the industry were illegal immigrants, the Asians working in Birmingham are largely British citizens. They consequently constitute a potentially sizeable minority of the electorate, which the national and local authorities would not want to alienate. Thus illegal work practices in clothing manufacturing may be ignored at times if it is felt that the local and national economy would suffer otherwise. This claim was one of the newspaper allegations concerning the persistence of sweated labour in Birmingham during 1996 (*Financial Times,* 3 October 1996).

## Conclusion

This chapter has sketched out the harshly competitive market environment that Asian entrepreneurs and workers find themselves embedded in. Global trends towards the decentralization of clothing production have only served to heighten the pressures upon the High Street retailers who have long dominated the British clothing industry. In turn, these retailers have sought to impose even more exacting terms and conditions on the usually larger clothing manufacturers who have trad- itionally been their main suppliers. Greater outsourcing, intense price competition from newly industrializing countries, and fast-changing customer preferences have threatened the viability of many traditional garment manufacturers. Further down the production chain, clothing firms in the West Midlands have felt the chill wind of rapid market changes and the ensuing fickleness of customer allegiances. The sector survives because the unpredictability of the market still provides sufficient opportunities that can be exploited by manufacturers who, in turn, draw upon a vulnerable co-ethnic workforce.

This case study has three broader implications involving its theoretical contribu- tion, the prospects for the continuation of the sector, and the pragmatic steps that can be taken to support the firms. In terms of its theoretical import, the case demon- strates the utility of a 'mixed embeddedness' perspective (Kloosterman *et al.* 1999) that recognizes the economic and social aspects of ethnic minority entrepreneurship. Hence, the international reconfiguration of clothing production has produced constraints as well as opportunities for British garment manufacturers. Shorter production runs, more style changes and keener prices were needed. The changing nature of the West Midlands urban and labour market context was conducive to these developments. De-industrialization produced a major 'shake-out' of male Asian workers from large 'metal-bashing' factories. These workers were able to draw upon social networks clustered in their neighbourhoods and localities for

financial support and sources of labour. Sexist immigration legislation has channelled Asian women into the sector; and a less than rigorous regulatory environment
appears to have had little success in curtailing 'informal' industrial practices.

Despite its apparent resilience, the interaction of these multi-faceted processes
has cast some doubt on the future of the West Midlands clothing industry. Foreign
competition and the progressive relaxation of the Multi-Fibre Agreement (MFA)
present a significant threat. The dwindling supply of Asian female workers appears
to be exacerbating the widely publicized 'labour shortage'. It is also felt that second-
generation Asians might be more intent on pursuing professional careers than
perpetuating the small business tradition of their parents (Metcalf *et al.* 1996).
There is also the prospect that regulators might follow the Amsterdam example
and enforce the rules much more scrupulously than they have to date. However,
this is not an inevitable trajectory. As was noted above, earlier predictions of the
demise of the clothing sector have proved to be premature. Clothing manufacturers
in the West Midlands have been adept at responding quickly and cheaply to customer requirements. The case study clearly illustrates that outsourcing from abroad
and reliance upon local producers like the ones in the West Midlands for the less
predictable market demand can be complementary strategies. Moreover, despite
the labour market aspirations of second-generation Asians, discrimination and
disadvantages continue to affect this ethnic group (Modood 1997). As Kloosterman
*et al.* (1999: 263) note: 'Changing the mix of embeddedness is an open, contingent
social process in which many social actors may take part and on which the insertion
of immigrant entrepreneurs depends.'

On a more practical and pragmatic level, a number of actions are recommended
to reinforce the sector:

1. A recognition by all the major political parties of the inherent problems faced
   by minority workers in the clothing industry, culminating in long-term funding
   and strategies targeting specific city locations.
2. The co-ordination of aid agencies by one central body.
3. Tightening the policing of the industry to aid firms that work within the law by
   reducing the competition and removing the association with 'sweated' labour.
4. Introducing legal contracts to prevent retailers from swapping suppliers midway
   through an order.
5. Strong moves to halt the influx of cheap imports into Britain.
6. National and local clothing unions to maintain continuous pressure on successive governments to terminate poor working conditions and make sure legislation
   is acted upon.

# Notes

1. In Cut, Make and Trim (CMT) operations, the manufacturer is generally supplied with the fabric and the required design by an agent or middleman.
2. Make-through production involves the firm being involved in all the aspects from design through to the sale of the product.
3. Much of the information for this section of the chapter is based upon interviews with key informants in Birmingham City Council, AEKTA and the Health and Safety Executive.
4. Officials at the West Midlands Low Pay Unit, AEKTA and the Health and Safety Executive have been consulted for information for this section.
5. For more information refer to the chapter on Amsterdam in this volume.
6. The West Midlands Low Pay Unit is funded by local authorities and publishes leaflets giving advice to workers and reports and statistical information on employment in the region. The Clothing Industry Action Research Project is an independent voluntary organization that disseminates information on employment rights, and gives advice and assistance in pursuing cases of breach of employment law. It is also actively involved in research into various aspects of the industry.
7. See the chapter on Los Angeles in this volume.

# –5–

# Amsterdam: Stitched up

*Stephan Raes, Jan Rath, Marja Dreef,*
*Adem Kumcu, Flavia Reil* and
*Aslan Zorlu*

## Introduction

In the Netherlands, as in other industrialized countries, immigrants have played a significant role in the development of the garment industry. In Amsterdam, the industrial production of garments was stimulated in the nineteenth century by the arrival of Roman Catholic immigrants from Westphalia and Jewish immigrants from Eastern European countries. They laid the basis for a flourishing Dutch garment industry that reached its a peak in the early 1960s. As in other industrialized countries, garment production declined after that, due to growing international competition and increasing wage costs. However, in the 1980s, the industry itself and the role of immigrants in it both made a significant comeback. Immigrants, mostly notably from Turkey, set up numerous sewing shops and employed up to 20,000 workers. Unlike similar cases described in the other chapters of this book, immigrant entrepreneurship in the garment industry came to an abrupt end in Amsterdam after 1993, due to a combination of policy interventions and market developments.

In this chapter, we describe, analyse and explain the rise and rapid fall of immigrant contractors in the Amsterdam garment industry in the 1980s and 1990s using a simple analytical framework. First, we focus on the supply side of the fictitious entrepreneurial market (Light and Rosenstein 1995). We examine the entrepreneurs and their businesses, and discuss a number of characteristics. Secondly, we turn to the environment these contractors operate in, i.e. the opportunity structure these entrepreneurs are facing. We analyse how a set of variables in the social, economic and political environment have influenced the opportunities of small contractors, how these variables have changed over time and how they have impacted on entrepreneurial strategies and success. This framework structures our thinking on the issue, and the format of this chapter. After a short historical prelude we give an empirical description of the sector and its factories, entrepreneurs and workers.

Then we discuss the aspects of the environment they operate in. In conclusion, as in the production of garments, we bring together the various parts of our argument, sewing them into a whole that will hopefully enable us to identify the pattern of cause and effect of the striking fluctuation of immigrant contractors in the Amsterdam garment industry.

## The Production of Ready-made Garments in the Netherlands

The production of ready-made garments started in the second half of the nineteenth century (see Raes 2000a). Westphalian Roman Catholic fabric pedlars like Lampe and the Brenninkmeyer brothers, founders of the renowned multinational C&A, established wholesale fabric shops, which they afterwards expanded into shops for ready-made garments (Miellet 1993: 22–7). Their activities made the town of Groningen in the north of the Netherlands an important centre for clothing production (de Leeuw 1991: 116). Tailors and traders in used clothing also shifted to ready-made clothing production. During the slack off-season periods, some tailors started producing clothing they then sold as ready-made garments. Jews especially, historically present in the Dutch textile industry (de Vries 1989), got involved in the production and distribution of ready-made garments. The inflow of Jewish immigrants from Eastern Europe in the second half of the century stimulated this process, with Amsterdam as the main centre of these (Wolff-Gerzon 1949: 36).

Both developments led to an increase in the production of ready-made garments after 1870 (Jansen 1991). In 1911, there were seventy-five garment factories in Amsterdam, nine of which employed more than nine workers. Only thirty-one of the factories worked with mechanical power. In addition, there were 109 larger garment factories, 48 contractors and 1,021 registered small firms or homeworkers (de Leeuw 1991: 185).

After the First World War the number of garment factories grew substantially, many of them having been started by retailers (Wolff-Gerzon 1949: 85). In the 1930s, when the Depression deepened, the Dutch government introduced measures to protect the domestic market, especially benefiting the manufacture of women's wear (Wolff-Gerzon 1949: 100). During this period, many German Jews fled to the Netherlands, bringing valuable experience in the garment industry and trade. Their arrival helped modernize the industry and heralded the rise of Amsterdam as the centre for the Dutch garment industry after the Second World War (Jansen 1991: 142).

The Second World War had a huge impact on the industry and distribution. Presser (1965: 190) reports that at the beginning of the war, 1,043 of a total of 32,319 entrepreneurs in the garment and cleaning industries in the Netherlands were Jewish, and so were 5,301 out of a total of 102,848 workers in these sectors. But in Amsterdam, the city with the largest concentration of Jews in the country, their role was far greater. In Mokum, the Jewish nickname for Amsterdam, there were 13,500 workers in garment production, 11,000 of them women, a substantial proportion of whom were Jewish (Heertje 1977: 123). In fact, 20 per cent of the Jewish population in Mokum worked in the garment industry (Leydesdorff 1987: 195). The Nazis started raiding Jewish firms in Amsterdam in February 1941. The vast majority of the Jews in the industry were eventually deported and killed in concentration camps.

After the destructive effects of the war the Dutch garment industry experienced a sharp growth, albeit not as sharp as in other industrial sectors (Brandsma 1970). Despite the murder of most of its workforce in the Holocaust, there was initially no shortage of workers. The low wage policy agreed upon by the business associations, trade unions and the state secured the profitability of the garment industry, keeping wages below those in neighbouring countries. In the early years of post-war reconstruction, immigrants as such barely played a role in the Dutch garment industry. In 1950 the industry employed approximately 60,000 workers (Jansen 1991: 260), and by 1960 there were 66,800 workers (Broer 1977: 91). The index for the value of production increased from 100 in 1953 to 167 in 1961 (Jansen 1991: 272). In 1953, 63 per cent of all the workers in the industry were concentrated in the large cities (Broer 1977: 86). In 1960, Amsterdam alone accounted for 21 per cent of all the workers and 29 per cent of all the firms (Broer 1977: 88). The role of the large cities in employment nevertheless decreased over the 1950s to 41 per cent in 1963, reflecting a shift to the countryside where labour was more widely available. This indicates a process of decentralization.

From the early 1960s the Dutch garment industry as a whole began to decline due to international competition and rising wage costs. In 1961 there were still 898 firms with more than ten workers in the industry, but in 1972 only 609 of them were left, and in 1980 only 321. Of the 63,000 workers at these firms in 1961, only 41,000 were employed in 1972, and only 17,680 in 1980 (excluding homeworkers) (CBS s.a.). In 1970 and 1971 the employment figures declined by more than 10 per cent, and from 1973 to 1975 the yearly decline in the number of jobs was more than 15 per cent! This decline hit the larger cities hard, especially Amsterdam. Between 1963 and 1967 alone, Amsterdam lost a quarter of its jobs in the garment industry!

## An Unexpected Recovery after 1980 and a Sudden Fall: Facts and Figures

Like a phoenix, the Amsterdam garment industry rose from the ashes after 1980. This recovery was manifested as an extension of the tier of contractors and particularly affected the lower end of the industry. As in the late nineteenth century, to a certain extent immigrants drove this development. From 1980 onwards, growing numbers of immigrants set up sewing shops (Bloeme and van Geuns 1987; van Geuns 1992; Tap 1983). From 1993 a rather steep decline set in, eventually leading to the decimation of a large part of this sector.

According to the Trade Register of the Amsterdam Chamber of Commerce, the official number of contractors steadily rose after 1980, reaching a peak in the second half of 1992.[1] However, the Trade Register of the Chamber of Commerce does not always provide reliable and complete data, since numerous contractors failed to register. Our own interviews and other estimates show there were up to 1,000 firms in the city at the peak of the sector in 1992/1993. After that, when the decline set in, there was some over-registration of firms that were still on the Trade Registers but had actually closed down. According to our own estimates, only forty to fifty firms were left in 1997. Figure 5.1 presents the official number of firms and the estimated number of firms, based on our research.

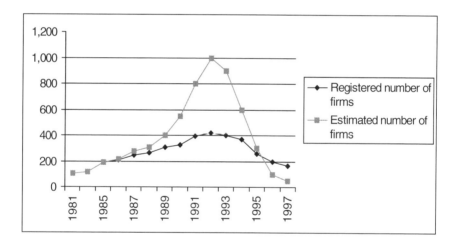

**Figure 5.1** Registered and Estimated Number of Contractors in the Amsterdam Garment Industry. *Source:* Raes (2000a: 73)

What looks in the first instance like a relatively steady development is in fact a more volatile phenomenon. First, many firms were only around for a short period of time, often less than a year, in some cases even less than a day. There was, in fact, an extraordinarily high turnover of firms. In 1990, for instance, according to the Trade Register, almost 250 new firms were set up, approximately a quarter of the total. To some extent these fluctuations follow the fashion calendar: the number of firms declined during the low seasons from December to February and from July to September, and increased in the high seasons. However, the fluctuations also reflect efforts to remain invisible to official agencies such as the Tax Department, the Aliens Police, the Industrial Insurance Administration Office (GAK) and the Labour Relations Service (DIA).

With the rise in the number of factories, the number of workers increased as well – to about 20,000 in 1992 (see Table 5.1).[2]

**Table 5.1** Number of Workers Employed by Contractors in the Amsterdam Garment Industry

|  | *Number of workers per firm* | *Total number of workers* | *Source* |
| --- | --- | --- | --- |
| Early 1980s | 12 | 1,304 | Tap 1983 |
| Mid-1980s | 15–16 | 1,920–3,052 | Zorlu 1997 |
|  |  |  | Bloeme & van Geuns 1987 |
| Early 1990s | 19–20 | 19,000–20,000 | Zorlu 1997 |
| 1996 | 17–18 | 680–900 | Zorlu & Reil 1997 |

Contractors and workers combine to account for a substantial value of production. In the beginning of the 1980s, the total turnover of the Turkish sewing shops amounted to 25 million Dutch guilders (NLG) (Tap 1983: 26), and some ten years later the figure had risen to roughly NLG1 billion (Zeldenrust and van Eijk 1992: 11).[3] These are very rough estimates, which do not provide much insight into the development over time. That is why we have calculated a minimum and a maximum value of production at different points in time. The maximum value was estimated by multiplying the number of workers at each firm by the average value of production per worker of registered contractors, and the sum of all the labour costs – which is the most important cost of production for the contractors – was taken as a proxy of the minimum value. Our research showed that the average worker worked eight months a year, six days a week and ten hours a day, and was paid an hourly wage between NLG10 and 12. The minimum value of production per worker would then be NLG20,800 to 24,960 (see Table 5.2 for an overview).[4]

The firms mainly produced lower- to medium-quality, medium-fashionable women's wear. When competition became stronger at the beginning of the 1990s, more firms started accepting orders in the less fashionable market segments as well. As was previously noted, the firms operated as contractors, with assembling clothing, sometimes combined with cutting and ironing, as the core activity. Throughout the 1980s and 1990s an increasing number of firms started to engage in other activities in wholesaling or import–export. In the 1980s, around 30 per cent of the firms in our database reported other activities, and by the 1990s this figure had risen to 60 per cent. It is important to emphasize that a substantial

**Table 5.2** Maximum and Minimum Value of Production of Contractors in the Amsterdam Garment Industry (in Millions of Dutch Guilders)

|            | *Minimum*     | *Maximum*         |
|------------|---------------|-------------------|
| Early 1980s | 27.1          | 52.2              |
| Mid-1980s   | 39.9–63.4     | 78.7–125.1        |
| Early 1990s | 474.2–499.2   | 1,083.0–1,140.0   |
| Mid-1990s   | 17.0–22.5     | 438.6–580.5       |

*Source:* CBS, our own Table 5.1, our own research

share of the production of the firms (up to 50 per cent) was for export, mainly to Germany.

As to the location of the firms, these activities were largely an Amsterdam-based phenomenon. Amsterdam is the centre of the Dutch Fashion industry, as is most clearly illustrated by the presence of the World Fashion Center, the heart of garment trading in the Netherlands. According to Tap (1983: 25), this concentration of native Dutch and immigrant contractors in Amsterdam was 'dependent on the importance of Amsterdam in clothing sales'. The City of Amsterdam ascertained that 65 per cent of clothing contracting in the Netherlands took place in Amsterdam (Burgers 1996). Tap (1983: 21) also reports that 60 per cent of the contractors were located in a number of specific Amsterdam neighbourhoods such as the Pijp, the western part of Oost, the Jordaan, the western part of the downtown canal district, and the southern part of Oud West. They were mainly residential areas. Rents were cheaper, particularly for residential premises – a mere NLG500 a month compared to over NLG6,000 for business sites – even though the gravitation of contractors to residential areas pushed the rents up. However, residential premises were not designed for manufacturing garments and were therefore less suitable. As the sector expanded during the 1980s, contractors also ventured into industrial districts. Over time, there was a westward shift in the location of the factories as is shown in Figures 5.2, 5.3 and 5.4.

In this period, home-based work seemed to grow too, with fifty to eighty firms, in sewing shops with two to five sewing machines, employing three to six workers. The shops were usually not registered and were located in 'hidden' premises (Zorlu 1997: 121). After 1996, most of the factories were located at business sites again.

## Characteristics of Entrepreneurs and Workers

We identified 2,524 entrepreneurs who operated as contractors from 1980 to 1997 in the Amsterdam garment industry.[5] The vast majority of these, that is five of every six entrepreneurs, were male. The share of female entrepreneurs, already

| | |
|---|---|
| None | (53) |
| 1 to 5 | (45) |
| 5 to 10 | (13) |
| More than 10* | (2) |
| (*) less than 15 | |
| Total 208 | |

**Figure 5.2** Contractors in Amsterdam, per Neighbourhood, 1986. *Source:* Amsterdam Chamber of Commerce Trade Register

| | |
|---|---|
| None | (44) |
| 1 to 5 | (46) |
| 5 to 10 | (13) |
| More than 10* | (10) |
| (*) less than 25 | |
| Total 372 | |

**Figure 5.3** Contractors in Amsterdam, per Neighbourhood, 1992. *Source:* Amsterdam Chamber of Commerce Trade Register

| | |
|---|---|
| None | (48) |
| 1 to 5 | (48) |
| 5 to 10 | (13) |
| More than 10* | (4) |
| (*) less than 17 | |
| Total 243 | |

**Figure 5.4** Contractors in Amsterdam, per Neighbourhood, 1995. *Source:* Amsterdam Chamber of Commerce Trade Register

low, decreased in the 1980s, but increased afterwards to 31 per cent in 1996. We found several cases of married couples running a factory together. In the beginning of the 1980s, new entrepreneurs were mainly recruited from the ranks of the older men. Their success encouraged an increasing number of youngsters to follow suit. Halfway through the 1990s, the average age was 35. After the crackdown in the sector, on average the entrepreneurs who managed to stay in business were older. This change is reflected in our data. The share of 20 to 25-year-olds starting out as entrepreneurs whose dates of birth we knew increased from 14 per cent of the total in 1986 to 28 per cent in 1992, and then decreased to 18 per cent. The 25–30 age group decreased from 41 per cent of the starters in 1986 to 31 per cent in 1992 and again to 22 per cent in 1996. The percentage of starters older than 30 was higher in the mid-1990s.

Most entrepreneurs registered at the Chamber of Commerce were of Turkish descent, i.e. either with Turkish nationality or with Dutch nationality after naturalization. This category includes ethnic Turks, Kurds, Laz or other ethnic subgroups from Turkey.[6] The ethnic or national profile changed over time. In the beginning, there was still a relatively strong presence of Dutch contractors, but the share of Turkish contractors increased in the 1980s, partly because Dutch contractors left the sector. From the mid-1980s onwards, immigrants from other national backgrounds had the same success as the Turks, the latter consequently decreasing among the starters. In 1993, the share of Turks amounted to almost 60 per cent (see Figure 5.5), a percentage that gives a flattering picture of the situation, since Turkish entrepreneurs were less likely to register at the Chamber of Commerce than Dutch ones (Zorlu 1997: 142). The share of Turkish entrepreneurs is therefore probably higher. But in the mid-1990s their share strongly diminished. These changes indicate that immigrants from one particular national category dominated the sector for a long time, as is also the case in other industrialized countries. However, the developments also show that, in contrast to findings elsewhere, a substantial spill-over occurred to immigrants from other national backgrounds (see Table 5.3).

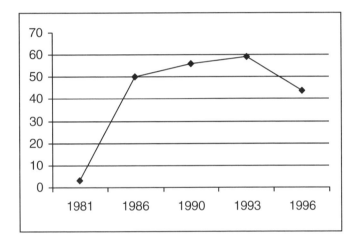

**Figure 5.5** Turkish Contractors in the Amsterdam Garment Industry. *Sources:* Chamber of Commerce Trade Register, and own database

The overwhelming majority of entrepreneurs from Turkey were first-generation immigrants, and this continued to be the case in the 1990s. Second-generation immigrants from Turkey hardly figure in our database. The main sending areas were the provinces of Konya, Karaman, Yildizeli and Kirsehir, and the regions of south-east Turkey and the central and eastern parts of the Black Sea region. It is striking that only very few entrepreneurs came from major Turkish cities such as Istanbul and Ankara, or from any of the garment-producing centres in Turkey such as the cities of Bursa, Mersin, Adana, or Istanbul. It is possible, though, that some of them migrated to the Netherlands via one of these cities (Zorlu 1998: 149–50).

The average length of their stay in the Netherlands was fourteen to seventeen years. This figure only refers to legal residents and is based on observations in 1997. But, as previously noted, many entrepreneurs operating in the 1980s and

**Table 5.3** Top 10 Nationalities of Contractors in the
Amsterdam Garment Industry

| Nationality | Number |
| --- | --- |
| 1. Turkish | 1,423 |
| 2. Dutch* | 338 |
| 3. Egyptian | 35 |
| 4. Moroccan | 25 |
| 5. Indian | 20 |
| 6. Pakistani | 12 |
| 7. French[†] | 8 |
| 8. British[‡] | 8 |
| 9. Iranian | 4 |
| 10. Cyprus | 4 |

* 92 of Turkish, 4 of Moroccan and 6 of Egyptian descent

[†] 3 of Turkish, 1 of Morocan and 1 of Syrian descent

[‡] 3 of Indian and 3 of Pakistani descent

early 1990s did not reside legally in the Netherlands. Numerous immigrants had entered the country without valid documents and many found employment in the garment industry, particularly in the periods from 1983 to 1985 and 1989 to 1991 (Zorlu 1998: 151; Zorlu and Reil 1997). A substantial number eventually set up shop themselves – especially the ones who had worked as *ayakçıs* (factotums) in sewing shops. Some of them managed to obtain legal residence status by the time they started their own firms, but others remained illegal. Their shaky legal status, the relative short duration of their stay, and their lack of familiarity with Dutch society impacted on their entrepreneurial opportunities. Their level of education was poor. Half the entrepreneurs had had no formal education after primary school. Most of them had job experience – some as self-employed tailors in Turkey, others as entrepreneurs in the Netherlands or workers in the garment industry. In the 1980s, the workers' qualifications became lower and lower until over 80 per cent of them had no experience whatsoever in the Turkish garment industry. This resulted in a mixed population of entrepreneurs: some contractors were experienced entrepreneurs, and others were skilled workers but lacked experience as entrepreneurs. When the sector collapsed in the mid-1990s, it was especially the latter who lost their businesses.

The story of the workers largely mirrored that of the entrepreneurs. Turkish entrepreneurs tended to hire Turkish workers (Zorlu 1997: 90). Their share increased throughout the 1980s from 25 per cent in 1981 (Tap 1983) to 72 per cent in 1986 (Bloeme and van Geuns 1987), and to 75 per cent in the mid-1990s (Zorlu 1997). However, they recruited workers from other nationalities as well – especially in the high season. We observed a substantial number of Egyptians, many of whom had become proficient in the Turkish language, working in Turkish factories (Zorlu 1997: 115). Promotion prospects within the firm were generally rather poor, since the entrepreneurs tried to keep the wages down and the workers docile. In practice, however, workers could get a pay rise by moving to another factory. There was, consequently, high worker mobility between factories. Firms with a good reputation in terms of labour conditions were able to keep qualified workers, but they were not very common before the crackdown in the mid-1990s.

A striking fact in the case of Amsterdam is the heavy under-representation of female workers. Whereas the workforce in most other cases is predominantly female, the workforce of Amsterdam immigrant contractors is predominantly male. Bloeme and van Geuns (1987: 114) observed that 56 per cent of the workers were women, but ten years later Zorlu and Reil (1997) only found 20 per cent women. Women involved in the sector, usually as seamstresses, tended to be of non-Turkish descent. The low percentage of Turkish women seemed to be linked to the relatively low percentage of Turkish women migrating to the Netherlands for employment reasons, and the relative ease with which Turkish men could migrate (illegally) to the Netherlands to work in the industry. To some extent, these processes rendered female labour superfluous.

Until 1993, a substantial number of workers were employed without the required residence or work permits, leading to estimates of more than 10,000 illegal workers. The files of the Public Prosecutor show that in the mid-1990s, 61 per cent of the workers did not have the required working permit. This practice became even more widespread in the 1980s. The number of illegal workers found by official agencies at sewing shops increased from 121 at 36 shops in 1988 to 209 at 22 shops in 1990 (van Geuns and van Diepen 1994: 27). After 1993, there was a sharp fall in the number of undocumented workers.

## Environmental Dynamics

Garment contractors, like any other entrepreneurs, do not operate in a vacuum but are influenced by the environment they operate in. Changes in the environment impact on their enterprises, and the entrepreneurs develop strategies to make optimal use of their environment. Explaining the rise and fall of the Turkish garment industry in Amsterdam thus requires an analysis of the environment the contractors operated in, and the way they dealt with its dynamics. We first discuss the social environment of the contractors, and then the market and its governance.

### Social Networks[7]

The presence of Turks in the Amsterdam garment industry can be traced back to the 1970s. Unlike other declining industries in the Netherlands, the Dutch garment industry did not embark on a large-scale recruitment of Mediterranean guest workers. A handful of Turkish guest workers nevertheless found jobs in Dutch garment factories. In the late 1970s, they quit the jobs and set up their own factories. Experienced in the Dutch garment industry, they had the relevant knowledge and skills and maintained relations with the customers, which enabled them to give their ventures a flying start. But this alone did not suffice. Unlike Dutch manufacturers, they were connected to skilled workers from their own group, and recruited them through informal channels, which gave them the edge. At the time, skilled workers were readily available in Amsterdam and Turkey alike. Workers from Turkey would simply come to Amsterdam on a tourist visa and stay until the high season was over and there were fewer orders. The recruitment of labour through their own social networks was not the only competitive advantage of the Turkish entrepreneurs. Business ventures normally require capital outlays, but financial institutions like banks have generally been reluctant to give credit to small starters, especially in unstable and risky sectors of the economy like the garment industry (Kumcu *et al.* 1998; Wolff and Rath 2000). Turkish entrepreneurs, however, were not put off by reluctance, since they financed their ventures with their own personal savings or loans from relatives and friends. The new entrepreneurs kept the costs, including the labour costs, down, delivered just in time, and were able to establish long-term and trustful relationships with their customers, generally manufacturers or (larger) retail stores.

In the 1970s and early 1980s, the level of immigrant employment in the Amsterdam labour market declined sharply, as was also the case in the rest of the country. Since then, immigrants have generally been unemployed more often and longer than native Dutch workers. The deteriorating situation of the labour market had two important effects: a growing number of redundant immigrants were looking for new job opportunities, and there was growing pressure on their social networks to circulate information about job opportunities and to ensure that the opportunities materialized. The activities of the new garment contractors were obviously noticed, and they encouraged others to follow suit. A growing number of garment workers decided to become self-employed. So one after the other, even people with little experience in the garment industry, or no entrepreneurial experience, started to set up their own garment factories. The market was obviously favourable, but the fact remained that each new venture nurtured new start-ups and this contributed to a mushrooming of small sewing shops in an increasingly competitive environment.

Undocumented immigrants were more than willing to accept any job at even the lowest wages, and in the 1980s there was an abundance of them in Amsterdam. Many of them came to the city precisely because they expected to find jobs at the Turkish garment factories. Even Turkish immigrants without any friends or relatives in Amsterdam were able to settle; they just approached a Turkish-looking person on the street and asked him to show them the way. Some five or six Turkish coffee houses served as informal labour offices operating on a labour spot market, each catering to different ethnic or religious subgroups (Zorlu 1998). Garment workers looking for a job would sit down, have a cup of tea and chat with their country-men until they were called for a job. A contractor in need of workers would simply call the coffee shop owner and ask for machinists or ironers. When the garment industry collapsed, a number of these coffee houses disappeared as well. Another less 'unobtrusive' job allocation system involved applying for work at the factory premises.

Not every sewing shop worker was equally important for the entrepreneur. Some could easily be replaced, but others occupied a more central position and became more or less indispensable. They performed key tasks such as bookkeeping, raking contracts, and organizing the production process. These key tasks, which in practice could be performed by one and the same individual, were often allocated to people who were well trusted, especially family members. On average two to five family members worked at the factories and were entrusted with various responsibilities. For the rest, the contractors preferred workers from their own social networks or, at any rate, their own country. The advantages were evident; this type of hiring practice diminished the communication problems on the shop floor, allowed man-agers to trust to their own cultural codes when workers needed to be prompted to work harder or be laid off, and provided some security in terms of not washing dirty linen in public. This became increasingly important when more and more of the production took place outside the formal economy. Hiring undocumented workers, paying them off the books, withholding fringe benefits, having them work under hazardous or unhealthy conditions, and so on, all involve risks. Discontented workers may betray their boss and tip off law enforcement agencies. Hiring people who can be trusted can reduce these risks. Of course, entrepreneurs and workers were violating the law and were dependent on each other, and this meant it was in both their interests to keep quiet. As for that, it was a question of one hand washing the other. Some entrepreneurs tried to hold on to their personnel and create loyalty by giving them sweets and other gifts, or discounts on garments (Reil and Korver 2001). Having said that, undocumented immigrants were often in a very weak position, unable to lodge complaints and secure their rights. No wonder some job disputes ended in violence. In the late 1980s and early 1990s, when the proliferation of sewing shops peaked, contractors found it harder to recruit workers from their own networks and consequently worked less critically.

## The Market

After a decline in demand due to the economic recession in the early 1980s, apart from a strong drop in 1989, demand rose considerably up until the early

1990s. In 1990 even, just before the Turkish contractor sector reached its peak, demand grew by 8 per cent. As such, the rising number of immigrant contractors in Amsterdam largely followed the pattern of the demand for garments.

The demand for garments also impacted on the rise and fall of Turkish contractors in a more qualitative way. It is here that we enter the realm of fashion. From the 1970s onwards, the importance of fashion for the clothing market started to change (new retail outlets, individualization, fragmentation of tastes). This was reflected in the increased number of retailers' collections every year: from two to four in the 1960s to over twenty collections nowadays. Initially, these changes did not affect the mass market; that did not happen until the 1980s (Scheffer 1992). The changes had important consequences for producers and retailers, particularly the increased risk related to stocks. With consumers becoming more volatile and less predictable in their behaviour, there was more of a risk of not being able to sell large stocks. In response, retailers embarked on just-in-time logistics, lowering batch sizes and minimizing stocks. To assure that the supply of clothing would still be available in the shops in time under this system, retailers started to look for production facilities closer to the consumers. This was particularly important, since the import of garments from, for instance, East Asia was largely done by ship and often took more than half a year.[8] This created an interesting opportunity for contractors in Amsterdam as well as in the Mediterranean and Eastern Europe. Consequently, they were able to carve out a niche.

The impact of the fashion cycle, and the concomitant changes in the demand for garments, not only helps explain the rapid rise in the number of contractors but also their decline. Over the 1980s, retailers gradually learned how to combine just-in-time logistics with imports via various innovations to improve information flows on consumer behaviour. As a consequence, they became less dependent on the supply of garments from 'around the corner'. In combination with the increased competition from Eastern Europe after 1989, this meant a deathblow for contractors in Amsterdam (Raes 2000a).

The contractors usually did not supply directly to retailers, but worked via intermediaries. Most of the intermediaries operated from the Amsterdam wholesale centre, the World Fashion Center. It comes as no surprise that many of the contractors settled around this hub of Dutch fashion logistics. But during the fall of the sector, the number of wholesalers at the World Fashion Center fell from 1,200 in 1990 to 550 in 1994 (*NRC Handelsblad*, 8 October 1994).

One category of wholesaler was of particular importance to the Turkish contractors. From 1985 onwards, Indians and Pakistanis from Britain entered the low end of the market. To these wholesalers, the price of garments was more important than their quality or quick delivery, and they consequently exerted great pressure on the making prices. Their squeezing forced contractors to tender at unrealistically low prices and this pushed them further into the informal economy. In fact, the jobbers and contractors operated on spot market. The contractors from the very beginning were able to establish stable and long-term business relationships with their mainstream clients. But the contractors who worked for Indian and Pakistani wholesalers were unable to establish relationships of this kind. The wholesalers preferred casual relationships that would give them even more market power. They played contractors off against each other, offered squeeze contracts and left ever-smaller profits, if any, to the contractors. The latter responded by transferring the costs to their workers, who were increasingly undocumented immigrants who were paid off the books.

It is important to emphasize that the clothing market in the Netherlands, as well as in some other countries such as the UK, has been a buyers' market where retailers hold a strong position towards suppliers.[9] Large retailers (including the three largest chains Vendex/KBB, C&A and P&C) and large discounters account for almost half the clothing sales. These retailers control the demand for garments and were thus able to squeeze the profit margins of their suppliers, a position that became even stronger when new supply-via-imports alternatives emerged. Numerous manufacturers went bankrupt from the 1960s onwards or converted into 'head–tail' manufacturers concentrating on design and marketing, and transferring or outsourcing labour-intensive parts of their production (assembling in particular) to low-wage countries. Since the 1980s, as has been noted previously, retailers have been looking for shorter supply lines. Immigrants with their relatively high unemployment rates and limited upward social mobility options in other sectors were just about the only ones willing to try their luck in the garment industry. The emergence of immigrant contractors in Amsterdam can thus be seen as filling a temporary niche in the supply chain for garments. Changing retail logistics and increased competition in the early 1990s made outsourcing to local contractors a non-viable option again, even for immigrants, and the niche eventually collapsed. It is clear that in many respects market developments paralleled the rise and fall of sewing shops in Amsterdam. As such, market forces constitute an important element of the explanation of the contractors' fate.

## *Regulation*[10]

Social and economic factors were not the only causes. Institutional processes and arrangements played an important role as well. Students of the garment industry often discuss the importance of trade policy, and rightly so. The textile and garment industries are notorious examples of sectors where industrialized countries have imposed import barriers on Third World products. In the Netherlands, and in fact the European Union as a whole, a more protectionist attitude emerged in the early 1980s, with the signing of the second Multi-Fibre Arrangement. Only in the 1990s did this restrictive attitude diminish. The proliferation of Turkish contractors in

Amsterdam thus parallels a more protectionist stance towards clothing imports, providing more leeway for domestic suppliers. The steps towards liberalization in the 1990s targeted the countries that were the major competitors for these contractors – the Mediterranean non-member states and Eastern Europe – and this dramatically changed the opportunity structure for Turkish contractors in Amsterdam (Raes 2000a: 155–62).

There is more than just trade policy. Let us first examine how the Dutch welfare state allocated economic citizenship rights to its residents. Despite cuts during the 1980s and 1990s, a central element in the Dutch welfare state is a substantial and continuing social safety net for insiders, i.e. Dutch citizens and immigrants who have resided in the country for more than five years. The existence of this safety net has not put an end to the social differences along ethnic or national lines, in particular with respect to unemployment,[11] but it has prevented what some would call an 'ethnic underclass'. The rise of immigrant entrepreneurship in the garment industry is not just a matter of survival, as seems to be the case elsewhere. Immigrants were not forced into marginal entrepreneurial activities for lack of subsistence alternatives. Nonetheless, many entrepreneurs started a business to escape from unemployment and the limited choices open to them. What is important is that at least in the Dutch case the notion of impoverished migrants engaging in Third-World-like activities as entrepreneurs is too simplistic. This also applies to workers who are entitled to social security arrangements as immigrants with residence permits. This mitigated the pressure to accept unpleasant jobs at sewing shops. From this perspective, it is hardly surprising that new, undocumented immigrants rather than legal residents got the lousy jobs. Various immigrants moonlighted at the sewing shops even though they were getting welfare.

As the welfare state came under pressure and steps were taken to change the welfare system and keep it affordable, this weakened the position of outsiders, i.e. people whose presence was considered illegitimate. However, as immigrants with residence permits maintained relations with their friends and relatives back home, and border control was far from perfect, international migration continued. Newcomers managed to enter the country without the proper documents and, of course, the first thing they did was look for a job. These new undocumented immigrants were increasingly excluded from the social safety net of the welfare state and were much more willing to do poorly paid, hard work. That is why the growth of the sector coincided with a rise in the number of undocumented immigrants. The Dutch welfare state may have done its best to keep an underclass of legal immigrants from developing, but in the 1980s and early 1990s the combination of open borders and lax law enforcement had led to a growing reserve of undocumented workers.

So far, we have mainly addressed the impact of welfare state arrangements in general. We would now like to examine the impact of the various political and legal regimes, and how changes in these regimes affected the opportunities for the contractors. In tackling this issue, it is useful to draw a distinction between rules and regulations as such and their implementation and enforcement. When it comes to enforcement, the Dutch claim to be specialists in dealing with awkward situations where conflicting interests are at stake. A common option is to refrain from inter- ference, even in the face of violations of the law (Blankenburg and Bruinsma 1994). The way the Dutch enforce their soft drug laws is a case in point.

For a long time, Dutch authorities failed to take a firm line regarding informal activities in the Amsterdam garment sector. The central government hardly took any notice of the developments in the Amsterdam garment industry, and the City of Amsterdam was facing a dilemma. Should the violation of immigration, labour and tax regulations be viewed as undermining the morals of the welfare state and as a threat to fair economic traffic, and therefore be strongly opposed? Or should these informal practices be seen as a promising strategy on the part of under- privileged immigrants for coping with the threat of unemployment, achieving upward social mobility, and moving towards better integration in Dutch society? Initially the City of Amsterdam opted for a policy of *gedogen* or leniency towards the fledgling entrepreneurs.

The role of contractors in illegal activities did not go unnoticed by the public. In the public eye, 'illegal' was automatically associated with the Turkish sewing shop. Still, the use of the word 'illegal' requires some clarification, since there are many ways entrepreneurs can violate the law (Kloosterman *et al.* 1998). First, many entrepreneurs did not adhere to the Law on Labour of Foreign Workers (WABW), later revised as the Law on Work by Foreigners (WAV), which stipulates that non-European Union citizens can only be employed if employers cannot find a suitable European Union citizen to do the job. In these cases, the employer has to request a work permit at the Central Employment Exchange, which is not a mere rubber stamp process. Many Turkish contractors failed to obtain these permits, perhaps because they did not have them themselves. Secondly, the salaries, working hours and conditions were often in violation of collective labour agreements (CAOs) or the Labour Law (Arbo). Thirdly, contractors did not always pay pre- miums and social security payments. Lastly, the entrepreneurs could be engaged in other activities, such as illegally tapping electric power.

In the beginning of the 1980s, very few official steps were taken to enforce the various rules and regulations. In 1985, the supervisory agencies only went to fourteen sewing shops (Bloeme and van Geuns 1987: 144), in 1988 they went to thirty-seven, and in 1990 to a mere twenty-two. This lax law enforcement gave many contractors leeway to grow. They were, of course, aware of the illicit nature of their activities, but since the government did not seem to care much these activ- ities came to be regarded as *de facto* legal.

This changed around 1990. At first, the sector itself (i.e. the leading business associations) introduced a programme to reduce irregular activities, especially in the area of taxation and social security premiums. The basic philosophy was that the law should not be primarily enforced by the state, but by the people themselves. These programmes targeted retailers, wholesalers and other clients of the contractors who were expected to engage in voluntary self-regulation. However, they were not very enthusiastic about this approach, for obvious reasons, and played the waiting game. The first measure was the introduction in 1989 of the Certificate of Guarantee. This certificate, which stated that the contractor had worked according to the rules, was to be handed by contractors to their clients. The second measure was the Certificate on Payments. This stated that the contractor had paid for his workers' social security benefits. The responsibility for checking these certificates was in the hands of the clients who gave orders to the contractors. Neither of these measures was compulsory, and neither of them had much effect (van Geuns and van Diepen 1994: 25).

Despite the lip service paid to the law, officials did little to obstruct garment entrepreneurs who wished to continue informal production. In fact it was only the poor results of this self-regulation that made the new central government shift to a higher gear. The new Cabinet of Social Democrats and Christian Democrats that replaced the old Cabinet of Liberals and Christian Democrats in 1989 made the battle against fraud, the improper use of welfare benefits and illegal residence a top political priority. It was felt that stricter law enforcement would result in public spending cuts. If successful, welfare state reforms, which were unpopular among Social Democrats, could be avoided. The Minister of Social Affairs and Employment led the way, and the others followed suit. The Minister of Justice, who had primary responsibility for law enforcement but also for immigration, gave this shift an extra moral twist. The dramatic events following the crash of a cargo plane in an immigrant neighbourhood in south-east Amsterdam only served to increase public support for the policy shift. A number of undocumented immigrants were victims of the crash, and this provoked a moral panic about their presence in the Dutch welfare state (Husbands 1994). So as of 1989, a new policy was designed, encompassing a package of repressive as well as supportive measures. One of them was the introduction in Parliament of a bill to extend the workings of the Law on Chain Liability to the garment sector. This law would make retailers formally responsible for their contractors' illegal practices.

In February 1994 the bill was passed. Under this law, contractors had to open a G-account, where their clients had to deposit 35 per cent of the price of each order as a guarantee that this sum would be paid to the tax and social security services. Furthermore, a number of law enforcement agencies such as the Public Prosecutor, the Labour Relations Service (DIA), the Tax Department, the Aliens Police and the Industrial Insurance Administration Office (GAK) started working together in the Clothing Intervention Team (CIT) to clear the Amsterdam garment industry. The Clothing Intervention Team paid numerous visits to Turkish sewing shops, organizing raids. In particular, it targeted violations of the Law on Work by Foreigners. A number of contractors were brought to trial and prosecuted for hiring undocumented immigrants, and some undocumented immigrants were deported. Many entrepreneurs, whose economic position was already severely undermined by the saturation of the sector and the changing outsourcing practices of retailers, quit the industry as things were now getting too hot for them. This played an important role in the collapse of the Turkish garment industry.

As the situation in the garment industry deteriorated, efforts were made to set up formal organizations to promote the interests of the contractors, especially the Turkish ones. Only two Turkish contractors were members of the regular association of garment manufacturers (FENECON). Most of them did not feel represented by this large Dutch organization, which had lobbied against illegal Turkish contractors. Furthermore, the trade unions had little to do with the Turkish factories, and only a few native Dutch self-appointed spokesmen were interested in promoting the interests of undocumented garment workers. A couple of Turkish entrepreneurs who, interestingly, had past experience in a national organization of Turkish communist workers took the initiative to organize the entrepreneurs and a number of action committees were set up. At best, they reached a hundred entrepreneurs, mostly from their own social network (Rath 1999). The vast majority of the entrepreneurs were not really involved though. The fact that it was so hard to establish formal organizations or to mobilize politically the entrepreneurs through their networks thwarted the development of political clout. This eventually impinged on their very existence when it came to making political decisions regarding the crackdown on illegal practices. The entrepreneurs had been unable to establish strong relations with the relevant political actors except for a handful of left-wing politicians in the Amsterdam City Council, and this further undermined their position.

## Conclusion

'Amsterdam is the casual clothing capital, a perfect place to escape the obligations of fashion' (*de Volkskrant*, 19 October 1996). Indeed the Dutch capital and its residents reflect the legacy of what Schama (1987) called 'the embarrassment of riches'. As the Dutch themselves say, 'act normally, that is crazy enough'. This Calvinist aversion to showing off goes with relatively low clothing expenditures in general, and a lack of interest in *haute couture* in particular. However, even in Amsterdam, the incorporation of short-cycle fashion into the mass garment market in the 1980s contributed to an important transformation of garment logistics, in which immigrant contractors played an important role. The sewing shops, mainly run by Turks, grew in importance during the 1980s, reaching a peak in 1993, only to fade away almost completely in the following years. In this chapter, we have analysed this rise and fall of immigrant contractors in Amsterdam and tried to explain why this process took place. As is indicated in Table 5.4, the process consisted of three main stages.

In the first stage (1980–1987), an increasing number of new garment factories arose in Amsterdam out of the ashes of the Dutch garment industry. They steadily grew in number up to 1987. Although a substantial number of Dutch entrepreneurs were still active in the sector in this first stage, Turkish immigrants played a growing role. These new entrepreneurs had frequently lost their jobs in the recession of the 1970s and early 1980s, and now started to work for themselves. The first of these entrepreneurs were immigrants with legal residence permits who often had some experience in Dutch garment manufacturing beforehand. Starting off as very small enterprises financed by their own or family savings, they gradually grew to employ around twenty workers each. The contractors produced short-cycle women's outerwear of lower to medium quality. Demand conditions for this merchandise became

**Table 5.4** The Rise and Fall of Contractors in the Amsterdam Garment Industry

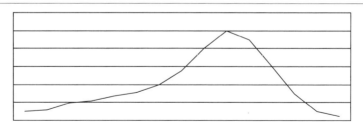

This figure represents the estimated number of contractors in the Amsterdam garment industry 1980–1997, see Figure 5.1

|  | *Rise* | *Boom* | *Fall* |
|---|---|---|---|
| Stage | 1980–1987 | 1987–1993 | 1993–1997 |
| Size | Slow but steady growth | Explosive growth | Rapid decline |
| Entrepreneurs workers | Increasing role of Turks | Increasing role of Turks and other nationalities | Decreasing role of Turks |
|  | Overwhelmingly documented entrepreneurs and workers | Many more undocumented entrepreneurs and workers | Overwhelmingly documented entrepreneurs and workers |
|  | Experienced entrepreneurs | Experienced entrepreneurs and, increasingly, also rookies | Experienced entrepreneurs |

**Table 5.4** The Rise and Fall of Contractors in the Amsterdam Garment Industry *(continued)*

| | *Rise* | *Boom* | *Fall* |
|---|---|---|---|
| Social networks | Temporary recruitment of skilled workers via social networks | Structural inflow of undocumented workers | End to undocumented worker recruitment |
| | Contractors maintain relatively stable relations with Dutch retailers | Emergence of Indian and Pakistani wholesalers; contractors maintain mainly casual relations with contractors clients | Contractors have relatively stable relations with retailers |
| | No political organization and mobilization | Various attempts to establish advocacy organizations and to mobilize social networks for political reasons | No political organization and mobilization |
| Market | Retailers need local contractors for short-cycle fashion | Retailers start to learn to combine short-cycle fashion with imports | Retailers combine short-cycle fashion with imports |
| | Steady growth of demand for ready-to-wear garments | Steady growth of demand for ready-to-wear garments | Declining demand for ready-to-wear garments |
| | Limited competition among contractors | Cut throat competition among contractors | Growing competition from Eastern Europe |
| Institutional arena | Restrictive trade policy | Restrictive trade policy | Liberalized trade policy |
| | Ignorance at level of central government, tolerance at level of local government | Continuing tolerance at level of local government, but preparation for stricter law enforcement at level of central government. Meanwhile attempts at voluntary regulation by the sector itself | Strict law enforcement at all governmental levels |

increasingly favourable throughout the 1980s. The entrepreneurs used their existing networks with jobbers as a stable channel for their output. The official agencies were usually willing to overlook the illegal practices in the sector, and the increasingly protectionist stance in trade policy diminished competition from imports. These factors joined to produce a fertile breeding ground for new sewing shops.

In the second stage (from 1987 to 1993), it seemed as if factors fertilized this breeding ground for new contractors. The growing number of new sewing shops reached a total of 1,000 in 1992 and a value of production of over NLG1 billion.

Although most of the entrepreneurs were still of Turkish descent, immigrants of other nationalities also entered the sector, and various forms of illegality increased. Numerous undocumented workers found employment and many of them set up their own shops. Growing competition among the contractors led to a decline in the profit margins and an expansion of the activities to less fashionable market segments. The enormous growth of the sector reflected a further improvement of the general market conditions the contractors operated in. Demand grew, in particular for short-cycle fashion. Competition from imports in these market segments remained relatively limited, in part due to import restrictions, although competition among the contractors themselves increased. New jobbers emerged, particularly wholesalers of Indian and Pakistani descent, contributing to a squeeze of profit margins for the contractors. Government intervention remained lax, allowing for the growth of illegal employment in the sewing shops. A shift in governmental policy was being prepared as of 1989, but it would take some time before it materialized. However, the growth in activity reflected a process of emulation with an increasing number of fledgling entrepreneurs following the example of their predecessors. As such, the growth in the number of contractors increasingly exceeded the demand for contract activities in the market. This meant that at its peak in 1992/3, the sector already exhibited some of the weaknesses that would soon contribute to its downfall.

In the last stage (1993–1997), the sector collapsed almost completely. In 1997 there were approximately only forty to fifty contractors left. This was due to four main factors. First, retailers managed to combine imports and high collection turnover and decreasingly needed local contractors for their short-cycle clothing supply. Second, there was an increase in competition from Eastern Europe and Turkey after the fall of the Berlin Wall and the liberalization of the trade policy. Third, competition became stronger because as a result of the emulation process the number of contractors started to exceed the market demand. And fourth, a much stricter approach by the government made many contractors close their shops. Stricter enforcement of the rules and regulations regarding immigrant work made the main asset of immigrant entrepreneurs – the recruitment of cheap and flexible immigrant labour though their own social network – obsolete. As a consequence, immigrant contractors disappeared again from the streets of Amsterdam.

## Notes

1. By law, all the firms in the Netherlands have to be registered in this Trade Register.

2. This is estimated on the basis of the average number of workers at each sewing shop, as by various sources and our own research at different moments in time.

3. NLG0.45 = one Euro.

4. We took into consideration the wage changes that place in these periods and used a lower wage rate for the early 1980s and a higher rate for the later period.

5. However, not all the people who were registered as entrepreneurs in the Trade Register of the Chamber of Commerce have actually been active as entrepreneurs. From our interviews it is clear that in some cases a firm was registered under the name of someone who was not really the entrepreneur (for example, the spouse). This was done to enable the entrepreneur to remain less 'visible' to the authorities. Since most factories were run by only one entrepreneur, the number of entrepreneurs over time parallels the data on the number of firms in Table 5.1. The fact that we found many more firms than entrepreneurs is partly due to the lack of data about entrepreneurs for some firms, but it also shows that many entrepreneurs have set up businesses several times.

6. To give an impression of the ethnic profile of the City of Amsterdam, we present the situation on 1 January 1996 (x1,000): Surinamese 69.6; Dutch Antilleans 10.5; Turks 31.0; Moroccans 48.0; South Europeans 16.3; Non-industrialized countries 59.7; Industrialized countries 69.5; Dutch 413.6. This gives a total of 718.2 (Hoolt and Scholten 1996: 15).

7. This section is partly based on the dissertation by Adem Kumcu (forthcoming).

8. It is surprising that even though the air transportation of garments has grown considerably, the percentage of garments imported by air has remained relatively constant (Raes 1995).

9. Only the producers of branded clothing have a relatively strong position *vis-à-vis* retailers.

10. This section is partly based on the dissertation by Marja Dreef (forthcoming).

11. Some would argue that it is the social security net in the first place which has been responsible for rising unemployment.

# – 6 –

# New York: Caught under the
# Fashion Runway
*Yu Zhou*[1]

## Introduction

New York City has been the centre of fashion in the United States since the late
nineteenth century. As ready-made clothes became more accepted and celebrated
as part of a way of life in the New World, New York rapidly became the indisputable
centre for factory garment manufacturing. Immigrants have shaped the garment
industry in New York City from its very start. Many immigrant groups in New
York were involved in this trade, including Jews and Italians at the turn of the
century, and newer Chinese and Dominican groups since the 1960s. The earlier
immigrants, particularly Russian and Eastern European Jews, laid down the organizational structure of New York's garment industry, which continues to shape the
participation of new immigrants today.

New York's garment industry has suffered a precipitous downturn since the
late 1950s in terms of total employment in the five-borough area, as well as its
relative position among other major metropolitan centres within the country. Yet,
the industry remained the largest manufacturing sector in New York City at the
end of the 1990s. It has continued to be defined as the quintessential immigrant
trade, a magnet attracting waves of new immigrants.

Closely associated with the immigrant nature of this industry is the prevalence
of ethnic entrepreneurship and ethnic networks. Earlier immigrants, particular
Eastern European Jews, used their ethnic network to build up and organize the
ready-made clothing industry. Like their predecessors, more recent Asian and
Hispanic immigrants entered this industry through a heavy reliance on ethnic entrepreneurship and networking (Waldinger 1986; Wong 1987). Ethnic networks not
only serve as the infrastructure to recruit, train, and discipline labour, they are
also instrumental for entrepreneurship, collecting capital, gaining on-the-job
training, and forging business connections (Bailey and Waldinger 1991; Waldinger
1996b; Wong 1987). While recognizing the key role of ethnic networks, in this
chapter I would like to highlight the limitations of networks.

Over the past 150 years the garment industry has evolved into a sophisticated network of specialization characterized by a two-tier system. The upper tier, mostly consisting of manufacturers, jobbers, and retailers, requires high education, financing capacity, designing, marketing, and management skills, and extensive industrial connections. It is dominated by established native-born capitalists, many of whom are descendants of Jewish and Italian immigrants. Newer immigrants, by contrast, are severely limited by their poor English skills and educational background, making it hard for them to contend for activities in the upper tier. Instead, they tend to be concentrated in the lower tier, consisting of contractors, subcontractors, and small manufacturers of various sorts. If trendy design and professional management characterize the upper tier, fierce price competition and acute time pressure characterize the lower one. The borderline between the two tiers is a well-guarded one entailing class, language, cultural, social, and educational privileges and barriers. Ethnic networks, prolific among immigrant firms, provide few channels for forging durable vertical linkages with the upper tier. This dual structure has become a major impediment for immigrants in mastering more profitable strategies and controlling their market conditions. Facing intense international competition from Third World countries and soaring real estate costs at traditional garment industrial locations, most ethnic entrepreneurs are struggling for survival. This has led to the proliferation of non-unionized factories and sweatshop conditions in New York City. The same ethnic networks that introduce immigrants to the garment trade also relegate them to the margin of this industry. The upward mobility that was feasible for Jewish immigrants when the industry was still in its infancy no longer seems to work for newer immigrant groups. This chapter reviews the development of the garment industry in New York and examines its current organizational structure. I will use the Chinese, the most established and largest new immigrant group in the garment industry in New York, to illustrate the major barriers that keep immigrants from moving to a higher level of the garment industry.

## Development of the Garment Industry in New York City

The dominance of New York over the American garment industry emerged in the nineteenth century. As in other manufacturing sectors, New York outperformed other East Coast cities such as Boston, Philadelphia and Baltimore because of its location, with deep sea ports and access to the vast hinterlands of the Great Lakes region. Yet, the garment industry became far more concentrated in New York City than other sectors of manufacturing in the United States. By 1890, 44 per cent of all ready-made clothes in the United States were manufactured in New York, and 53.3 per cent of all the women's garment industry employees worked there. The concentration intensified until the Second World War, with 65 per cent of the women's garment industry workers concentrated in New York City (Green 1997). This level of concentration is largely due to the specific characteristics of the garment industry, which has persistently resisted the standardization and mass production that occurred in other industries. Instead, such features as small factories, wildly fluctuating seasonalities, and poorly paid labour have been the hallmark of garment manufacturing since the emergence of ready-made clothing.

In response to the flexibility requirement, Waldinger (1986) and Green (1997) argue that the garment industry became a textbook case of spatial agglomeration. The volatile fashion demands, in conjunction with the finer division of labour-forced fashion-makers to seek proximity to associated businesses such as fabric suppliers, designers, cutters, contractors, and accessory suppliers. As a result, the Manhattan fashion district, which extends between Sixth and Ninth Avenue from 35th Street to 41st Street, became a magnet for a variety of garment-related activities. Spatial proximity facilitated and encouraged the finer division of labour, which gave the New York fashion industry a high level of flexibility and efficiency.

The prominence of New York's garment industry also stemmed from its position as the immigration gateway. The growth of the industry was based on a willing supply of cheap labour provided by new immigrants. As the immigration gateway to the United States, New York attracted multifarious poor and industrious workers. As the children of earlier immigrants gradually moved up the social ladder and out of garment manufacturing, new immigrants filled the vacancies, becoming the workers and small factory owners.

Historically, Jews were the most significant immigrant group in the garment industry around the turn of the century. Italian women also constituted a major workforce, although in far smaller numbers than the Jews. From 1880 to 1920, an estimated 460,000 Eastern European Jews poured into New York City (Moore 1981; Waldinger 1986). Many of the Jews had been tailors back in Europe, and many others also claimed to be tailors, since it was known to be an occupation that could get them admitted at Ellis Island. Their poverty, the language barrier, and fictional and real skills steered many Jews into the emerging ready-to-wear garment trade. They supplied the cheap labour and entrepreneurs for the industry. Most importantly, Jewish involvement reconfigured the garment production system in New York in two ways. First, Jewish immigrants introduced numerous organizational innovations to shape the institutional structure in the garment industry. Rather than working at large factories, Eastern European Jews opted to work for smaller contractors who lived and located their shops in the tenement buildings with immigrant residents (Waldinger 1986). Between the wars, a manufacturers–jobbers system also emerged and expanded, with the sewing subcontracted out so fashion-makers could concentrate on designing, financing, and co-ordinating the various components of garment production and marketing (Green 1997). Ethnic networks were prolific in the industry to recruit workers, collect start-up capital, and forge business linkages with the upstream and downstream of the production. This subcontracting system not only laid down the framework for the industry's flexible production, it also opened the door for the involvement of later immigrant groups in the subcontracting business.

Secondly, Jewish immigrants were instrumental in the emergence of garment workers' unions, which transformed New York into the most organized and union-ized garment industrial centre in the United States. Since the International Ladies' Garment Workers' Union (ILGWU)[2] was founded in 1900, it has engaged in organ-izing strikes and collective bargaining with the industry to improve working conditions. The union gained strength during the First World War, and had 129,000 members in 1918. Its membership declined precipitously in the 1920s, with only 23,800 members in 1929. However, after 1932 the membership rose to reach a quarter of a million in 1940 (Green 1997). After the Depression, the powerful union was able to guarantee social benefits ranging from health care, housing, unemployment benefits to day care. The benefits appealed to many new immigrants and remain one of the union's main selling points in attracting members (Kwong 1997).

Employment in the New York garment industry peaked during the Second World War when New York produced 70 per cent of the unit-priced dresses in the United States (Green 1997). Global ILGWU membership rose to 430,000. This was the heyday of organized labour. In an industry characterized by volatility and frag-mentation, the union successfully organized the industry with union-approved contractors, supervised industrial linkages, and regulated wage and working conditions.

Yet the higher wages and unionized workers also contributed to the garment industry's decline in New York. Although it was not clear until the late 1950s, New York's dominance in the garment trade had in fact been eroding since the 1930s (Green 1997). The restriction of immigration after the 1920s and the success of the garment workers' union both led to a steady wage rise in New York. The standardized and mass production end of the garment industry left New York and went in search of cheap labour locations – first to the surrounding states and then to the South, where labour was thought to be docile and in abundant supply. Since the 1960s, mass garment production has further internationalized to Asia and Latin America (Petras 1992). Imported clothing accounted for less than 15 per cent of the United States market in the 1960s, but grew to over 80 per cent in the 1980s (Waldinger 1986). Nowadays, clothing sold in the United States bears labels from Third World countries all over the world. There were also steep declines in garment employment, and the total number of New York garment workers on the payroll declined in 1998 to less than 40 per cent of what it was in 1973 (see Table 6.1).

A sizeable section of the fashion industry is still in New York City however, especially the more fashion-oriented segments – in particular women's and girls'

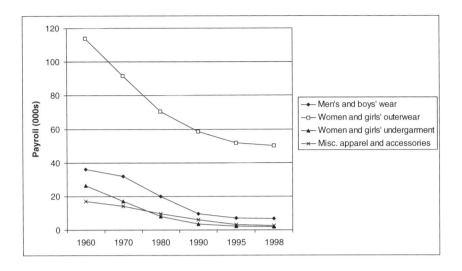

**Figure 6.1** Decline of New York City Garment Employee Payroll

outerwear (see Figure 6.1). The rapidly changing fashion cycle, the small and fragmented demands and short lead-time, make women's clothing less prone to mass production, and thus less likely to move offshore (Petras 1992; Taplin 1996). Women's outerwear has become an increasingly central part of the New York garment industry, employing about seventy per cent of the total garment labour force in 1998, compared to the 45 per cent in 1970 (see Table 6.1). The garment industry was still the number one manufacturing sector in New York at the end of the 1990s. In 1998, the industry employed 132,900 people in fashion-related firms, from designing to retailing in the five-borough area. About 74,000 were in apparel manufacturing and another 10,400 in textiles. Apparel and textile manufacturing firms together accounted for 31.6 per cent of all the manufacturing firms in the city in 1998 (Bowles 2000). New York City continues to occupy the top position in garments produced within the United States. Eighteen per cent of all the women's outerwear produced in the United States was made in New York in the mid-1990s. More than one in every four dresses made in the United States was manufactured in New York City (GIDC 1995). In dresses and women's sportswear, New York City actually became even more prominent in its share of total United States employment (GIDC 1992). Green (1997) also argues that the decline, although real for production, is not reflected in the product value. The total value added more than doubled in Manhattan from 1958 to 1977. From another angle, this indicates that the role of New York in the garment industry has disproportionately moved to the high-value-added fashion section.

**Table 6.1** Employees on Non-agricultural Payrolls in New York City (× 1,000)

|                                    | 1960  | 1970  | 1980  | 1990 | 1995 | 1998 |
|------------------------------------|-------|-------|-------|------|------|------|
| Men's and boys' wear               | 36    | 31.9  | 20    | 9.7  | 7    | 6.7  |
| Women's and girls' outerwear       | 113.8 | 91.6  | 70.4  | 58.7 | 51.7 | 50.3 |
| Women's and girls' underwear       | 26.3  | 17    | 8.2   | 3.4  | 2.3  | 1.8  |
| Misc. apparel and accessories      | 17.2  | 14.2  | 9.7   | 6.2  | 3.1  | 2.6  |
| Apparel and other textile products | 267.4 | 203.9 | 139.6 | 94.7 | 75.2 | 70.1 |

The resilience of New York's garment manufacturing depends, as in the past, on spatial agglomeration and immigration (Waldinger 1986). The striking agglomeration of fashion-related industries and services in New York City provides a unique milieu that is unmatched anywhere in North America. Within Manhattan there are over 5,100 showroom facilities, and eight schools for fashion design and training. The Fashion Institute of Technology (FIT) is the world's largest school for fashion, and graduates 11,000 students each year for careers in the fashion industry. Figure 6.2 portrays the finer division of the labour and specialization in the garment manufacturing networks with the jobbers (and/or manufacturers) at the centre. The presence and proximity of designer houses, educational institutions, fabric suppliers, manufacturers, various contractors, accessory suppliers, and distributing or marketing firms clearly constitute an extensive web of information and exchange networks that are central to the garment industry. Researchers on the garment industry frequently stress the key role of spatial agglomeration (Bowles 2000; Green 1997; Taplin 1996; Waldinger 1986). Bud Konheim, the CEO of New York's designer firm Nicole Miller, was quoted in a research report released in March 2000 (Bowles 2000: 11): 'There's nothing like controlling the quality of goods that are being made across the street. When it's across the street, the lapse time is just a few minutes. The quality gets immediately better. What it means to your business is that you're not making mistakes and you don't have to give away any garments.'

According to the New Industrial Space thesis forwarded by Scott (1988 and 1993), spatial agglomeration provides substantial transactional advantages of players of all sizes in all the industries defined by unpredictable and rapid market cycles, which arguably characterize the garment industry better than any other. The spatial concentration of New York City's garment industry is currently threatened by the soaring real estate prices of the late 1990s. Due to the demand for office space in Manhattan, the rent in the garment district has risen to a level unaffordable to many garment makers. According to the report by the Center for an Urban Future (Bowles 2000), for the first time ever, in 1998 fashion industry employees no longer constituted a majority of the employees in the midtown

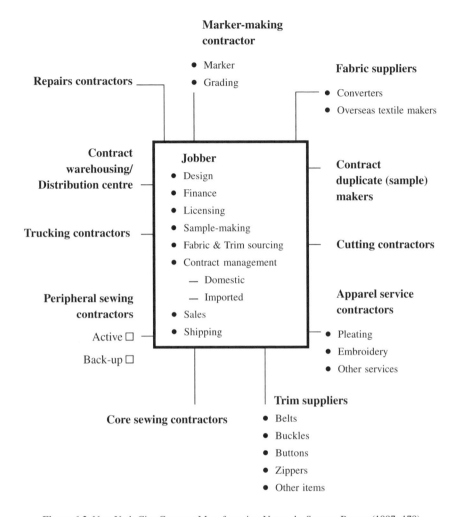

**Figure 6.2** New York City Garment Manufacturing Network. *Source:* Proper (1997: 179)

fashion district. Chinatown, another centre of garment manufacturing, faces similar real estate pressure (Oser 1998). As a result, many garment firms moved out of Manhattan to outer boroughs like Queens and Brooklyn or out of state to New Jersey (Bowles 2000). This spatial diffusion might well give a fatal blow to New York City's competitiveness in the garment industry, although it is still too early to assess its overall effect.

Another factor in the persistence of the garment industry in New York City is, of course, the renewed supply of cheap immigrant labour. The surge of immigrants since 1965 provided a fresh inflow of labour from Asia and Latin America. With the decline of other manufacturing sectors in the city, the garment industry has become all the more attractive for unskilled immigrants. The industry has low skill and language requirements and can absorb a large number of female workers who have trouble finding other jobs. The subcontracting system developed by Jews facilitated the entrepreneurial activities of more recent immigrants. According to the GIDC estimate (1992), in the early 1990s immigrants owned more than 30–40 per cent of the contracting facilities and over 75 per cent of the New York City production employees were immigrants. Of the garment workers, 70 per cent were members of minorities, 33 per cent were Hispanics, 27 per cent were Asians and 9 per cent were African-Americans. The leading national groups were the Chinese, Dominicans, Italians, Mexicans and Koreans. Women were and are the main force in this business: 67 per cent of the employees in the garment industry are women.

Different immigrant groups tend to be introduced into different areas of the industry by their ethnic networks. The Chinese are known to be one of the largest and most established groups, and are fairly well-documented. After 1960, the number of Chinese-owned garment firms increased from eight to 480 (Waldinger 1986; Zhou 1992). Most of the Chinese contractors tend to concentrate on women's sportswear. About 20,000 Chinese women are members of UNITE, Local 23–25 (women's sportswear). This does not include the non-unionized factories, which have also rapidly increased. Chinatown has become New York City's largest concentration of garment manufacturers and contractors. Koreans are more likely to be involved as garment contractors than as workers. Dominicans, according to Waldinger (1986), tend to be involved in the garment industry more as workers. Dominican-owned firms also tend to be smaller than Chinese ones. The garment industry is the largest employer of Dominican women in New York City (Pessar 1994). The involvement of Hispanic immigrants is less documented, since most of the Hispanic-owned firms are non-unionized. Interviews with a UNITE official indicate that they disproportionately concentrate on children's wear and the under-wear sector, which are more standardized and less volatile than women's outerwear.

Statistics on the garment industry can be gathered from different sources, such as the Census of Economics, County Business Patterns, the Bureau of Labor, and the United States or New York State Department of Labor. A general shortcoming of these statistics is that they rarely draw structural distinctions between contractors and manufacturers. These statistics are also likely to under- or over-count small firms, since they have such a short lifespan. The information in this chapter is from secondary sources such as existing statistics, published books, articles and research reports, official websites, and interviews with people involved in the garment industry, including the director of the Chinese contractor association (the Greater Blouse, Skirt & Undergarment Association, Inc.), staff members in the Garment Industry Development Council and UNITE. Garment factory owners and employees also contributed their insights into the trade. The fieldwork was conducted between 1996 and 1998.

## Division of Labour and Restructuring in the Garment Industry

The garment industry, particularly women's clothing production in New York City, should be viewed as a well-established, yet ever-changing network of specialization. The upper tier of the network consists of manufacturers, jobbers and retailers. Manufacturers purchase material, design, cut, assemble and finish the final product, and market it for retailers. Jobbers are outsourcing manufacturers, doing everything manufacturers do except assemble and finish the garments. This is contracted out to contractors who cut, make, trim and do the finishing (see Figure 6.1). Since manufacturers also frequently subcontract the garment assembly to contractors, the difference between manufacturers and jobbers is primarily in their production capacity rather than in their practice. The retailers are usually the major fashion chains or department stores who do the marketing and final sales. The retailers trace the fashion cycles and submit orders to the manufacturers and jobbers. Slightly over half the garment revenue is absorbed by the retailers (Proper 1997). Since the 1980s, mergers and acquisitions have reduced the number of retailers; as a result they have gained a great deal of authority as regards dictating the prices paid to manufacturers. Some major retailers such as Macy's also started their own private labels in addition to selling an assortment of other manufacturer's labels, so in fact they too have become manufacturers. Manufacturers or jobbers may transfer the price pressure from the retailers further down the chain onto the contractors (Bonacich 1994; Bowles 2000). Manufacturers, jobbers, and retailers combine to occupy the professional and most profitable end of the industry, which takes about 88 per cent of the revenue from each garment (Proper 1997). Contractors are at the lower tier of the industry, which takes about 12 per cent of the revenue.

Garment contracting factories are the sites of high concentrations of immigrants as factory owners and workers. The sewing jobs require little language proficiency. The skills are something many immigrant women have already obtained in their home countries, or can be learned rather quickly through on-the-job experience. The work also offers the flexible (albeit long) hours that are important for women with young children. Working at garment factories gives immigrants an opportunity to acquire experience and inside knowledge of the sector. Some of the more successful ones later become entrepreneurs. Becoming a contractor involves only a low entry cost. The factory space can be rented, and used sewing machines can be cheaply purchased. Green (1997) estimates that one can become a contractor with as little as $25,000 in initial capital. In addition, connections with jobbers or manufacturers can be inherited from the previous owners or otherwise through personal contacts with other contractors, truckers, etc. Once some immigrants have gained a foothold in this industry, others are introduced into the trade through informal ethnic networks (Bailey and Waldinger 1991).

As more and more immigrants crowd into the field, an oversupply of contractors inevitably intensifies the competition and generates a downward price spiral. Pitting one contractor against the other, the retailers, manufacturers, and jobbers depress the piece rate and reduce their responsibilities, at the same time ensuring a larger labour pool and at a lower risk. This competition has been seen as the primary cause of the poor working conditions at garment factories (Bonacich 1994; Buford 1999). The marginal profit also causes high failure rates among garment factories, discourages capital investment for technology and personnel training, and thus generates a vicious cycle preventing contractors from advancing their businesses.

Entering the 1990s, the garment industry in New York City was faced with unprecedented pressure from a stagnant domestic market and intense international competition. Slow population growth, the gradually ageing American population, and the trend towards casual wear in women's and men's clothes led to a dearth of practical growth in apparel purchasing (GIDC 1992). On the other hand, the improved transportation and communication, trade deregulation, and better business infrastructure, distribution networks and services increased the competitiveness of offshore producers. They were increasingly capable of producing sophisticated fashion-oriented clothing in a shorter time and at a lower cost. When Waldinger (1986) first wrote the book on the garment industry in the mid-1980s, the orders to offshore producers took about a year to turn around. Nowadays it takes as little as three months or even six weeks, particularly in Asia, according to my interviews with a garment import company in New York City. The gap in timing, service, and quality between offshore and domestic producers has narrowed considerably. These developments have forced New York garment makers to focus even more on the higher-value-added products, striving for shorter lead-times, more styles, higher quality, and better services in an environment characterized by an accelerated life cycle of fashion products.

In addition, information technology has revolutionized the garment industry and further reduced the manoeuvring room for lower-tier producers. In large facilities, computer-aided design (CAD) has changed the design and cutting process, so fabrics can be used more rationally. Bar-coded shipping containers speed up the distribution process. The electronic point of sale (EPOS) system helps retailers trace sales and restock faster. In contrast, basic garment assembly has not changed that much since the nineteenth century, with human labour over the sewing machines still the mainstay (Abernathy *et al.* 1995; Taplin 1996). Different segments of the market have somewhat different technology dynamics. According to Taplin (1996), men's and boys' wear are the most standardized and therefore more easily automated. They have the highest capital–employee ratio and depend on a highly skilled and well-paid workforce. Women's and children's underwear also tend to be standardized, but are often made in Third World countries. Women's and girls' outerwear, the bulk of New York's garment industry, is the least capitalized sector.

Rapid fashion changes and small batch production make the sector the least conducive to mass production. The lower value of women's dresses as compared to men's suits leaves the workers the lowest paid in the United States garment industry.

Given the market dynamics and technology changes, one of the main responses of the New York fashion industry has been to adopt the 'just-in-time' or 'quick response system' (QR). This system involves a reorganization of the production, marketing, and inventory management operations to create closer, more efficient linkages between fabric suppliers, contractors, jobbers, manufacturers, and retailers. To avoid fashion risk, retailers try to place orders 'closer to the season', start with a smaller volume, and reorder the items that become hot on the market. A Department of Labor research report shows that retailers are moving towards continuous restocking, with daily or weekly replenishment shipments constituting more than 66 per cent of the 1992 shipments.[3] This pressures all the upstream suppliers into ever-shortening lead-times, forcing them to adopt the quick response system. Although the spatial proximity has substantially reduced the transaction and turn around time, and the subcontracting system can expand or shrink at short notice, quickening the response any further would require far more structural adjustment. According to the assessment of GIDC, the QR system can only be developed with efficient decision support systems, durable relationships between the suppliers and customers, electronic data interaction, and a strong upper and middle management.

This kind of ideal corporate strategy becomes highly problematic in a situation with a large number of immigrant contractors. The vast majority of them do not have the technical and management expertise envisioned by the industrial leaders. In addition, the networks developed by immigrant firms tend to be most intense within specific ethnic groups. Many of these firms depend on word of mouth, ethnic networking, and the transfer of former contracts to new firms to gain their work orders. Language barriers, a lack of connections with powerful players among the entrepreneurs, and the shorter lifespan of the sewing factories serve to further inhibit immigrant firms from using a more direct approach to locate work and nurture high quality and enduring relations with manufacturers or retailers. The spatial dispersion of garment factories from Manhattan has made it even more difficult to stay connected, though truckers and unions can provide a certain degree of assistance on job orders. GIDC (1992) found in its research that contractors often complain about how difficult it is to locate customers, and manufacturers and retailers have a hard time identifying appropriate supply sources.

## Sweatshop Resurgence

Unable to adopt a more sophisticated management strategy, most immigrant contractors resort to price competition as their only option. Faced with intense competition from low-wage Third World countries and rising numbers of illegal immigrants into New York City, many social science analysts, government agencies, and the public fear a major resurgence of sweatshops (Kwong 1997; Portes and Castells 1989; Sassen 1989; USGAO 1989 and 1994). Whether or not this fear is warranted is hard to tell, as the definitions of the term 'sweatshop' vary a great deal. The United States General Accounting Office developed a working definition of a sweatshop as 'an employer that violates more than one federal or state labor, industrial homework, occupational safety and health, workers' compensation, or industry registration' (USGAO 1994: 1, n1). Waldinger and Lapp (1993) use the OECD category of 'concealed employment' as the definition for a sweatshop on the grounds that it is better defined, and USGAO's definition would even categorize some of the union factories as sweatshops. By analysing employment against production data, they found no evidence of a sweatshop resurgence in New York City. There is also a sharp disagreement on the effects of sweatshops, and on whether sweatshops serve as a much-needed stepping-stone for new immigrants (Buford 1999), or deprive them of a basic livelihood (Kwong 1997). Yet most analysts agree that garment workers earn very low wages and survive in conditions not much better than at the turn of the century, with rampant violation of labour and health standards. The downward price pressure that manufacturers, jobbers, and retailers exert on the contractors is inevitably transferred to garment workers, who already earn meagre wages. Another even more problematic factor is that in order to meet more stringent deadlines, more work is subcontracted down the chain, so the payment delay to the workers at the bottom of the chain is lengthened, leading to serious backwage problems (Buford 1999). According to the United States Department of Labor, which conducted 262 investigations in 1998, 111 violations of the Fair Labor Standards Act were observed, a total of $800,000 in back wages were collected, and $124,715 in civil fines were issued in New York City alone.[4] Bowles (2000) cites a United States Labor Department report issued on October 1999 that only 35 per cent of the New York garment shops that were surveyed were in compliance with federal minimum wage and overtime laws.

The sweatshop phenomenon is also closely linked with the influx of illegal immigrants. Kwong (1997) argues that the 'employer sanction' provision in the Immigration Reform and Control Act (IRCA) passed in 1986 worsened the bargaining power of illegal workers. The IRCA granted amnesty to illegal residents in the United States and held employers accountable if they knowingly hired illegals after the IRCA was passed. Although well intentioned, Kwong charges that the provisions can be easily evaded and the Act makes illegal workers even less likely to complain about violations. The increasing numbers of illegal Chinese immigrants from Fujian Province since the late 1980s, as part of human smuggling operations, brought an influx of Fujianese into New York City's Chinatown. Desperate for jobs to pay back the debts they incurred in the journey, the illegal Fujianese greatly depressed the wages of the garment workers in Chinatown (Kwong 1997).

The proliferation of sweatshops was the target of growing public criticism in the 1990s as more and more brand names were found to be made in the sweatshops, and illegals were found to be held under slavery like conditions. The criticism became even sharper in 1997 after it was revealed that some of Kathie Lee Gifford's line of clothing was made in sweatshops in New York and Central America. Kathie Lee was a popular network talk show host. She broke down on television and turned herself into a campaigner for the no-sweat movement. The public outcry even compelled United States President Bill Clinton to set up a presidential task force in 1996 to work towards eliminating sweatshops. Known as the White House Apparel Industry Partnership, the task force consisted of companies, trade unions and human rights and religious groups. After two years of negotiations, a Workplace Code of Conduct was signed by some of the participants. The Code requires companies voluntarily to adopt and have contractors adopt standards including a maximum work-week, a stipulation that employers pay the minimum or prevailing wage, and a prohibition of child labour. It also set up a special apparel industry association to make sure companies lived up to the Code and to develop ways to share information with consumers, such as labelling. UNITE, the AFL-CIO and a large union of department store workers, however, refused to sign the deal, charging that it did not establish a 'living wage' and there was insufficient independent monitoring (Greenhouse 1998a,b).

The fact that the Code of Conduct was voluntary rather than mandatory indicates the United States reluctance to play a stronger role in industry and labour relations. The government indeed has taken other law enforcement actions such as frequent raids in conjunction with the Immigration and Naturalization Services at suspected sweatshop sites. The Department of Labor has also issued a quarterly Garment Enforcement Report since March 1995 to publicize labour code violators on their Internet site (see note 3). Public anti-sweatshop campaigns have also gathered force, especially at colleges and universities. Despite the campaigns, labour code violations have not fundamentally improved. Major corporations, mindful of their public image, often pull their contracts from suspected sweatshop sites, such as in New York's Chinatown. Yet the downward structural pressure on small contractors has not been addressed. So although the anti-sweat campaign has shut down a number of violators, on the whole the non-union factories continue to proliferate, especially in boroughs like Brooklyn, as was observed by a number of my interviewees. Pressured by the anti-sweat campaign and the rapidly rising rents in Manhattan, many contractors have closed their Chinatown shops and moved to Brooklyn. Since most of the Chinatown shops are unionized and most Brooklyn factories are not, the migration implies a reduced monitoring system.

In short, the sweatshops have been widely criticized. Although there is a great deal of debate on the definition of sweatshops and on whether they are on the rise and what effect they have, there is widespread agreement that the conditions of garment workers are often unacceptable and labour violations are rampant. However, the current measures of curtailing sweatshops are either poorly enforced, or fail to address the underlying problem of industrial structure and international competition. The continued influx of new immigrants into New York City from Asia and Latin America does nothing to improve the wages of the garment sector. The wages in the United States have become so low that some garment makers were prompted to return to the United States from Third World countries in the early 1990s to increase the turnaround speed and get around the quotas (Petras 1992). Meanwhile, measures to assist the garment industry – such as rent control, technology support for contractors and worker training – have received little attention, or even witnessed funding cutbacks (Bowles 2000).

One way fundamentally to enhance the garment workers' situation is by improving the capability and position of immigrant-owned contracting firms so that they can move into more profitable parts of the operation. The benefit of the industry would be more equally distributed. The following section examines the development of Chinese entrepreneurship in the garment industry. As one of the largest and most established immigrant groups in New York's garment industry, the experiences of Chinese entrepreneurs demonstrate the difficulties confronting immigrants moving in this direction and prospering in today's industrial environment.

## Chinese Immigrant Entrepreneurs in the Garment Industry

Since the 1960s, Chinese involvement in the garment industry has grown at a rapid pace. As suggested by Waldinger (1986), starting in the 1960s, the previous generation of Jewish contractors either died out or moved to different industries, leaving ample vacancies for new immigrants, especially the Chinese ones. The influx of unskilled immigrants from mainland China since the late 1970s fuelled the industry with inexpensive and disciplined labour. After working in the industry for some time, many immigrants used their savings to become self-employed, which turned Chinatown into the largest concentration of garment shops in New York City. Many shops owned by the Chinese also opened in midtown, Queens, and Brooklyn. With real estate values going up in Manhattan in the late 1990s, the most desirable site in the outer boroughs became Sunset Park in Brooklyn, which, not accidentally, is the third largest concentration of Chinese in New York City after Chinatown in Manhattan and Flushing in Queens (Bowles 2000).

Chinese-owned garment factories are typical of immigrant businesses: small, highly competitive, and with a short lifespan. According to the estimate of the director of the Chinese contractors association, 30–40 per cent of the firms would either close down or change their names within the first year. Changing the firm name is a common strategy to escape debts, since debtors may decide the small amount of money owed is not worth the pursuit. Owing back wages is another reason for closing an operation. Most Chinese immigrant owners were generally poorly educated and spoke little English, and they gained their experience by working in other garment factories. Up until the mid-1990s, a vast majority of the Chinese garment factories were unionized, with 20,000 Chinese women belonging to UNITE. However, as intensified competition made conditions worse, more and more non-unionized shops opened in the outer boroughs and unionized firms become a minority among the Chinese-owned factories. Even worse problems were reported among the factories hiring the most recent illegal immigrants from Fujian Province, such as extremely low wages and slavery like working conditions (Kwong 1997).

Despite a presence in the New York garment industry of more than two decades, Chinese firms continue to occupy a marginal position. The vast majority of Chinese firms are new and were established after large flows of immigration from mainland China became possible at the end of the 1970s. A good share of the entrepreneurs are inexperienced and lack capital. There are very few signs of upward mobility from the lower to the upper tier. Based on the discussion above, unless immigrant entrepreneurs can move to the upper tier of manufacturers or jobbers they stand little chance of gaining more than survival space in this trade. Yet moving up the established industrial hierarchy means overcoming formidable odds. Even for the earlier Jewish immigrants, it took more than one generation for many of them to move into positions as manufacturers, jobbers, designers or retailers. Today, the barriers have only become steeper in a hyper-competitive environment. My research in the Chinese community suggests that although some immigrant entrepreneurs have indeed moved in this direction, for the vast majority of the immigrant contractors this strategy is out of reach, although not out of mind.

The key step towards becoming a manufacturer or jobber is to own a private label. This can significantly upgrade a contractor's position or at least allow him to circumvent the usual jobbers. It will increase his profit margin by internalizing the higher end of the industry, and also reduce the seasonal factor since producers are able to plan production according to their own pace and capacity. This theory is well understood by many Chinese factory owners, but owning a private label also entails some major difficulties.

The first question is how to acquire financial capital. To become a jobber or manufacturer means to be able to purchase the fabric prior to production. Along with a private label comes the need to hire professionals, such as designers, managers, and highly skilled workers including sample makers, models, and cutters. This kind of operation thus requires a substantial capital investment before the garment is sold to the market. As a result, the producer runs a significant financial risk. Most immigrant contractors operating on a razor-thin profit margin are incapable of assuming this kind of risk.

Second, being a manufacturer or jobber makes it necessary to co-ordinate and streamline the specialities in the garment trade and requires an ability to meet the stringent deadlines, which in turn require planning and management expertise that can not be acquired simply by working on the factory floor. For most of Chinatown's contractors, whose only experience in business came from working in the factories, a sophisticated business operation on this scale is beyond their reach.

Third, moving into the upper tier of the garment industry means adhering to the mainstream regulations and laws and thus avoiding legal troubles. Most Chinatown contractors, however, operate on a cash basis. Cash transactions make it easy for the owners and workers to evade taxes, yet it also leaves the owners with highly problematic accounting books. Sometimes the books show fewer workers than there really are, so each worker's pay appears higher. On other occasions, the books only show the paycheck portion of the salaries of their workers, who also receive partial cash payment. As a result, the pay on the books is below the minimum wage, and the owners would appear to be committing labour code violations. A union official familiar with various violation cases in Chinatown commented that it is extremely difficult to sort out what exactly had been paid to the workers. Many contractors argue that they were forced to engage in illegal practices to save costs. But the illegality also cost them legitimacy, making it difficult to establish a solid reputation and expand into major and formal operations.

Fourth, in order to gain a foothold in the garment industry firms have to be around for a long period of time. Yet most Chinatown firms have a very short lifespan. It is practically impossible to know how many firms there are in the Chinese community. The official statistics are highly unreliable and a third of the firms disappear in their first year. The director of the garment contractor association estimated that a third of the firms that had disappeared really failed, but the majority simply changed their names to avoid their debtors and either started operating at a different location or remained at the same address. Needless to say, frequent changes are not conducive to establishing a stable relation with manufacturers or jobbers, and are disastrous for formal business operations.

Finally, a jobber's key role is to co-ordinate different networks and specialities in a garment factory (see Figure 6.1). Yet most immigrant entrepreneurs concentrate on a narrow segment of garments with few outreach channels. The most efficient networks Chinese entrepreneurs depend upon – namely the ethnic networks – are hardly a useful mechanism when it comes to contacting the mostly white upper tier. To get better orders, Chinese entrepreneurs would have to intensify their marketing efforts and have more intimate interactions with the professional class. Their poor mastery of the English language obviously gets in the way of making these social contacts.

Given these barriers, most factory owners are relegated to the contractor sectors and only compete on prices. This creates a vicious circle in which the lower the profit, the less stable the enterprise, and the more the illegal practices become a way of operation the less likely an enterprise is of having any long-term planning, investment and education. An official from GIDC commented that so many Chinese contractors are trying to survive until next week, there is no way they can think about next year or about making long-term plans.

The general lack of Chinese participation in the upper tier of the garment industry does not mean they are totally absent there. And there are a few success stories. In fact I spoke to one highly successful Chinese garment manufacturer. I visited the firm site and discussed the firm's history with the owner and manager. His success story is not representative of Chinese garment operations, but this exception demonstrates the daunting distance immigrant entrepreneurs have to travel to reach a higher level.

Mr Siu is the owner of a very large garment factory at the edge of Chinatown, and employs nearly 400 people. He was born in China and migrated to Hong Kong before he came to the United States in the 1960s. He entered the garment business in the mid-1970s, so his firm was one of the earlier ones in Chinatown and is now one of the largest. Like other contractors, he had been doing contracting work for a number of major brands such as Liz Claiborne and Anne Klein. The superior quality gained him a good reputation with these jobbers. In 1995, an Asian designer left Liz Claiborne and invited Mr Siu to create a private label. Seeing an opportunity to have better control of the line and to raise the profit margin, Mr Siu agreed to give it a try. The label is Lafayette 148, his street address. It is a relatively high-end fashion line for women's clothes, with most of the dresses selling for between $200 and $400. Since then, he has hired a number of professionals to do the designs, samples and management. The business has expanded substantially and has an on-site retailing store, although it mainly functions as a showroom because of its out-of-the-way location. Several upscale department chains such as Saks Fifth Avenue carry the Lafayette 148 brand. The factory, however, still does contracting from other jobbers to maintain its business stability. It is the chief domestic contractor for Anne Klein and has a military contract for the women's uniform jacket for the United States Air Force.

The factory was cited as one of 'the best' shops in the city by a UNITE official (Proper 1997: 190) – quite a contrast to most of the Chinatown factories which tend to operate in basements or upstairs with boarded-up windows. The factory occupies an entire thirteen-floor building, with spacious working areas on the top floors and bright daylight. A large cutting room occupies one entire floor, a rarity among factories in Chinatown. It also has showrooms and professional offices where several whites and Asians work. Some of the subcontractors work in the same building.

Mr Siu's story is unusual for several reasons. First, his background differs from that of most Chinese entrepreneurs. He did not go into the garment industry after working in garment shops. Instead, he switched to this field from a business background. He previously owned a successful plastic bag factory in Chinatown, but switched to garments as a more profitable trade at the time. He had strong business management skills and experience, and is committed to hiring other professionals. He is particularly proud of the fact that he has hired a dozen managers with Master's degrees. One of the managers I spoke with was a daughter of one of his subcontractors, and she got her Master's degree under Mr Siu's sponsorship. Secondly, Siu himself is also much better educated than most of the immigrant entrepreneurs, having a Master's degree in engineering from a United States university. A good share of the contractors in Chinatown did not even finish high school. Siu was far more technologically aware and often spent his time at equipment shows in the United States and abroad. Thirdly, his operation was established in the early 1970s, when contractors were in short supply and much of the clothing was still made in the United States. Buford (1999: 136) quotes one Chinese contractor, who described the situation in the 1970s as follows: 'I was like Hong Kong boss, show up at noon. Manufacturers begging for work. They sent me turkeys at Thanksgiving, gift baskets at Christmas and trips to Florida in the winter.' It is not hard to imagine how easy it was for Mr Siu to form respectable relations with some of the best designer houses and jobbers under these circumstances. With his contractor work, he accumulated the knowledge and experience in high-end fashion products that made it possible for him to try a private label. Even so, Mr Siu commented that maintaining a private label is still an uphill battle for him. To reduce his risks, he continues subcontracting work from other jobbers. Fourth, his factory does the cutting work internally, which gives him more control over the garment production and enables him to hire some highly paid skilled workers. Most Chinatown factories do not have cutting facilities. Fifth, unlike most contractors who engage in various illegal practices, Mr Siu insists on having his operation legitimate so 'everything is on the books'. This, according to him, is the only possible way to mainstream his business. He suggests that profit can be made even if you conduct a business legitimately. Yet this may have a great deal to do with the fact that he has an established niche in the high-end fashion market, something that cannot be said of most Chinatown contractors.

People like Mr Siu are making efforts to establish more respectable operations. Together with half a dozen of the largest and oldest contractors in Chinatown, he founded the Made-In-New York group. By sticking to legal operations and providing streamlined services, from purchasing fabrics to retailing, they hope to establish a more profitable and legitimate path for Chinese contractors.

Siu's success and his experiences certainly have a potential for providing a role model for the newer Chinese entrepreneurs wishing to break into higher levels of the garment business. However, there are several reasons to doubt the long-term prospects of Chinese firms in the garment industry. The Chinese generally tend not to view garments as a long-term business, but as one that offers a quick start and serves as a stepping stone to other types of business. One of the major attractions of a garment factory is its low entry cost – about half of what would be required for a restaurant. If the entrepreneurs are successful and accumulate some capital they are more likely to move out of the garment trade and invest their money in a less risky and more profitable business like a restaurant or real estate. Thus the prevailing mentality among Chinese garment factory owners is one of survival, not of development. In addition, the second-generation Chinese seldom gravitate to garment-related fields, since other professional fields have become more accessible to them. Secondly, although white owners largely abandoned the subcontracting segment of the garment industry after the 1960s there are a very few signs of this happening in the upper tier of the garment industry, which continues to be the most lucrative part of the business. Breaking into a well-established and profitable sector is a far more difficult process now than at the turn of the century when the garment industry was still evolving.

The garment industry is polarized to an extreme degree, with one of the highest-paid professional workforces, including fashion models and designers, and the poorest-paid sewing workers. There are few intermediate steps between the two poles that immigrants can readily take. In contrast to the case in Miami described in this book, where Cuban immigrants were able to carve out niches of their own and move to more profitable areas of the industry before it was well established locally, New York's garment industry is too deeply entrenched and institutionalized for a large number of immigrant entrepreneurs to work into the process.

## Conclusion

The garment industry has been the most important manufacturing sector in New York City since the mid-nineteenth century. Over the last 150 years it has evolved into a highly flexible, competitive and polarized trade with highly paid professionals and poorly paid labour. Throughout its evolution, immigrants have always been a vital force in garment production as workers as well as entrepreneurs. During the post-war era New York's garment industry suffered a major downturn, with a substantial loss of employment. Women's garments, especially the most seasonal and fashionable part of the industry, have disproportionately remained in New York City.

The polarized nature of the garment industry and its recent response to intensified global competition generated disproportionately more pressure at the lower end of the industry. Contractors face reduced profit, shorter lead-times and higher risks. As a result, the number of non-union firms soared and illegal practices abounded. Sweatshop conditions have proliferated. More importantly, as the garment industry becomes more and more flexibly organized it becomes difficult for immigrant owners to move up the industry hierarchy. The required financial capacity, education, professional and managerial expertise, and the extensive connections that are needed, all present formidable barriers for immigrant owners who are trying to surviving at marginal profit levels.

Unlike Jewish immigrants who gradually established, penetrated, and controlled the full line of the garment trade, today's immigrant enterprises in New York City tend to be locked into the contractor section and compete on few fronts other than labour costs. Their reliance on ethnic networks, their inability to make long-term investments and plans, and their poor education and limited English effectively keep many entrepreneurs from adopting profitable strategies. They are also unable to gain better control over the trade. Harsh reality impedes Chinese entrepreneurs in their long-term interests and commitment in the garment industry, and this further reduces their chances for upward mobility. Ethnic networks and a hardworking ethic may be the most important assets for immigrants in the garment industry, but they are not enough in the competitive world of fashion and, with some noticeable exceptions, may doom the vast majority of immigrant firms forever to the margin of fashion production in New York City.

## Notes

1. The fieldwork of this research was supported by two Vassar College summer research grants (1996, 1998), two Ford Scholarships for undergraduate research assistants (1996, 1998), and a planning grant from the International Migration Program of Social Science Research Council, 1997. I want to thank the Institute for Migration and Ethnic Studies (IMES) at the University of Amsterdam, the Netherlands for providing the opportunity of international exchange among scholars working in the fashion industry. I am also grateful for two of my Vassar student research assistants, Siu Sue Mark and Christina Eng, for their diligent efforts in interviewing Chinese entrepreneurs and workers in the garment trade in New York City. In the process of writing this manuscript I received insightful comments from Deborah Dash Moore in the Religion Department of Vassar College.

2. The union merged in the mid-1990s with the male garment workers' union. Now it is called the Union of Needletrades, Industrial, and Textile Employees (UNITE).

3. The data was from a report published by the United States Department of Labor (2000) as part of the Fashion Industry Forum. See website at http://www.dol.gov/dol/esa/public/forum/report.htm

4. The data have been compiled from the *Garment Enforcement Quarterly Report* published by the United States Department of Labor. See website at http://www.dol.gov/cgi-bin/consolid.pl?media+reports

# –7–

# Miami: Ethnic Succession and Failed Restructuring

*Guillermo Grenier* and *Alex Stepick*[1]

## Introduction

Behind tall fences and barren walls in the north-west section of Greater Miami there are numerous small apparel firms, the epitome of Sunbelt industry. There are no smokestacks or grimy buildings, just low-lying concrete-block rectangles joined by acres and acres of pavement covered with thousands of cars. Inside the buildings is the Sunbelt's most attractive economic asset: abundant, mostly non-union, mostly female, low-wage immigrant labour.[2] In Miami, nearly 15,000 women, almost all immigrants and primarily Cuban, cut and sew the latest fashions.

When the national Chicago-based corporation bought the Miami apparel firm, they had big plans. They intended it to be at the cutting edge of the industry, technologically as well as in labour–management relations. Internally, they originally called it the Saturn plant, named after General Motors' still-experimental Saturn car plant. Borrowing somewhat from Italian manufacturers and adding some of their own innovations, they conceived of a new way of producing a man's sports coat, formally called the two-shell construction and informally known as the 'sixty-minute coat'. Some lower-quality materials were used, but the real saving was to be in labour, in deskilling the most skilled apparel product, a top-quality man's sports jacket. These $400.00–$600.00 coats would be made on two parallel assembly lines, one for the inner part and another for the outside shell. The two parts of the coat would proceed down the two parallel assembly lines, merge about halfway through and emerge, on average, ninety-five minutes later (in spite of the 'sixty-minute' name tag) compared to the 135 minutes of the old, more skill-intensive way. The process would be the same as the one used to produce low-end dresses and jeans for K-Mart, but the quality, they anticipated, would be comparable to a tailor-made sports jacket.

Competition prompted the innovation – not from the offshore assembly plants of Asia or Latin America that compete with most of the United States apparel industry but from Italian companies that capture the high end of the men's clothing market by combining quality and, as one of the company managers put it, 'charisma', the prestige of clothes made in Italy. The corporate headquarter gurus figured they could not hope to compete with the 'charisma' factor, but they could redesign the product to compete in quality and undercut the Italians in cost. The manager appointed to head the experimental plant attributed the Italian high quality to a craftsmanlike devotion to production that permeates all the levels of the workforce. He claimed that this type of attitude is regrettably and noticeably absent among United States workers. He incidentally mentioned that Italy was 'quasi socialistic' with long vacations and high benefits, and found it inexplicably curious that 'quasi socialism' should exist in conjunction with craftsmanship. The United States corporation presumed that restructuring production through deskilling was the only way to beat the Italian competition.

They primarily selected the Miami plant because of its immigrant labour, Cuban women, whose deft and quick hands had created Miami's apparel industry in the 1960s. They had the kind of reputation all employers like: they were good and they were cheap. The plant would be far from the rest of the corporation's production facilities, which are located primarily in the triangle of Chicago, south-eastern Missouri, and Georgia, thus adding at least an extra dollar in transport costs to each coat. But in the end, the corporate headquarters could not ignore the advantage of low-wage, skilled labour, and they began their experiment with enthusiasm and great expectations in the mid-1980s.

Their plans failed. In 1992 the corporation announced the imminent closing of the Miami plant. At the last moment they found a buyer who promised to preserve at least some of the plant's approximately 250 jobs. But the men's sport coat Saturn plant dream dissolved, and not because the plant could not produce quality coats. Everyone agreed the quality was no lower than in their other plants. The two-shell method worked fine. It was the sixty-minute part that was the problem. They could not produce the coats fast enough to keep the labour costs per coat as low as they wanted.

The immigrant workers quietly but determinedly resisted the management's plant. This chapter recounts the failed experiment, and examines the restructuring of Miami's apparel industry since the 1960s and the venture at this one plant.

## Immigrants Recreate the Industry

The garment industry in Miami bears resemblance to others in Chicago, Los Angeles and New York (Fernández-Kelly *et al.* 1991; Waldinger 1986). It is dominated by females; the work is considered unskilled machine labour, and it provides basic job opportunities for new immigrant workers. As in other garment towns, new immigrants continue to be the preferred workforce. While the garment industry is traditionally unionized, in the Sunbelt and elsewhere it has suffered deunionization in the process of economic restructuring.

Miami's apparel industry has its roots in the 1940s diversification of the local economy, but its biggest boost came in the late 1960s. Many, primarily Jewish, manufacturers from New York relocated in Miami in the face of threatening union-ization in the north-east, attracted by the labour force made available by waves of Cuban immigration. The manufacturers soon found that the middle-class Cuban women made excellent employees. Firm in their belief that their stay in the United States would be brief and eager to maintain the family living standards until their return, these women accepted harsh working conditions without complaints. The union fervour felt in New York in the 1960s pushed numerous employers south at just the right time to contribute to the reinforcement of the Cuban exile economy. As Portes and Stepick report:

> A typical mid-sixties Cuban household in Miami featured a husband who had been a member of an anti-Castro organization and now strained to find employment and a wife who had never worked outside the home before but now sewed full time in a Hialeah factory. The large-scale employment of Cuban women in the needle trade had two important consequences. First, it allowed families to stay in Miami and bought time for husbands to learn English and find some local business niche. And second, it itself created some of these niches through independent subcontracting. (Portes and Stepick 1993: 128)

Overall employment rates in the industry peaked in the late 1970s, but earnings continued to increase even after the number of employees declined (Table 7.1). Miami's apparel firms are almost all small, family-owned enterprises. Today, only 29 per cent of the approximately 625 firms have more than twenty workers, and the average number of employees is twenty-six.

While overall employment has remained relatively steady, the ethnicity of the workforce has changed dramatically. As Figure 7.1 indicates, forty years ago employees were nearly 95 per cent white; many of them, although by no means most of them, were unionized. Today's apparel workers are 85 per cent Hispanic women, and far fewer shops are unionized.

Ownership patterns were also changed by the Cuban influx. A former Needle Trade Association official reports that a division of labour in production began to develop during the 1960s: 'In the beginning [of the Cuban influx] all the factories were Jewish-owned but by the mid-seventies there was a division of labor. The manufacturers were still Jewish, but most contractors were Cuban. Cuban garment "factories" usually started in the owner's garage, with the wife, the mother, and other women in the family as operators' (quoted in Portes and Stepick 1993: 128).

By the mid-1980s, Miami manufacturers were having difficulty finding new workers to replace their ageing and retiring female Cuban workers. The economic success of the Cuban community allowed the second generation of Cuban women to abandon the law wages of the apparel industry, while the virtual elimination of

**Table 7.1** Miami's Apparel Industry, 1973–1995: Employment, Earnings and Firms

| Year | No. of employees | Total earnings | No. of firms |
|------|------------------|----------------|--------------|
| 1973 | 20.567 |         | 532 |
| 1974 | 22.346 | 113.707 | 572 |
| 1975 | 18.846 | 111.363 | 595 |
| 1976 | 21.064 | 125.571 | 606 |
| 1977 | 23.006 | 147.626 | 702 |
| 1978 | 24.819 | 160.082 | 724 |
| 1979 | 24.441 | 169.496 | 693 |
| 1980 | 23.697 | 169.739 | 670 |
| 1981 | 20.707 | 174.839 | 671 |
| 1982 | 20.618 | 175.351 | 634 |
| 1983 | 20.278 | 192.191 | 708 |
| 1984 | 21.536 | 192.061 | 718 |
| 1985 | 19.546 | 192.315 | 724 |
| 1986 | 20.160 | 198.146 | 717 |
| 1987 | 18.982 | 216.369 | 702 |
| 1988 | 18.429 | 224.085 | 687 |
| 1989 | 19.019 | 237.231 | 670 |
| 1990 | 18.572 | 236.934 | 695 |
| 1991 | 17.940 | 233.360 | 661 |
| 1992 | 19.667 | 243.837 | 702 |
| 1993 | 17.651 | 239.424 | 697 |
| 1994 | 16.543 | 227.915 | 663 |
| 1995 | 16.124 | 213.432 | 625 |

*Sources:* County Business (Dade County); Bureau of Economic Research, Gainesville, Florida; Annual Reports 1974–1995

Cuban immigration reduced the new supplies of workers. Although Haitians and black Americans provided a potential solution, manufacturers were reluctant to incorporate them. Instead, by the late 1980s newly arrived Central and South Americans replenished the supply of women willing to work at tedious, repetitive tasks for low wages.

In response to the challenge of Third World imports, Miami firms restructured by dividing into three types:

1. completely above-board, legal firms with factories obeying all or most of the labour laws;
2. firms with factories that do their best to evade labour laws; and
3. firms that specialize in putting-out, or homework (see Fernández-Kelly and Garcia 1989; Stepick 1989 and 1990).

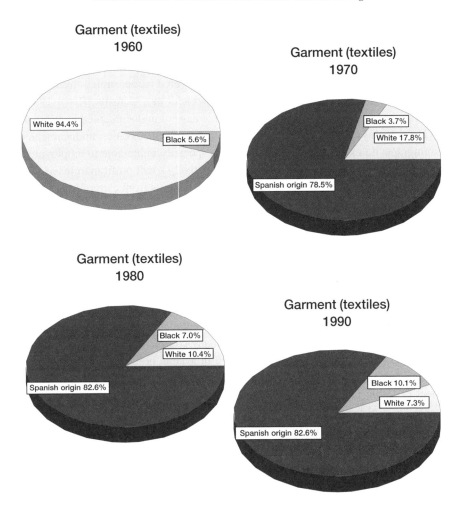

**Figure 7.1** Ethnic Employment Percentages in Miami's Apparel Industry, 1960–1990. *Source:* US Bureau of Census, Florida

The firm we studied falls into the first category: the legal firms. Foreign competition and the New York Chinatown garment district hit these firms the hardest, especially the ones that concentrated on children's or women's wear. Many of them closed down in Miami, some completely terminating their operations and others resettling abroad. Union membership, which was concentrated in the largest firms, fell from 5,000 in 1978 to 1,000 in 1986 and hovered just under that figure for over a decade.

The other two types of firms not only survived, they even flourished through the 1980s and into the 1990s. In 1980, the United States Department of Labor, stating that Miami was swiftly becoming one of the sweatshop capitals of the United States, appointed a strike force that discovered labour violations totalling $80 million in owed wages to over 5,000 workers in 132 firms (Risen 1981). Although Miami does not have as high a percentage of undocumented immigrants as Los Angeles and many other south-western United States cities, undocumented immigrants do exist in Miami and they are especially vulnerable to employment exploitation. Garment factories operate on relatively small profit margins as they try to compete with offshore production, which benefits from extraordinarily low wage rates. An easy cost-cutting move for garment manufacturers is to violate wage labour laws, usually by paying piece rates so low that workers cannot earn the minimum wage. Workers are entitled to a minimum wage regardless of how many pieces they produce, but unscrupulous employers commonly pay only the piece rate, even if the resulting wage is below the minimum.

Many of the violations pertain to homework, which is illegal in the United States garment industry. United States labour legislation specifically bars homework in the garment industry because it was the source of abuse at the beginning of the twentieth century and later. Nevertheless, many contractors farm out production to women who do the work in their homes. In Miami, homework is estimated to cover between 30 and 50 per cent of local production. The United States Department of Labor claims Miami homeworkers actually earn at least the minimum wage.[3] It is also said that garment workers prefer homework (Fernández-Kelly and Garcia 1989). Nevertheless, homework in the apparel industry is illegal in the United States, and it does lower overhead costs even if workers do receive the minimum wage.

## Plant History

The apparel plant we studied is a subsidiary of the largest United States clothing manufacturer, which purchased it in 1985. Previously owner operated, the plant has been in existence since the early 1960s. At the time of the research in the late 1980s it employed approximately 250 operators, most of whom were older Cuban women. The number of Haitian workers has been increasing since the early 1980s, and more recently Central Americans, especially Nicaraguans, have been hired. There are also sprinklings of black Americans and other Latins.

The Amalgamated Clothing and Textile Workers Union (ACTWU) has represented the workers since the plant's opening. The ACTWU had been associated with the Chicago-based corporation that owned this plant since the early twentieth century when the two organizations joined ranks to develop some of the most progressive collective bargaining agreements of the time. Since that time, the union has also been one of the most active organizers of immigrant and female workers – groups that are widely considered the most difficult to organize. Perhaps because of this long tradition with female immigrants, all of the employees at the three ACTWU plants in Miami belong to the union. This level of voluntary membership in a labour organization is a notable anomaly in a right-to-work state.

We conducted extensive interviews with all the managerial personnel, interviewing the regional vice-president and the regional division chief. The managerial interviews each lasted from forty-five minutes to three hours. We also participated in various plant rituals and regularly walked the floor, talked to operators, and went to the lunchroom during the three lunch periods. In addition, two research assistants worked as operators in the plant. Bernadette is a middle-aged Haitian woman with some experience in the apparel industry; Aline is a Jewish American woman who speaks fluent Spanish.

In 1982 it seemed that the plant would have to close. Mr Elman, the owner and manager at the time, addressed the workers and supervisors and suggested that they work without benefits for a certain amount of time. In an emotional appeal from the steps to the production floor, he informed the workers that they had a choice. Their benefits could be paid for the current period, but it would mean the plant would have to close for a while as a result. However, if the workers agreed to work without benefits for an undisclosed period of time, the plant could continue to operate. He put the issue to a vote, vowing to comply with the majority decision. With the union's approval, all the employees, including the non-union management employees, voted on the issue. With only twelve opposing votes, the employees voted to work without benefits.

In spite of the evident sacrifices the workers endured, they cherish these memories, referring to Mr Elman's tenure as the period of *huevos de oros*, 'golden eggs'. The workers uniformly remember Mr Elman fondly as an accessible man who knew the names of all his employees, who cared if someone was sick, who would always keep his door open to workers, and who attended to his workers' concerns beyond the workplace. He created a flexible and warm working environment. Workers could have their own radio and hotplates or enjoy a snack at their machine. After hours, they could use the company presses or sew for themselves. As the production control manager put it: 'Mr Elman knew the names of all the workers. He talked to every new [employee] . . . People worked because we wanted to protect him . . . He had charisma.'

Initially owned by a Venezuelan Jew, the plant was part of a local manufacturing process and survived largely on individual contracts established with outlets, the retail trades and specialized customers. This type of contract work continued into the tenure of the subsequent owner, a Colombian, and the immediately previous owner, Mr Elman. During the Elman period from 1974 to 1985, the plant was a flexible production plant. Contracts for nuns' habits, children's clothes, and other items were produced for as many as twelve contractors at a time.

The previous plant management had exercised direct, personalistic control. One supervisor who had worked at the plant since 1965 maintains that the Colombian owner had a very 'familial managerial style'. Subsequent owners preserved this style, culminating in the period of the illustrious Mr Elman, the last owner before the present management, who seemed to have elevated paternalism to an art form.[4]

In exchange for certain personal considerations from their employer, the workers were loyal and dependable, and understanding when it came to the firm's needs. This trade-off between personal considerations and company commitment appealed to the largely Cuban workforce. As the union representative reported, Mr Elman knew how to treat Latins: 'Sabia como pasarles la mano.' ('He knew how to pat them.') This 'patting' included sending employees to his personal physician when they needed medical care.

When Mr Elman sold the plant to the present conglomerate, the management–labour relations changed entirely. As regards what the arrival of the new management meant to all the employees who had been accustomed to Mr Elman's style, one supervisor reported: 'It was like giving children a new father.'

## Restructuring the Plant

After approving the plans for the innovative Saturn-like apparel plant, the Chicago corporate headquarters hired a well-known apparel management consulting team and assigned two of their own industrial engineers to implement their ideas. Their initial impression of the plant disenchanted the visionaries. One of the corporation's industrial engineers, who later became the in-plant industrial engineer, bluntly called the plant 'a pigsty'. The other industrial engineer, who became the plant manager, described it as 'filthy, disorganized . . . with not clean engineering and off-standard discipline'.

They envisioned a thorough restructuring of the labour process, putting an end to the flexible production system and replacing it with their innovative two-shell process. This would also incorporate many of the labour relations methods that were popular in the 1980s, including work teams, quality circles, and the abandonment of piece rates (an unprecedented step in the modern apparel industry). The corporation had already created work teams and quality circles in other plants, thus achieving higher output levels with acceptable quality.

While the two-shell process was an innovation, assembly-line construction is not at all new in the apparel industry (Lamphere 1987; Waldinger 1986). It has dominated the apparel labour process for over a hundred years, and the previous management had employed it at this particular plant from its beginnings in the 1960s. An extreme division of labour characterizes the process. Each worker repeatedly performs a minute task, hundreds of times a day. Almost all the workers are paid a piece rate. The more they produce, the more they earn.

The task of the new corporation and its management team was to adapt the entrenched assembly-line method to their product. This required three kinds of changes: reconfigured tasks and piece rates appropriate to the high-quality sport coats that would be produced, some new state-of-the-art machinery and, most important, the replacement of the simple, paternalistic relations the previous management had enjoyed with the plant's workers by bureaucratic labour–management control.

The industrial engineers intensively analysed all the operations required to produce the coat, designed new operations and revised the piece rates earned by workers. The constructing of the new sewing operations for the two-shell design deskilled the process into simpler, more repetitive tasks. The workers, however, did not necessarily consider the tasks simple. Our research assistant Aline trained on one of the new machines, the 'chopper':

> The 'chopper' sews as it cuts, they said. Until I saw it work, I was completely baffled by the apparent paradox. But it does just that – it cuts off the ragged sides of the seam that is being made. I will be sewing an inside part of the shoulder of the jacket . . . First, A. had me learn how to thread the machine, by watching her, then by doing it myself over and over again several times. Then she showed me the way to put the piece in the jacket. But she had me simply practice using the machine on pieces of plain cloth, without the chopper. I had a terrible time the entire day getting control over the foot pedal – it is delicate enough that with a not-so-delicate touch of the foot, the thing flies. All the jokes from everyone not to get my fingers sewn together and not to get my fingers under any needles really weren't funny today. It all seemed very possible.

Even while she was still in training, Aline described the work process as a demanding physical task. Operators are required to be at their machines when the break-bell rings, 'not running back'. The constant reminder by her supervisor that she was working too slowly combined with the physical demands of the machine to make the production process 'totally nerve-racking. My shoulders are aching – and so is my ass from sitting on this hard chair the whole day.' Talking and looking around were discouraged. Everything was focused on the task at hand: *dominar* (dominating or mastering) the machine. The training director walked the floor-timing new and old operators to 'save the company money and help the workers'.

Helping the workers meant helping them operate the machine faster, thus increasing production. To this end, the workers were not taught to sew but to operate a specific machine that performed a specific task. Each machine had a different 'personality' and it was the operator's job to get to know it. After the training period, the operator and the machine were moved out to the floor together, each aware of the other's quirks.

Each job was learned as a series of distinct steps to be mastered. After two weeks on the job, Aline had developed a list in her head of the 'little shit' that had to be done perfectly:

1. smooth the lining and continue to do so before each section is sewn;
2. go around the little curve slowly at the top;
3. the piece being inserted is a little longer than the shoulder because it is supposed to make the shoulder full – so you have to push the piece gently to add fullness;
4. but it can't be pleated;
5. going around the curve, the material can't be cut, just the leftover edges;
6. sew in the middle of the foot, not too far to the edge or the inside;
7. don't catch up the inside of the material as it rolls up.

Aline found that each step had to be done perfectly, otherwise the operation would not come out right. And if it did not come out correctly, 'you have to do it again and again and again'. To make money, she learned you have to also do it very fast. During the training period Aline had time to chat as her quality was being checked, but this kind of 'down time' was almost nonexistent for the operators on the shop floor. Bernadette, our Haitian research assistant, had previously worked in other Miami apparel plants, but she found this work more demanding.

She described the conditions as follows:

> I do not have the time to talk to people because I am worrying about the job, so that I can make more. Well, I can do it. But when I see people working, they are going fast. I would like to work like them, so that I can make a lot, too. I am rushing, I want to make a lot, too. But Fritz, the Haitian supervisor, said no. If you are rushing to make a lot, you are not going to make them well, because you don't know the work yet.

As Bernadette said to a co-worker: 'The work is easy for you, but it is difficult for me.' The co-worker replied: 'Don't worry, don't trouble yourself because you are going to find that the work is not easy until you have been doing it for three months.' Bernadette thought to herself, 'After I have been doing it for three months, that is when I will find it easy. I told myself, three months! After three months.'

Along with devising the new set of supposedly deskilled operations, the engineers determined how much the workers would be paid for each operation. The piece rates under the previous management were chaotic, according to the new management. They seemed to bear little relation to the work performed, since similar and sometimes even identical operations were paid at different rates. In fact, there were almost as many piece rates as there were workers. By re-engineering the tasks, the new management tried to standardize the work and wages using methods common throughout the industry. A 100 per cent 'base rate' would be established for each of the 130 operations in the new two-shell method. It was the rate of an average worker expressed in terms of how many pieces should be produced in an hour or day. If workers performed at 100 per cent, they would earn the standard hourly rate, which in this plant in 1988 was slightly under $5.00 an hour.

All the workers nevertheless believe that the 'average' base rate is too difficult to obtain and that the piece rates are correspondingly too low. Moreover, some material is easier to work with and thus faster, yet the piece rates only recognize one distinction – the one between plain and plaid material. Workers vie to obtain bundles of easy material that are paid at the same rate as bundles of slightly more difficult materials. It is the responsibility of the supervisor to regulate this competition among the workers. Although workers who perform the same operation compete to obtain easier-to-work-with material, the ones who do the subsequent operations depend on others to work efficiently enough to supply them with a constant stream of bundles. As one of the researchers reported: 'There's a lot of discussion about whose job is the hardest and how fast people are working.'

Usually under the guise of equity and improving working conditions, the management bureaucratized the worker relations. Whenever the workers had a problem under the previous owner, they would walk directly into the owner-manager's office. He was the only boss. There was no personnel manager or payroll clerk, just one manager assistant who checked the time cards, processed the production sheets, and cut the checks. Under the new regime labour relations became considerably more complex, with a many-levelled hierarchy. Directly above the shop-floor operators, the new plant appointed supervisors who had almost exclusively worked their way up in the same factory. They spoke Spanish or, in one case, Haitian Creole, and presumably the workers could relate to them better.

The workers could no longer address the manager directly. He no longer listened to the workers' work-related or personal problems. From now on they had to go through the floor supervisors, then the area supervisors, perhaps the personnel manager, proceeding to the union representative, a filed grievance, and finally to an audience with the plant manager who might still defer a decision 'upstairs' to the corporate headquarters in Chicago. Chicago was even in charge of many of the accounting and inventory details, transmitting the results back to Miami by computer.

The chain of command was now clearly hierarchical. The union grievance procedure was presented as the method all the workers had to use if they wanted to voice a complaint. This significantly enhanced the roles of the union and management supervisors. Indeed, the plant manager viewed himself as one of the strongest supporters of the union because he emphasized the union as a stabilizing force within the production and organizational structure.

Snacks at the machines were no longer allowed, nor were hotplates. The company put a new microwave in the lunchroom and encouraged the workers to use it during their breaks. Individual fans and radios were replaced by plantwide air conditioning and piped-in music. (According to the production manager, the station alternated between American and Latin songs. 'You can't please the Haitians on this one.' The radio, however, is only played on Saturdays when a few people come in to do makeup work.)

The management was convinced that these changes would be beneficial to them as well as the workers. Consistent rules that applied equally to everyone and working through the union were 'fairer'. Hiring Spanish-speaking supervisors fostered better communication. Banning fans would keep fire from spreading and keep pieces of material from blowing in a worker's eyes. Prohibiting food on the floor would keep mice away.

The workers, however, resented the changes and their resentment stimulated them to sabotage the ideas adhered to at the corporate headquarters. The workers produced acceptable-quality coats, but they did not produce them quickly enough; the overall output met no more than 80 per cent of the management's goals. According to the quality-control manager, who had worked for nine years at other plants for the corporation, 'The people [at other plants] are more easy to control than here.' The highest management official we interviewed, the Chicago-based executive vice-president, believed that workers deliberately resisted change by way of work slowdowns. One of the locally promoted Spanish-speaking supervisors claimed that the low production resulted from the management's bureaucratiza- tion. 'People are still pissed, even three years later.' Some of the workers referred to the new management rules as 'totalitarian'. Two other respondents mentioned that the new management was making the factory 'just like Cuba' and that 'this is becoming like a dictatorship'.

The workers commonly ignored the bureaucratic procedures. The payroll manager, another locally promoted Spanish speaker, still had Haitians storm directly into her office whenever their cheques did not match their expectations. The workers did not care whether the floor supervisor spoke their language. They wanted to address the plant manager directly. Moreover, the management unwit- tingly selected floor supervisors who were not really representative of the majority of workers. Many were Spanish speakers, but either non-Cubans or from earlier waves of slightly higher-class Cuban immigrants, and had a condescending attitude to those under them. Whereas the workers had previously volunteered to do over- time for Mr Elman, under the new management absenteeism became a recurrent problem. Some workers smuggled in radios under their blouses and listened to them through a small earphone.

The workers, resistance was not organized by the union, but more informally. Some of it, such as sneaking in radios, was individual but much of it was a collective effort by informal social groups, such as women who worked in the same area or had worked together for numbers of years. As in other apparel plants and female- dominated workplaces (Lamphere 1987), informal social interaction commonly focused on celebrations such as birthdays, showers, and retirement parties. The intensity of the work limited socializing during working hours, but during the breaks (one in the morning, lunch, and another in the afternoon) the workers would gather in small groups. These activities served as the basis for resistance. They were the context in which the workers remembered and reconstructed their relationship to Mr Elman, a relationship that admittedly exploited labour more but assumed more positive tones in their restructuring. At the same time, the workers critiqued the new management, especially the revised piece rates that could not be adjusted simply by going to the manager's office but had to be addressed by way of a complex multi-staged grievance procedure.

All the managers felt that the new owners imposed their 'northern, Anglo' management techniques too quickly and brusquely on an immigrant workforce that had been accustomed to and worked well under the paternalistic, less bureaucratic approach of the previous owner. The on-site Anglos assigned to Miami by the corporate headquarters tended to recognize that they had made mistakes in implementing the changes, but they were still convinced that things would be better overall if the Latins and Haitians became more like them instead of returning to the former paternalistic management styles.

The Latin managers, in contrast, believed that not only did the new Anglo managers make mistakes, they also changed and became a lot more like the Latins. By 1990, the plant manager had learned that he had to talk to people at all levels to get them to work for him. In the first year, he rarely communicated with the workers and did not take much of the advice of the older, middle-management group. Perhaps learning from the personalistic practices of his predecessor, he allowed a supervisor to use his condominium while he was out of town. His adaptation, however, was too little, too late. The impatience at the corporate headquarters about achieving the dream plant finally force the management to abandon the Miami experiment.

## Conclusions

The structure of Miami's apparel industry, the nature of the work there, and the ethnic composition of the workforce are all similar to the past and present patterns in the apparel industry throughout the United States. An abundant supply of immigrant Latin, non-unionized women attracted manufacturers from the northeast. As a result of these women's long hours and quick hands, the industry flourished in the 1960s and 1970s. The 1980s brought competition that restructured the local industry, closing some shops, forcing others abroad, and driving still others to bend the labour laws or go underground.

The shop we studied sold out to a national firm with ambitious ideas about restructuring. Their strategy included incorporating new machines and it also sought to recast labour relations in a different way than the general restructuring trends in the industry. Flexible specialization was abandoned and replaced by concentration on a single product: men's sports jackets. The management eschewed the trends towards deunionization and informalization. Instead, they dismissed the allegedly inefficient prior paternalism and imposed a rigid, hierarchical bureaucratic structure, which one supervisor referred to as the 'Americanization of the plant'. One middle-level manager who had worked under both regimes succinctly expressed the nature of this dynamic interrelation:

> I have fewer responsibilities now. Part of the reason for this is that the company produces less variety of products. Mr Elman had to hustle whatever work we could get. When [the new management] came in, we were producing twenty-one different types of garments! Everything from nuns' habits to flight attendants' uniforms . . . Also, Mr Elman had no personnel department. We all got involved with the workers.

Under the new regime, the division of labour and responsibilities became much more specific and rigid.

For the workers, the new rules meant a depersonalization of control through integration into a rationalized, bureaucratic management structure that limited the interaction between managerial and floor employees, restricted shop floor behaviour (no radios, hotplates or fans), and increased production requirements (higher quality was demanded, even if the units per hour remained approximately the same).

Not only did the workers now have to adhere to a variety of new rules and regulations, the on-site management also had to defer the major decisions to an office in Chicago. As one supervisor said: 'Mr Elman was the only boss. He never told us he had to check with "upstairs" to make a decision.'

The workers resisted, complaining about and refusing to obey the new rules. The management soon abandoned any hope of forming quality circles and concentrated on more traditional bureaucratization. But the workers never met with the management's production expectations, and the management ultimately conceded defeat. In 1992, seven years after launching the experiment, the management announced the closing of the plant, which was subsequently sold to a local investor.

The unusual aspects of this case – a unionized apparel plant that tried to comply with all the labour laws and fulfil the American ideal of bureaucratized labour relations – reveal the force of macrostructural factors as well as the power of local labour resistance. The recession of the early 1990s damaged all of Miami's apparel industry. The plants most able to survive relied on a combination of flexible specialization and the informalization of work relationships, particularly the use of homeworkers. Although the working conditions are uncertain and pay is low, workers may actually still prefer these conditions to the bureaucratized relations at the plant we studied. Homework allows women to combine domestic chores with earning money, and the direct control of nonbureaucratic relations in Miami, and apparently in southern California (see Fernández-Kelly and Garcia 1989), makes for more personal relationships with employers.

The workers in the plant we studied resisted quietly and indirectly. There were no strikes or formal work slowdowns. Informal social groups articulated their grievances, and individual workers complained to the management and failed to work as quickly as the management desired. The force of the macro factors, particularly the recession of the early 1990s, nearly cost them their jobs, and still might. The workers and management found themselves caught in the same vice, with structural factors pushing for lower wages and harsher working conditions and a management incapable of realizing the dream of a Saturn apparel plant.

Unfortunately the workers had little chance of creating a working environment that satisfied their needs. Under Mr Elman's warm paternalism they had more individual freedom and were better able to balance work with domestic responsibilities. However, Mr Elman could barely keep the company afloat in the midst of the industry's restructuring. The competition from offshore production meant contracts were uncertain and usually short term. He eventually gave up and sold the firm. The new owners thought they could create a niche in the restructured industry, but the resistance of the Latino workers undermined their strategy.

## Notes

1. The authors would like to thank the owners and managers of the apparel plant we studied. We would especially like to thank Tom and Frank, whose openness and generosity far exceeded our expectations. Without their assistance this study would have been impossible. We would also like to thank all the workers, in management as well as on the floor, who co-operated with us. Our two research assistants, Aline and Bernadette, both deserve to be co-authors. Bernadette, however, prefers to remain anonymous.
2. Low corporate tax rates are another attractive feature of the Sunbelt states.
3. Since wages are based on piece rates, and garment homework is illegal, it is impossible to verify this claim.
4. Paternalism is understood to mean a system of control where the owner-manager has final and arbitrary authority although his actions are constrained to some extent by an implicit understanding of the rights and obligations of the employees. One important characteristic of paternalism is the personal relationship between the owner and the employee. The concept of paternalism dates from the Weberian presentation of 'traditional' authority (Weber 1947). Bendix expanded the concept to include the dynamics of worksite control by arguing that traditionalism 'frequently facilitated the management of labor' by establishing a familial structure of reciprocal loyalties (1956: 47). Bendix added

that because of its exploitative nature and inefficiency, paternalism would decline in importance in the course of capitalist development. More current studies, however, argue that paternalism is an important technique in controlling and motivating workers in small firms. These studies reveal that despite low wages and stagnant working conditions many workers exhibit a surprisingly low level of alienation or resentment and often express loyalty to the firm and high levels of identification with the interests of the firm.

# –8–

# Los Angeles: Wearing out Their Welcome
## *Ivan Light* and *Victoria D. Ojeda*

## Introduction

Immigrants dominated the Los Angeles garment manufacturing industry in the past, and they still do.[1] However, Los Angeles was not the United States' leading garment production centre until about 1989. In 1924 Los Angeles was the fourth largest garment manufacturing centre in the United States with an employment base of immigrant whites.[2] In around 1970, extensive immigration from Asia and Latin America began in the wake of the Immigration and Nationality Act of 1965, which eliminated the national origins quota. Liberal immigration gave Los Angeles access to foreign-born workers from Asia, Mexico, and Central America. Table 8.1 shows that the number of garment factories in Los Angeles County nearly tripled between 1970 and 1996, and the number of employees doubled. Mainly as a result of its superior access to immigrant labour, New York City had been the

**Table 8.1** Apparel Manufacturing* in Los Angeles County, 1970–1996

|  | *1970* | *1979* | *1989* | *1996* | *Index* † |
|---|---|---|---|---|---|
| Establisments ‡ | 2,332 | 3,759 | 4,960 | 6,364 | 273 |
| Employees | 73,926 | 120,255 | 133,299 | 149,969 | 203 |
| Mean employees per establishment | 31.7 | 32 | 26.9 | 23.6 | 74 |

*Sources:* US Bureau of the Census, County Business Patterns, California for 1970, 1980, 1996, and 1998. (Washington, DC: US Government Printing Office)

\* Apparel and other textile products
† Index = 1996/1970 × 100
‡ In 1970, data were collected for 'reporting units'. The reporting category was later changed to establishments. 'Each manufacturing location of a company is counted as a separate reporting unit. In manufacturing industries, reporting units are therefore conceptually the same as establishments in Census Bureau terminology.'

garment manufacturing capital of the United States until around 1989 when Los Angeles passed it (Kessler 1999; see also Zhou in this volume). Los Angeles has been the major United States garment producer ever since. In 1998, garment and textile manufacturing and wholesaling were the largest manufacturing sectors in Los Angeles, which was the top manufacturing region of the United States, not just the top garment manufacturing region (Scott 1996). Garment and textile manufacturing together represented almost 10 per cent of Los Angeles County's $282 billion economy (California Fashion Association 1999).

Los Angeles' vast garment and textile manufacturing industry employed as many as 140,000 workers in 1998. Even this generous estimate is conservative because the official figures do not include the garment industry's informal sector, which is known to be large (Sarmiento 1996: 38–9). Approximately 93 per cent of all the workers were foreign-born in 1990 (Table 8.2). Of the immigrants, an estimated

**Table 8.2** Place of Birth of Factory Owners and Seamstresses in the Garment Manufacturing Industry of Los Angeles, 1990

| Place of Birth | Owners (%) | Sewers (%) |
|---|---|---|
| North America | 35.3 | 59.7 |
| USA | 28.5 | 6.0 |
| Canada | 0.7 | 0.1 |
| Mexico | 6.1 | 53.6 |
| Caribbean | 4.7 | 0.8 |
| Puerto Rico | 0.0 | 0.1 |
| Cuba | 4.0 | 0.5 |
| Dominican Rep. | 0.7 | 0.1 |
| Haiti | 0.0 | 0.1 |
| Europe | 5.6 | 0.7 |
| France | 0.0 | 0.1 |
| West Germany | 0.6 | 0.0 |
| Italy | 0.4 | 0.2 |
| Poland | 0.7 | 0.1 |
| Romania | 0.0 | 0.1 |
| Spain | 0.0 | 0.1 |
| Sweden | 0.7 | 0.0 |
| England | 1.6 | 0.0 |
| USSR | 1.6 | 0.2 |
| Asia | 40.1 | 13.2 |
| Cambodia | 3.1 | 0.4 |
| China | 6.8 | 5.5 |
| Hong Kong | 0.8 | 0.6 |
| Japan | 0.4 | 0.2 |
| Korea | 19.3 | 3.1 |
| Laos | 0.0 | 0.2 |

## Los Angeles: Wearing out Their Welcome

| Place of Birth | Owners (%) | Sewers (%) |
|---|---|---|
| Philippines | 0.0 | 0.5 |
| Taiwan | 3.7 | 0.3 |
| Thailand | 2.1 | 0.5 |
| Vietnam | 3.9 | 1.9 |
| Middle East | 6.5 | 0.5 |
| Iran | 3.7 | 0.2 |
| Iraq | 2.1 | 0.0 |
| Lebanon | 0.7 | 0.2 |
| Turkey | 0.0 | 0.1 |
| Central America | 3.2 | 18.6 |
| Belize | 0.0 | 0.1 |
| Costa Rica | 0.0 | 0.1 |
| El Salvador | 1.4 | 11.0 |
| Guatemala | 0.0 | 5.4 |
| Honduras | 0.0 | 0.8 |
| Nicaragua | 1.8 | 1.2 |
| South America | 3.9 | 1.9 |
| Argentina | 0.0 | 0.1 |
| Brazil | 0.0 | 0.1 |
| Chile | 0.8 | 0.1 |
| Colombia | 0.9 | 0.3 |
| Ecuador | 0.5 | 0.7 |
| Peru | 1.1 | 0.5 |
| Uruguay | 0.6 | 0.1 |
| Africa | 0.7 | 0.1 |
| Egypt | 0.0 | 0.1 |
| S. Africa | 0.7 | 0.0 |
| Total | 100.0 | 95.5* |
| N | 3,181 | 67,883 |

*Source*: US Bureau of the Census 5% Public Use Samples

* Less than 100 due to rounding down

80 per cent were illegally in the United States. About 80 per cent of the garment industry employees were women. The *Los Angeles Times* acknowledges that immigrants provided virtually all the financial capital, human capital, social capital, cultural capital and labour power that the city's biggest manufacturing sector required (Dickerson 1999).[3] Indeed, as Zhou (1992: 169) observed of New York City, without the immigrant-created garment industry, Los Angeles would not have been able to absorb 140,000 more immigrants. In this sense, the Los Angeles garment industry is a product of immigrant entrepreneurs, immigrant workers, and the immigration process itself. The garment industry thus represents the kind of migration-caused increase in a destination economy's carrying capacity that the augmented migration network theory proposed.[4]

Prior to 1982, garment manufacturers were not required to register with the state, and many or even most employers ignored the labour code. Violators paid their employees less than the statutory minimum wage, gave out industrial home-work, maintained filthy and unsafe workplaces, and evaded taxation. In order to improve the enforcement of the labour code, California passed the Montoya Act in 1982, requiring garment contractors to register their factories (Bonacich and Appelbaum 2000: 224). Registered firms are subject to unannounced inspections by state authorities, whose agents seize the books and impound bundles. None-theless, non-registration is still widespread. The California Safety Compliance Corporation estimates that 40 per cent of the garment contractors are still unregis-tered.[5] It is not clear whether the Montoya Act even reduced the violations of the law, although it probably did (Bonacich and Appelbaum 2000: 235). Widespread violation of the law still persists. Registered and non-registered firms alike continue to pay less than the minimum wage, give out illegal homework, maintain unsafe and unhealthy working conditions, and evade taxation the same way they did before the Montoya Act (Lee 1994).

Why are labour laws *not* enforced? First, the jurisdictions are jumbled. The state and federal authorities share the responsibility for law enforcement. Every-one's responsibility becomes no one's responsibility. Second, law enforcement encounters powerful political, economic and cultural resistance. The economic resistance manifests itself as bribes to enforcement officers. These bribes pay for toleration. The political resistance to law enforcement, which is much more import-ant than the economic resistance, derives from the garment industry's political influence. The garment industry's paid lobby donates campaign funds to California politicians, including the Governor and Attorney-General (Bonacich and Appel-baum 2000: 125). This practice is completely legal under current American law. The donations elect neo-liberal politicians who reduce law enforcement staffs to below the minimum required for effectiveness. As a result, officials do not have the police needed to enforce the labour laws, and have no choice but to negotiate compliance agreements with garment industry associations. Under current federal law the government does not prosecute until the *fourth* time industrial violations come to its attention. Earlier violations are overlooked in the interest of industrial self-regulation (Bonacich and Appelbaum 2000: 235–6). A less explored but equally important issue is the cultural resistance to law enforcement. It derives from the ubiquitous belief, a product of the growth ideology, that any and all metropolitan growth is good for Los Angeles. Since the garment industry promotes population growth, so the thinking goes, it must be good and should, therefore, be tolerated (Logan and Molotch 1987).

A City of Los Angeles (1993) survey identified 3,642 registered garment factories in Los Angeles County, each with a mean of 27.1 employees.[6] The *Los Angeles Times* counted 5,070 garment manufacturing firms in Los Angeles County in 1996. This suggests a 40 per cent growth in the number of firms between 1993 and 1996. The *Los Angeles Times* estimated that these 5,070 firms employed 115,000 workers, a much lesser figure than Sarmiento's (1996: 38–9) estimate. The *Times* also estimated that garment manufacturing firms each employed an average of about twenty-seven workers (Lee 1998). Even using the *Times'* low estimates, the garment industry ranked fourth in Los Angeles County in 1996 behind engineering and management services, but ahead of the Hollywood film industry (Levy 1997: 8–10). The garment industry's 115,000 workers constituted 2.6 per cent of all the wage and salary employees in metropolitan Los Angeles in 1996.[7] In itself, the garment industry's labour force constituted 5.5 per cent of the immigrant labour force in Los Angeles County in 1990.

These figures do not indicate how much of the garment industry is the product of an ethnic economy, an immigrant economy, or the mainstream economy (Light *et al.* 1999). An ethnic economy consists of ethnic firms and their co-ethnic employees, an immigrant economy of immigrant-owned firms and their immigrant employees, and the rest is the mainstream economy. However, the literature reports that the immigrant economy accounts for the bulk of garment industry employment. Bonacich (1993a: 65, 1994: 152–3) reports that 51 per cent of the garment factory owners were Asians, and that most of their employees were Hispanic women. Lee's (1993) study of Korean garment factory owners notes that 85 per cent of their employees were Hispanic. Lee's estimate corresponds closely with that of Hess (1990: 94), who reports that Hispanics constituted 87 per cent of the employees of the Korean-owned garment factories he studied. It is clear from all these estimates that Asian employers were hiring more Latino than Asian workers (Kim *et al.* 1992: 74). Using this terminology, the garment industry of Los Angeles thus obviously required a large immigrant economy in which, as Appelbaum (1997) notes, Asian, European and Latin American entrepreneurs hired Mexican and Central American seamstresses. To illustrate this point with census-derived evidence, Table 8.2 compares the national origins of seamstresses and owners in the Los Angeles garment industry. Mexicans constituted 6.1 per cent of the owners and 53.6 per cent of the workers, whereas Asians were 40.1 per cent of the owners and only 13.2 per cent of the employees. Seventy-two per cent of the owners were immigrants, as were 93 per cent of their employees.

Garment industry employers have complained of labour shortage for a generation. Light and Bonacich (1988: 305–8) interviewed garment contractors in the late 1970s. Employers complained at the time that labour shortages were forcing them to hire inexperienced seamstresses.[8] In 1989, when Hess (1990: 95–6) interviewed them, Korean garment entrepreneurs stated that their industry was confronted with a 10–20 per cent labour shortage. Confirming this claim, the City of Los Angeles (1993) reported widespread employer complaints regarding the labour shortage at hotels and garment factories. In 1996 Light *et al.* (1999)

contacted the Korean American Garment Industry of America, a major trade association of garment contractors, to find out whether the labour shortage had been resolved. A representative insisted that there were still labour shortages in the garment industry. From a conceptual standpoint, the chronic labour shortage is important. It suggests that immigrant-owned firms attract non-coethnic immigrant workers to Los Angeles rather than just taking advantage of the unemployed immigrant labour already there. If so, the immigrant employers *increase* the number of immigrants who live in Los Angeles by increasing the city's absorptive capacity.[9]

Light *et al.* (1999) used census evidence to estimate the size of the immigrant economy, the ethnic economy, and the mainstream economy in the Los Angeles garment industry in 1990. They estimate that 30.3 per cent of the workers recruited from forty-five countries worked in the ethnic economy. Their employers were their immigrant co-ethnics. Table 8.3 shows estimates for the three employment sectors' contributions to the total employment in the garment industry. The estimate (30.3 per cent) is the percentage of the total garment industry employment that represents immigrant employers hiring co-ethnic immigrant workers. Similarly, the mainstream economy's contribution to garment industry employment was 22.5 per cent. This share strictly entails native-born employers who hire immigrant workers. From a technical standpoint, this sector represents the mainstream economy because native-born employers are hiring immigrants. The last sector is the immigrant economy, which arises when immigrant employers hire non-coethnic fellow immigrants. In the example already given, when Mr Kim from Korea hires Mrs Lopez from Mexico, the employment relationship is classified under the immigrant economy.[10] Our estimate of the immigrant economy, obtained by subtraction, is 47.2 per cent of the total employment in the garment industry. The immigrant sector is the sum of the immigrant economy plus all the various ethnic economies, only excluding the hiring of native-born Americans by other native-born Americans, as occurred in 6 per cent of the cases. We calculate that the immigrant sector accounts for 71.5 per cent of the total employment in this industry. In the Los Angeles garment industry, the immigrants created 71.5 per cent of all the jobs. This share is lower than the immigrants' share in the total employment in this industry (94 per cent) because native-born Americans were about a quarter of all the employers.

## Industrial Environment

The Los Angeles garment manufacturing industry consists of three hierarchical tiers. At the summit are the retailers, which are department stores like Macy's, the Gap, Nordstrom's, and K-Mart. With the exception of the Gap, which manufactures and produces its own clothing, all the retailers order clothing from independent manufacturers. Manufacturers design their own lines, to which they give fanciful

**Table 8.3** Economic Location of Los Angeles Garment Industry Personnel, 1990 (%)

| Sector | Personnel | Percentage |
|---|---|---|
| Mainstream economy | US native hires immigrant | 22.5 |
| Immigrant economy | Immigrant hires non-coethnic immigrant | 47.2 |
| Ethnic economy | Co-ethnic immigrant hires co-ethnic immigrant | 24.3 |
|  | US native hires US native | 6.0 |
| Total |  | 100.0 |

labels like Bugle Boy or Suzie Q. Since about 1970, manufacturers no longer produce the clothing they design and sell. When they receive a contract from a retailer, manufacturers subcontract the actual production to independent contractors. The numerous contractors actually produce the clothing in small, owner-directed factories. Thus, when Macy's orders 10,000 Bugle Boy slacks, Bugle Boy hires five to twenty contractors to make the pants from the patterns Bugle Boy provides. In short, retailers give contracts to manufacturers, who give contracts to contractors. There are about three contractors for every manufacturer in the Los Angeles industry.

The actual industrial power and business profits reside with the quasi-monopsonistic retailers who initiate the order chains. As the orders descend the hierarchy from retailers to manufacturers to contractors to workers, they move into ever more competitive economic environments that finally approximate what economists call price-taking markets. As a result, the higher levels appropriate the bulk of the industry's revenue. Bonacich and Appelbaum (2000: 2) show that at the top of the feeding chain retailers get half the gross revenue from the clothing they sell; below them, manufacturers get 35 per cent of the gross; and below the manufacturers, contractors get 15 per cent. Production workers only divide 6 per cent of the gross. In view of the poverty-level wages garment workers earn, this unequal division of the industrial revenues provoked and continues to provoke great civic and social outrage (Bonacich and Appelbaum 2000: chap. 10).

Despite this public outrage, the Los Angeles garment industry is thriving in the face of adverse trends in other local garment manufacturing sectors and in the national garment manufacturing industry.[11] In the period from 1993 to 1996, the number of garment manufacturers and contractors in Los Angeles County increased by 15 per cent. In approximately the same period, 1993 to 1997, employment in the Los Angeles garment industry expanded by 40 per cent, even though garment industry employment in the United States *declined* 17 per cent (Soja 1996: 439). The national reduction in garment employment resulted from the job export to Mexico. American garment manufacturers began to shift production to Mexico following the approval of the North American Free Trade Agreement in 1993

(Ching Louie 1992: 3–4). Los Angeles also witnessed an outflow of production jobs to Mexico in this period (Kessler 1999; Lee 1998). Two-thirds of the Los Angeles garment manufacturers with annual net sales of $10 million, the largest class, had some production in Latin America, mostly Mexico, by 1998. Just prior to implementation of the North American Free Trade Agreement, only 12 per cent of the garment manufacturers in Los Angeles had any production staff in Mexico. Five years later, a 1998 survey of all the manufacturers, not just the largest ones, reported that 43 per cent indicated that some of their production was now done outside of California (L. Wong 1998). At the April, 1999 'Sewn Products Expo' in Los Angeles, representatives of seven Mexican states were on hand to expedite and promote the relocation of Los Angeles garment factories to their states (Apparel Industry Magazine 1999). Were it not for the outflow of Los Angeles production to Mexico, observers claimed, the Los Angeles garment industry would have added even more employment in the five-year period than the 40 per cent growth it actually experienced (Lee 1998). However, observers expect the job export to continue because if they operate from Mexican plants, where labour costs one-tenth of the low Los Angeles price, manufacturers can still cut production costs by a third even after they pay higher costs for the transportation of the finished goods to the American markets. Moreover, the American tariffs were not removed from garment imports from Mexico until 1999, at which point Mexican plants became cheaper than ever.

Mexico's direct competition is the Los Angeles garment industry's largest problem, but it is not the garment industry's *only* problem. Three other threats have indirectly contributed to Mexico's growing popularity with local manufacturers. First, in the political aftermath of the Thai slavery case, when public indignation was fierce, President Clinton appointed the White House Apparel Industry Partnership in 1996 to pursue 'non-regulatory solutions' to industrial problems (Liebhold and Rubenstein 1999: 9). This voluntary partnership announced that the federal government was watching the garment industry, but did not impose any new statutory penalties or launch any new enforcement efforts. Second, Congress increased the national minimum wage in 1996. This Democratic legislation raised the minimum hourly wage from $4.25 to $5.15, and California's State Assembly subsequently increased the state's minimum wage from $5.15 to $5.75. The minimum hourly wage in California is thus now $0.60 higher than the national minimum, and $1.50 higher than it was in 1995. Since most garment workers earn the minimum wage increases in the statutory minimum wage make California less attractive as a production site. California's minimum wage is now so high, garment industry studies conclude, that garment manufacturing in Los Angeles can no longer rely upon cheap labour to maintain its international position (L. Wong 1998). Indeed, the latest press reports state that wages in the garment industry, already low, fell by 25 per cent after 1996 because of international competition and that garment industry employment fell more after NAFTA than was initially realized (Cleeland 1999; Dickerson and Cleeland 2000).

Third, the health costs of garment work, externalized to the public, have become a political issue in California and all across the United States. Garment work is unusually unhealthy for various reasons, only some of which are unavoidable. Sewing is hard and gruelling work. Studies have demostrated that garment operatives experience neck and upper limb aches, fatigue, sleeping disorders, anxiety, depression, and digestive problems. The repetitive motions they make on the job contribute to Carpal tunnel syndrome, a frequent complaint among garment operatives. In addition, workplace formaldehyde, flame retardants, lint, and dust create respiratory and skin problems.[12] Many if not most garment factories are unsafe and dirty (Silverstein and White 1996). Often, drinking water, clean toilets, first aid kits, adequate lighting and ventilation, and safety guards on machinery are all absent (Ojeda 1996). Garment factory managers routinely insult, belittle, grope, and even hit the female production workers, thus creating emotional as well as physical tension and hazards in the workplace (Loucky *et al.* 1994: 356). If the garment industry maintained ordinary working conditions, its health impact would be less serious. However, the garment industry's health conditions are notoriously substandard.[13] As a result, its operatives sustain a high volume of job-related tension, injury and emotional and physical disease.

California employers are not required to provide health insurance for their employees, and 97 per cent of the garment industry employers do not. Garment contractors work on margins too thin to permit health insurance premiums for their workers. Manufacturers and retailers claim they have no responsibility to pay health insurance premiums for someone else's (their own subcontractors') employees (Bonacich and Appelbaum 2000: 173). Admittedly, 40 per cent of all the workers in Los Angeles County do not have any employer-paid medical insurance (Hiltzik 1995).[14] But as regards employer-paid health insurance, garment manufacturing is among the worst industries in Los Angeles, and Los Angeles is the worst metropolitan offender in the state of California.[15] Nonetheless, due to its reckless indifference to occupational health, the garment industry has more than its share of diseased and injured people who, due to their low wages, cannot buy health care in the marketplace and, without health insurance, have no employer-paid access to it. Although fully employed, these workers are medically indigent. Large and growing members of medically indigent and diseased immigrants turn to public emergency hospitals for free medical care, imposing additional burdens upon these tax-supported institutions (Bonacich and Appelbaum 2000: 183). Los Angeles County spent $80 million on emergency care for the uninsured in 1997, as compared with only $62 million in 1992. In effect, as the press pointed out, tax-supported hospitals subsidize the health care of the garment industry's immigrant workers.[16]

This subsidy became a public issue in 1994. California's Republican Governor Pete Wilson campaigned for and induced voters to pass legislation (Proposition 187) that restricted the access of illegal immigrants to public schools and public hospitals in California. The Governor argued that illegal families imposed more costs on the educational system than the immigrants paid in taxes.[17] He went on the argue that immigrants used the state's free emergency rooms for their health care needs, omitting to note that the employers of these illegal workers were not providing medical care benefits for their full-time employees. Nearly two million children in California had no medical insurance in 1998, and nearly all were children of immigrants (Freedberg and Russell 1999).[18] Indeed, uninsured children and medically indigent children represented 7 per cent of the state population. Although research results have not been conclusive about how much the immigrants' health care and education actually cost California's taxpayers, the Republican Governor persuaded white voters, who represented 80 per cent of the electorate, that the state paid for the health care of illegal immigrants.[19] Proposition 187 was passed, but legal challenges have stymied enforcement (Skelton 1999). The California Democratic Party opposes enforcement because of its dependence upon Hispanic voters, who also oppose enforcement (Villaraigosa 1999). If enforced, the measure would strip illegal immigrants, many of them employees of the garment manufacturing industry, of the right to utilize public tax-supported hospitals, and deprive them of free medical care.[20]

California and federal authorities subjected the garment industry to more effective regulation in 1996. Before 1996, law enforcement had largely ignored the garment industry, maintaining just enough visibility to give an impression of vigilance without actually accomplishing anything. This feeble policy suited the business as well as the immigration lobby. However, in response to Governor Wilson's support of Proposition 187, law enforcement authorities began to police the garment industry in 1996. Since garment factories routinely ignored wage and hour laws as well as health and safety requirements, law enforcement authorities discovered that a great deal was amiss. The basic enforcement mechanism is the unannounced raid or 'sweep'. Agents descend upon a plant, seize its books, and question the employees about their immigration status. In one such raid, investigators turned up time card violations in the factories that produced Kathie Lee Gifford's line of women's clothing (Silverstein and Lee 1996). Gifford is a Hollywood celebrity whose image sells women's clothing. Her violations stirred a great deal of criticism in the press, capturing the public's attention.[21]

The most spectacular sweep raided the factory where Suni Manasurangkun and her five sons, two daughters-in-law, and two gunmen worked seventy-two Thai immigrants, mostly women, as industrial slaves in a guarded compound (Bonacich and Appelbaum 2000: 165–6; Cleeland 1999). Manasurangkun ran her factory in a seven-unit apartment complex at 2614 Santa Anita Avenue in El Monte, a western suburb of Los Angeles. Manasurangkun's factory recruited seamstresses in Thailand, where they signed indenture agreements. These agreements obligated each woman to pay $5,000 in 1997 dollars over three years. Manasurangkun's sons then smuggled the indentured women into the United States and transported them to the factory compound, a two-storey building surrounded by a high wall topped with razor wire. In this guarded factory, gunmen made the women work sixteen-hour days seven days a week. The seamstresses lived in crowded dormitories and were not permitted to exit the guarded building. The factory's canteen charged high prices for their food and supplies. Paid on a piece-rate basis, the workers earned an average of sixty-nine cents an hour, less than one-sixth the legal minimum wage. At this price, the workers would have to work 181 weeks to pay off their indenture.

Acting on a tip from a factory escapee, the police raided Manasurangkun's factory and arrested its operators on 2 August 1995. The factory's operators subsequently pleaded guilty in federal court to conspiracy, involuntary servitude, smuggling, and harbouring illegal immigrants. They received prison sentences ranging from two to seven years, plus a fine of $250,000. Manasurangkun's products had been marketed under various names, including SK Fashion, S & P Fashion and D & R Fashion. The publicity about the case embarrassed several important retailers, who had sold the slave factory's products. In 1999 eleven companies agreed to pay more than $3.7 million damages to 150 ex-slaves who had laboured in the El Monte factory and two affiliated front organizations also run by Manasurangkun. The retailers included Millers Outpost, Mervyn's, and Montgomery Ward. Of course, the retailers denied any knowledge of the conditions in their contractor's factories.

Some observers propose that enforcement pressure explained the abrupt growth in legal immigrant employment in the Los Angeles garment industry between 1993 and 1997. On this view, the sweeps compelled some previously clandestine plants to reopen in the formal sector, thus increasing the legally registered working population without necessarily increasing *the real* population at all. In principle, the enforcement sweeps might account for the *entire apparent increase* in garment industry employment. The actual share of the increase they explain is unknown. However, the issue is relevant to any interpretation of the garment industry's health. If the industry grew rapidly without any help from the enforcement sweeps, this growth might be attributable to the industry's economic viability. This is the view held by most authorities. If on the other hand the industry's growth resulted wholly or largely from the invasion of the informal sector and the subsequent normalization of the legal status by theretofore informal firms, then the industry's apparent growth really only reflected a deterioration of its political protection. Without political protection, garment manufacturing firms would have to meet the legal code's industrial standards. This obligation would increase their production costs, rendering the Los Angeles garment manufacturing industry less competitive with Mexico. If competitiveness declined enough, retailers would shift production to Mexico, and the garment industry of Los Angeles would cease to attract new immigrant workers or even to support the ones already in town.

## Management

Garment contractors utilize the progressive bundle system of production. Garments are tied into bundles, which are routed through a sequence of workstations. At each station, a seamstress performs a repetitious operation such as sewing on a pocket. After she has completed her operation on all the garments, she rebundles them and passes the bundle to the next worker. Garment workers are paid piece rates. At best, the piece rates are low. Bonacich and Appelbaum (2000: 181) estimate that the average garment operative in Los Angeles earned $7,200 in 1990, when the legal minimum wage would have yielded $8,840 and the official poverty level for a family of four was $13,359.[22]

Garment contractors often work at a sewing machine along with their workers for at least part of the working day. Many garment contractors allow their seamstresses to bring their children to the factory. Since they earn piece rates, the seamstresses do not cost their employers any money when they tend to their children instead of working at their sewing machine. This indulgence gives the seamstresses a chance to watch their children while they work. Although this practice is not universal in the garment industry, it is more common there than in other manufacturing industries in Los Angeles which simply ban children altogether. The advantages to the seamstresses are obvious. Employment in the garment industry allows the mothers of small children to earn some money, whereas other 'non-exploiting' industries exclude them altogether. In view of this advantage, many mothers view low-wage garment employment as their best *realistic* alternative for employment.

The Los Angeles garment industry probably does not have all the credit it could use. Small firms generally have less access to bank credit in the United States than they want, and the Los Angeles garment industry predominantly consists of small firms (Light and Gold 2000). However, the garment industry spokespersons who complain about labour shortages and government regulation do not complain about the credit shortage. The recent mushrooming of the Los Angeles garment industry is hard to reconcile with the notion that a lack of credit access is stifling the industry. One reason is the low cost of start-ups. A new contractor can start in the garment industry with six $300 sewing machines and two months' rent for a loft. Even immigrant entrepreneurs can raise these sums. In addition, Asian entrepreneurs, the dominant group in the industry, have more access to informal loans from their relatives and friends than non-Asians.[23] Asian entrepreneurs make extensive use of rotating savings and credit associations. When queried, 77 per cent of the Korean garment contractors indicated that they had participated in a *kye*, a Korean rotating credit association, since arriving in Los Angeles (Light *et al.* 1990). And the Asian communities have numerous banks of their own that support the business enterprises of co-ethnics (Flanigan 1998).

## Long-term Outlook

Despite some loss of production to Mexico between 1993 and 1998, the Los Angeles garment industry was still thriving in 1999. True, industry growth had peaked in 1997 and had declined 10 per cent by 1999. Nonetheless, this decline did not impose stagnation, much less ruination (Dickerson and Cleeland 2000). The unique survival of the Los Angeles garment industry is hard to explain. Since other American cities can also access cheap immigrant labour, cheap immigrant labour in Los Angeles cannot explain the unique viability of the city's garment industry. At this point, specific features of the Los Angeles economic environment hover into view. They need to be addressed to explain why Los Angeles flourished when the other garment centres of the United States declined. Observers usually attribute the unusual flourishing of the Los Angeles garment industry to two environmental factors. The first is the rapid start-up rates of new, immigrant-owned firms, a supply-side push (Light and Roach 1996). California has very high self-employment rates compared with other American states, and the Los Angeles self-employment rates are higher than California's (Light and Roach 1996). Thanks to the low start-up costs many immigrants already have, or can easily acquire, the capability to start a garment factory where the immigrant employees will not have paid medical insurance. Thanks to the huge immigrant population and continuing influx of new immigrants, many immigrants wish to start factories of this kind. They still have the American Dream. Even Bonacich and Appelbaum (2000: 154), harsh critics of the industry, acknowledge that many garment contractors earn tidy middle-class incomes: 70 per cent of the Korean immigrant contractors own their own homes and 61 per cent have moved out of the inner city to a suburb.

The second factor is the Los Angeles industry's unique market niche. Los Angeles apparel makers specialize in contemporary clothing and sportswear for the women's and junior markets (L. Wong 1998). Los Angeles sells the 'California Look', not just cheap clothing. True, California Look clothing is also produced quickly and sells at moderate prices to a trend-following market of young women (Kessler 1999). Sixty-one per cent of the Los Angeles industry's sales are in women's outerwear, a sector where rapid style changes discourage production in less fashion-conscious cities that lack Hollywood's glamour (Wolff 1995). Los Angeles has fashion cachet. Guess? Incorporated is an immigrant-owned Los

Angeles manufacturer that specializes in exactly these California Look youth styles. Its website listed the 'January hotpicks' for sale: drawstring cropped cargo pants, white peasant top, velcro wrap-around utility bag, and day-glo pink T shirt.[24] California Look clothing often bears the logo 'Los Angeles', and, thanks to the Hollywood film industry, this place name commands prestige and recognition from young women all over the world.

## Conclusion

The Los Angeles garment industry expanded enormously between 1970 and 1999, a period when garment production in the rest of the United States was decreasing. Cheap labour alone does not explain why only Los Angeles retained its garment industry.[25] The California Look does. In this fashion-driven environment, poor immigrant women found ample job opportunities in a dynamic and expanding clothing industry. By 1998, approximately 5 per cent of the employed immigrants in the City of Los Angeles were working in the garment manufacturing industry. At least three-quarters of the industry's expansion we attribute to new immigrant-owned businesses. These immigrant-owned businesses employ co-ethnic and non-coethnic immigrants in the formal and informal sectors. A product of immigrant social, human and cultural capital resources they brought with them to the United States, the expanded garment industry increased the absorption capacity of Los Angeles as an immigrant reception centre. Thanks to the expanded garment industry, approximately 5 per cent more immigrants were able to find employment in Los Angeles than could have been the case without the industry.

The past quarter century's expansion of the Los Angeles garment industry relied upon political protection of the low wages and substandard industrial conditions that always characterized these factories. Many of the garment factories were in overt violation of wage, health, and industrial standards for twenty-five years, but police ignored the violations. Given political protection, which was ubiquitous until approximately 1996, immigrant entrepreneurs could undercut normal and reasonable production costs, rendering their stylish garments competitive with Mexico's cheaper products. Substandard conditions were most prevalent in the garment industry's informal sector, of course, but they were also notoriously common in the formal sector. As the supply-driven influx of Mexican and Central American workers increased,[26] immigrant wages generally declined in Los Angeles, as did the social conditions in the garment industry. However, the declining industrial and labour conditions in the garment industry had by no means hit bottom in 1999. There was still plenty of room for additional decline before reaching Mexico's level.

However, ultimately the long-term growth of the resident immigrant population, coupled with the declining real wages in the garment industry and generally in Los Angeles, began to publicize the negative conditions in the industry. One troublesome area was health care costs. Their substandard wages and lack of employer-paid medical insurance made most full-time immigrant employees medically indigent. In effect, garment industry employers assigned the health care of their employees to the state's publicly funded emergency rooms. The garment industry's employers had thus obtained a taxpayer subsidy. This taxpayer subsidy rendered their low-wage firms internationally competitive. Other low-wage immigrant industries in Los Angeles obtained the same benefit, but political protection was not as essential or problematic to any of them as to the garment industry.[27]

If California had not had any publicly funded health care system at all, as was the case in Britain under the *laissez-faire* regime of the nineteenth century (Polanyi 1957: chap. 6), garment employers could have replaced dying seamstresses with healthy new immigrants at no cost to the public.[28] To have done so, however, would have repealed what Polanyi called 'the right to live'. Since the immigrants were using free, state-supported health care, employers paid nothing for worker health, and California did not repeal 'the right to live' until 1994 (Vernez and McCarthy 1996). Playing into a growing anti-immigrant backlash in the white electorate, Governor Wilson also elaborated the backlash.[29] The anti-immigrant political backlash reduced the reliable political tolerance towards illegal working and health conditions in restaurants, garment manufacturing and other immigrant-dominated industries in Los Angeles. This decreased political tolerance reduced the size of the vast informal sector of the garment industry, and pressured the formal sector to actually pay the increased minimum wage rather than evade payment, as in the previous status quo. Political intolerance meant that, at last, the political structure of California had begun to monitor the working conditions of immigrants and the number of immigrants in Los Angeles and, indeed, in the entire United States.

Admittedly, the movement towards state regulation collided with an adventitious and unique condition non-existent anywhere else in the United States: the California Look. The Los Angeles garment industry owed its success to Hollywood's worldwide visibility as much as to its low-wage workforce. Without the cinematic visibility, which lent prestige to California Look clothing, the garment industry of Los Angeles would have failed to develop as rapidly or extensively as it actually did, and would have declined more rapidly after the North America Free Trade Agreement was passed. Additionally, the increase in the federal minimum wage and the state's subsequent increase and the signing of the North American Free Trade Agreement all harmed the Los Angeles garment industry even if they did not kill it. One cannot credit all these changes to the negative externalities of the garment industry.

Nonetheless, important as they were to the actual status of the garment industry, the topic of this inquiry, these environmental changes do not obscure the underlying issue of how much immigrant poverty welfare states can tolerate. Even in Los Angeles, the historical home of the open shop, the political system began to restrain a wave of immigration that was still expanding. The main reason had to do with the negative social externalities that the immigrant garment industry created. Living as they did below the legal survival minimum, low-wage immigration imposed negative externalities that impacted state finances. The voters discovered that immigrant-owned garment factories had given the taxpayers the responsibility for the health care of the industry's immigrant workers. Simultaneously with leftist political attacks on the industry, the right wing's intolerance of immigrant poverty reduced the Los Angeles tolerance for garment factories. In the political reaction that followed Proposition 187 and the Thai slavery case, which still has not run its course, the industry's previously reliable climate of political protection deteriorated. The enhanced enforcement of the existing wages and hours legislation, and that of industrial health and safety, detrimentally affected the competitiveness of the garment industry, encouraging the relocation of threatened plants to Mexico even without NAFTA. If the industry left Los Angeles, as it has already left other American centres of garment production, fewer immigrants could live in Los Angeles and the growth machine ideology, a sovereign touchstone of American opinion, would register a failure.

## Notes

1. For a personal account of the early garment industry in Los Angeles, see Orfalea (1999).
2. In Los Angeles, Asian and Latin American immigrants replaced the ethnic whites, a few of whom remain in the industry, usually in executive positions. This also occurred in Toronto (see Gannagé 1989–1990: 49; see also Loucky *et al.* 1994: 346).
3. On the important role of social capital in garment manufacturing, see Uzzi (1996: 677–83).
4. On migration networks among Mexican immigrants in California, see Orrenius (1999: 5).
5. Other authorities confirm this estimate (see Lee 1996).
6. Lee (1992) found that Korean garment factories in Los Angeles employed an average of thirty seamstresses.

7. The *Los Angeles Times* estimated the workforce of the Los Angeles garment manufacturing industry at 132,000 in 1997.
8. Unpublished field notes in the possession of Ivan Light.
9. The London garment industry also witnessed labour shortages. 'In the London sample, a general fear of "losing" women machinists during "slack periods" and complaints over labour "disloyalty" were frequently expressed by contractors. "Finding machinists" was cited as the single largest problem confronting employers' (Panayiotopoulos 1996a: 455).
10. All the women whom Kim *et al.* (1992: 74) interviewed had 'obtained their jobs by being introduced by a friend' who worked for their new employer.
11. Manufacturing industries in Los Angeles have generally been in decline for thirty years (see Scott 1996: 224; see also Ong and Blumenberg 1996: 310–14).
12. Opera fans are certain to know that in *La Bohème*, Puccini's overworked and underpaid heroine, Mimi, dies tragically of tuberculosis, even then a common complaint among garment employees.
13. The Los Angeles restaurant industry has comparably harsh and substandard working conditions (see Kang 1998a,b). Other American cities' garment industries have equally substandard working conditions, coupled in some cases with organized crime domination (see Petras 1992: 77).
14. Schlauffler *et al.* (2000: 12) estimate that only one-third of the people in the 0–60 age group in Los Angeles County had no health insurance in 1999.
15. Construction and manufacturers such as furniture and garment makers have added thousands of jobs in recent years, but most do not offer health benefits (see also Nazario and Shutt 1995).
16. 'I'll tell you who gets the free ride in this, when you look at the UCLA data on the uninsured in the county', says Jonathan Friedman, chief of staff to Burt Margolin, the county health czar. 'When two-thirds of the uninsured work or are dependants of full-time employees, small business is getting a free ride' (Hiltzik 1995: 11).
17. Governor Wilson did *not* point out that the garment retailers and manufacturers were the main beneficiaries of this public subsidy. 'Thirty percent to 60% of all apparel manufacturing in Southern California is done by unregistered, untaxed, cash-paying shops', says Robert Walter, vice-president of Frank Walter Sportswear, a sewing contractor that produces girls' clothing. 'If all the sewing contractors and apparel manufacturers were registered and paid taxes, we wouldn't be having this health care problem' (Hiltzik 1995: 11).
18. Immigrant parents even resist state-subsidized medical insurance programmes which their children are eligible for because they are afraid that accepting public welfare will result in their citizenship applications being denied. The operative law is a 100-year-old federal law that denies citizenship to aliens who have received public welfare.

19. Although 77 per cent of the Latino voters opposed this measure, Latinos were only 8 per cent of the voters.
20. For example, 70,000 illegal immigrant women in California received free prenatal care in 1999 (Lindlaw 1999).
21. Wal-Mart is the major distributor of this line (Silverstein and Lee 1996).
22. These substandard wages are not necessarily illegal because workers may not have worked full time for an entire year.
23. Taiwanese immigrants have three times more business loans from their relatives and friends than white Americans; Chinese banks are also numerous in Los Angeles, and they aggressively promote Chinese businesses (Tseng 1997: 181, 185).
24. Visit their website: http://www.guess.com
25. 'Wherever the garment industry has taken root in the US, unlicensed, sub-standard sewing shops have sprung up by the hundreds. They are illegal, off-the-books, pay no minimum wages, unemployment insurance, or health benefits and ignore child-labor laws or overtime pay regulations' (Petras 1992: 77).
26. Network support is great, but *not* as great as the immigrants had expected (Hamilton and Chinchilla 1995: 32).
27. The restaurant industry was equally troubled. Post-1993 sweeps of this industry also turned up evidence of pervasive substandard and illegal industrial conditions (Kang 1998a,b).
28. 'The immigration crisis in Europe is connected with the issue of how to deal with the escalating costs of the social welfare state' (Martin 1994: 87).
29. The issue has now become national, not just regional. Health coverage is an important part of the entire reception context for immigrants. 'Many immigrants hold jobs that do not offer health insurance, and their comparatively low incomes make it very difficult for them to purchase insurance on their own' (Camarota and Edwards 2000).

# –9–

# Sewing up Seven Cities
## *Jan Rath*

## Introduction

The world is in a state of flux. Capital, goods and people move around the globe, generating vast changes and linking distant social, political and economic configurations. The creation and preservation of economic ties over long distances is intriguing, but in themselves nothing new. In days of yore, merchants in pursuit of market expansion ventured on to the silk route, sailed to Hanseatic towns, embarked on colonial projects, or travelled Europe's dirt roads as hawkers. The current internationalization of economic traffic is no more than another stage in a long historical process: the inexorable *longue durée*. What is unprecedented, though, is its speed and scale. If anything characterizes internationalization or globalization, it is the time–space compression. The shrinking of the world (Dicken 1992) does not necessarily mean the 'end of geography', as Raes (2000a) correctly observes, and the rag trade is a case in point.

Fröbel *et al.* (1980) expected processes of globalization to enhance the rag trade exodus to low-wage countries. These countries would become sites of global garment manufacturing, and the advanced economies would be the main setting for garment sales. These developments, it was argued, only served to strengthen the emergence of a New International Division of Labour. However, the spatial concentration of small garment factories in specific advanced countries, urban areas, neighbourhoods and sometimes even blocks of houses, has demonstrated considerable resilience and in some cases spatial reconcentration. Immigrants play a salient role in these processes. The simultaneous proliferation of immigrant garment factories in various world cities suggests that the industries there are on parallel tracks, although a close examination of these developments also reveals striking differences. General processes are taking place and produce effects, but location obviously still matters.

In the previous chapters we have explored this question by examining the cases of Paris, London, the West Midlands, Amsterdam, New York, Miami and Los Angeles. Each of these locations occupies a specific position in the global economy, is a major garment production centre, and has experienced a proliferation of small immigrant enterprises. Each chapter addressed questions pertaining to the performance of immigrant entrepreneurs, their position in the rag trade, the dynamics of their entrepreneurship, and the factors underlying these processes. As is noted in the introductory chapter, each drew from building blocks linked to the capacity of immigrant entrepreneurs to mobilize social relations, the significance of market structures and processes of restructuring for the creation of business opportunities, and the impact of various forms of regulation. In this final chapter I wrap up this study by presenting a number of observations that shed light on global processes and local differentiations.

It is a generally accepted view that advanced urban economies constitute nodal points of globalization and centres of political and economic power. Authors have examined the development of these centres and described the social, political and economic processes that account for their emergence and the implications for various segments of the population. They cite the degradation of manufacturing industries, the growth of the service economy, the increasing significance of flexibility and outsourcing, and the dialectics of gentrification and the informalization of different parts of the labour market. Sassen (1991) emphasizes the gravitation of multinational headquarters in the service industry to particular 'global cities', a process that reinforces the central position of these cities in the global economy. According to her, the old manufacturing industries continue to exist and provide opportunities for people who lack the resources to operate at the higher end of the labour market. The rag trade is one such industry in that it offers entrepreneurial and job openings to poor and unskilled Third World people. Numerous newcomers have surely been attracted by these low-grade opportunities and have subsequently been funnelled to sweatshops in the darker regions of the economy.

These views on economic restructuring enhance our understanding of the development of certain sectors of specific urban economies and the sorting out of immigrants over various sectors, but they are also contested. Some critics note the lack of empirical support or the idiosyncrasies of the cases studied, others criticize the underlying economism and lack of appreciation of regulatory matters, and others again object to the strong bias towards structural determinants (see Burgers 1996; Hamnett 1996; Waldinger 1996b; Waldinger and Lapp 1993). Light (2000) acknowledges the significance of globalization, but emphasizes that immigrants, particularly entrepreneurs, are not simply passive objects of economic restructuring, they are also agents of international change (see also Light *et al.* 1999). Waldinger (1996b) also criticizes structural approaches and favours an approach that takes the 'real dramatic personae' as a starting point. They both note that international migration, once set in motion, becomes network driven. The mobilization of networks reduces the costs and hardships of migration, expands the supply of immigrants, and lowers the costs incurred by immigrant-owned firms. Waldinger envisages the clustering of immigrants in economic niches and holds that the niches are involved in processes of ethnic succession, facilitating long-term collective immigrant incorporation and upward social mobility into the host country's economy. Light presents a slightly different view as he argues that social networks enhance the expansion of the economy. Many more businesses can exist as a result of lower wages and the exploitation of co-ethnics. Both approaches attempt to debunk globalization theory, which is part of the merit, but one cannot help feeling they are ignoring the good points. While arguing that immigrant absorption in the economy is fostered by the power of their social networks, it is suggested that social capital works wonders and produces business success irrespective of local or supra-local political and economic conditions.

These agency-oriented approaches are not isolated, they are simply specimens of a paradigm currently in favour with students of immigrant entrepreneurship (Rath 2000b; Rath and Kloosterman 2000). In this paradigm, the social and ethno-cultural features of ethnic entrepreneurs are the point of departure for research that subsequently focuses on the embeddedness of entrepreneurs in social networks. However, the political economy of entrepreneurship is not really addressed.[1] In the recent past an international team of researchers tried to construct an interactive model that would do justice to structure as well as agency (see Light and Rosenstein 1995; Waldinger *et al.* 1990). In practice, though, many of them zoomed in on the resources of immigrant entrepreneurs rather than their relations with the wider political and economic environment. This does not suffice (Rath 2000c). This is why the next stage is to give the study of immigrant entrepreneurship a twist and explore how the various aspects can be linked. The concept of mixed embeddedness indicates this new research approach (Kloosterman and Rath 2001 and forthcoming; Kloosterman *et al.* 1999). It acknowledges the significance of the concrete embeddedness of immigrants in social networks as regards economic transactions, and recognizes that these relations and transactions are embedded in a more abstract way in wider economic and politico-institutional structures.

## Made-to-measure

Before going into these matters, let us focus on the cities in question. There is the trivial but nevertheless important fact that Paris, London, Birmingham (the Midlands), Amsterdam, New York, Miami and Los Angeles differ sharply in terms of surface area and population, and the size of the local economy in general and the garment industry in particular. The City of Amsterdam, to mention one extreme, is the Dutch capital and, with approximately 730,000 residents, the largest city in the Netherlands. But compared to Los Angeles, Amsterdam is an insignificant provincial town. This still holds true even if the focus is expanded to include Greater Amsterdam, which has just over a million residents. The five-county Los Angeles region covers a vast area more than twice the size of the Netherlands and with almost as many residents (14.5 million compared to 16 million) (Allen and Turner 1997; Waldinger and Bozorgmehr 1996). It can easily take an hour and a half or even more to drive from one part of Greater Los Angeles to another, depending on traffic, but someone who starts in Amsterdam would cross the Belgian or German border by then. Paris, London and New York are more compact than Los Angeles, but still way larger than Amsterdam or Birmingham. These spatial dimensions affect the size of the local garment market, which in turn influences the opportunities for small garment firms. Garment and textile manufacturing in Los Angeles County alone amounts to $28 billion, which is almost a tenth of the total economy. At its peak in the early 1990s Dutch garment manufacturing amounted to NLG2.3 billion, thus roughly $1 billion, including informal production. These differences, to be sure, underscore immense quantitative differences in the opportunity structures.

Despite the differences, all the authors in this book report that the cities have long functioned as immigrant hubs. Immigration increased dramatically in the 1950s and 1960s following the break-up of the French, British and Dutch colonial empires, the influx of guest workers in Europe, and the 1965 changes in the American immigration laws. These processes have continuously altered the ethnic make-up of the urban population, as is reflected in the economy in general and the rag trade in particular. Since the late 1950s and 1960s, when the sector was in decline in most cities due to restructuring, large numbers of immigrants have entered the sector and halted or even reversed the decline. In Paris, London and New York, the involvement of immigrants boiled down to what Waldinger (1996b) calls a game of ethnic musical chairs. In other cases, there is not much evidence of ethnic succession (cf. Rath 2000a). Still, all the cases demonstrate how the industry has been affected by the input of immigrants.

At a juncture when de-industrialization is a buzzword, the resilience of the SME sector in garment manufacturing obviously stands out. At the end of the 1990s the garment industry was still the number one manufacturing sector in New York. In 1998, 132,900 people were employed by fashion-related firms, from designing to retailing in the five-borough area, most of them in garment manufacturing. Garment and textile manufacturing firms together accounted for almost a third of the manufacturing firms in the city. An estimated 30–40 per cent of the sewing shops had immigrant owners, 30–40 per cent of which closed down or changed their names in the first year. Los Angeles outperformed New York as the garment manufacturing capital of the United States around 1989; according to Ivan Light and Victoria Ojeda this was mainly as a result of its superior access to (illegal) immigrant labour. In the mid-1990s, when garment industry employment in the United States declined by 17 per cent, the number of garment manufacturers and contractors in Los Angeles County increased by 15 per cent, expanding the number of jobs by 40 per cent to roughly 140,000. Low estimates suggest that the Los Angeles garment sector included 5,070 firms. In London, the garment industry continued to have a significant presence despite the relocation of part of the garment production offshore or to regions in the United Kingdom like the West Midlands in the face of high unemployment a few decades ago. In the late 1990s, approximately 2,500 small firms in the London garment industry employed an estimated 30,000 predominantly female workers. In the West Midlands, many small garment factories had emerged since the mid-1970s. They were predominantly Asian-owned and mainly operated at the lower end of the market. There were about 500 of these firms in the area. In Amsterdam, between 1980 and the early 1990s, numerous mainly Turkish immigrants set up approximately a thousand small sewing shops, employing roughly 20,000 workers at the peak, and contributing to a temporary resurgence of the SME sector in the Dutch garment industry. Paris and Miami experienced similar developments.

The figures are impressive but their real significance is hard to assess. First, the actual situation is unclear because there are so many informal workshops and homeworkers. They circumvent or evade the official legal requirements, resulting in an unknown level of unreporting and unrecording. Secondly, the manufacturing of garments in advanced economies is subject to great pressure, for example from globalization, leading to ruthless competition with local and international producers. Under those unfavourable conditions entrepreneurs are quick to close shop, or are forced to do so due to violations of the law. All this contributes to an extraordinarily high fluctuation rate. The extreme case of Amsterdam shows that it is technically possible to wipe out a substantial number of contractors within a matter of months. The point is that a thousand firms seemed like a lot in the Lowlands, but in the bubble economy of the rag trade they vanished in no time. This illustrates their vulnerability as well as the arbitrary nature of the figures. Thirdly, the figures are not self-evident but contingent on local conditions. The 500 firms established in the West Midlands only represent 20 per cent of the total number of firms in London, and less than 10 per cent of the total number of firms in Los Angeles. Still, in the local context of inner Birmingham, Smethwick, Coventry, Wolverhampton, West Bromwich and Walsall, this figure means a lot, and this is even truer of the Asian communities that have entered the sector. In short, figures only make sense if they are linked to the specifics of the local situation. How different this situation can be was illustrated when American sociologist Ivan Light visited a Turkish sewing shop in Amsterdam. The plant was clean, brightly lit and pleasant and did not bear any resemblance to the sweatshops he had seen in Los Angeles.

## Social Networks

As is elsewhere the case, networks are referred to in an effort to explain the participation of immigrant entrepreneurs in the rag trade. The authors of this book maintain that social networks are important in explaining the formation of immigrant niches as well as individual entrepreneurs' everyday management, even if they do not always account for how the first immigrants found their way to the garment industry. Social networks provide entrepreneurs with essential information about business opportunities in the sector, access to informal financial capital and cheap and flexible labour, and actual support in the performance of a variety of tasks. Prodromos Panayiotopoulos and Marja Dreef (London) note the multi-faceted character of social networks and hold that there are complementary social networks involving kinship, ethnicity, caste, village or town origins, schoolboy friendships, and membership in political and cultural organizations. But as Nancy Green (Paris) puts it, networks are not the whole story. In addition to social networks, the limited skills and low capital needed to get into the business, and the poor options in the larger labour market, account for the continuing influx of immigrants to an industry characterized by cut-throat competition and difficult working conditions.

Immigrant garment entrepreneurs have exhibited multifarious labour market careers, but most start as wage labourers and become self-employed at a later stage. The specifics of their migration history and entrance in the host society's economy are crucial here. Immigrants did not move initially to Amsterdam or Birmingham because of the garment industry. In the 1950s and 1960s there was little evidence of the garment industry and little demand for migrant garment workers. Immigrants flocked into these cities because other industries offered them job opportunities, and in the Dutch case because they were recruited from their home country to do temporary work. Only when these industries declined and numerous workers, including ex-colonial and guest workers, were laid off did the garment industry emerge as an option. In this period of economic recession the unemployed immigrant could hardly find a regular job. This situation deteriorated due to factors such as educational deficiencies, the lack of relevant social networks, and racist exclusion. Under these conditions, self-employment seemed to be an attractive alternative. The rag trade was an obvious choice, since it was characterized by low entry barriers in terms of financial capital or skills. Immigrants who took this path seem to be a perfect example of the blocked mobility thesis, i.e. they became entrepreneurs in response to the lack of opportunities in the regular labour market. As the lack of opportunities was particularly high in times of economic decline, their entrepreneurship demonstrated contra-cyclical tendencies.

However, not all the entrepreneurs took this route and their entrepreneurship thus illustrates different path dependencies. Apart from a small number who migrated with the explicit purpose of setting up shop in the garment sector, such as the Indian and Pakistani wholesalers in Amsterdam, many garment entrepreneurs started as wage labourers employed by a garment firm. Newcomers were all too willing to become machinists, cutters, ironers or general garment workers. Information about job opportunities was widely available in the communities and often in the home countries as well, and was spread by word of mouth.

The authors demonstrate that these social networks extend over long distances and across borders. Stephan Raes *et al.* (Amsterdam) show that some garment workers from Turkey were explicitly recruited by co-ethnics to perform skilled tasks. Ivan Light and Victoria Ojeda (Los Angeles) and Yu Zhou (New York) describe how the very existence of clusters of ethnic enterprises fosters new international migration. Once they have been hired, these newcomers often turn out to be apprentices. Although some of the workers were tailors at home or had some other experience with sewing, as Green (Paris) writes, sewing *and* contracting are generally learned on the job. After a while, a number of workers resign from their jobs to set up their own factory. This process eventually contributes to the mushrooming, if not supersaturation, of small sewing shops in a hyper-competitive environment.

The different path dependencies are important since they help to explain why particular groups gravitate to the garment industry and others do not. Monder Ram *et al.* (Midlands) examine the presence of Asians and the absence of African-Caribbeans in the Midlands garment industry. African-Caribbeans have fewer class resources, are dispersed on a wider scale, have low home-ownership levels, which negatively influences their chances of getting bank loans, and gravitate towards public sector employment. These features combine to indicate a distinct path dependency that prevents the development of social networks that funnel African-Caribbeans to the rag trade, or any other SME sector for that matter.

Yu Zhou (New York) refers to intricate class-based network differentiations. She describes how Jewish and Italian immigrants in New York were able to achieve upward mobility by mobilizing their social networks, and argues that this is no longer feasible for newer immigrant groups since the industry has matured. The garment industry in the Big Apple has evolved into a sophisticated specialized network characterized by a multi-tier system. The upper tier is dominated by established native-born capitalists, many of whom are the descendants of Jewish or Italian immigrants. They constitute a tier of college-educated manufacturers, jobbers, and retailers well embedded in the industry. The lower tiers tend to consist of newer immigrants without educational qualifications, proficiency in English, and the right social connections, who have been relegated to work as contractors, subcontractors, and small manufacturers of various sorts. The upper tier has the profits and the prestige of the fashion industry, and the lower tiers are faced by fierce competition and low profits. Prodromos Panayiotopoulos and Marja Dreef (London) note similar differentiations in the London garment industry. They describe the Greek Cypriot entrepreneurs who have been active in the sector for a long time and have managed to link up with local political parties. This linkage has helped them move up-market. I return to this subject later.

Immigrant groups in the rag trade are often portrayed as exhibiting high levels of gender segregation: Asians in the Midlands, Greek Cypriots in London, the

Chinese in Paris and New York, Latin Americans in Los Angeles and Miami, and Turks in Paris. This in part informs a gender-specific division of labour on the shop floor. A number of chapters recount how married couples run a garment business, with the husband usually as the production manager and the wife dealing with the external contacts and doing the bookkeeping. Monder Ram *et al.* (Midlands) emphasize, however, that the role of wives goes beyond these more visible tasks, as they do the housekeeping, look after the children, and so forth. This domestic work may not always be recognized, but it surely enables the husband to run the show as entrepreneur.

Most immigrant entrepreneurs are male, and most of the sewing shop workers are female (except in Amsterdam). Women are usually employed as machinists or general workers and do unskilled or semi-skilled work. Immigrant entrepreneurship researchers commonly explain the role of women in cultural terms: ethno-cultural moral codes and practices funnel immigrant women to what seem to be sheltered sectors of the economy where these codes and practices are respected. The steady supply of reliable labour, allocated through co-ethnic and familial ties, gives immigrant entrepreneurs a competitive edge. Monder Ram *et al.* (Midlands), however, abandon these culturalist explanations and argue that the position of immigrant women in the rag trade needs to be viewed in a broader context of racism and sexism (see also Phizacklea 1990). Until 1988, racism and sexism were part and parcel of the British immigration legislation that treated women as dependants of men. Most women either entered the United Kingdom to join their family or on a voucher sponsored by a relative in business. According to the authors, this legislation helped perpetuate the cultural stereotypes of Asian women as weak and passive, thus lessening their chances in the general employment market, and has exacerbated their dependency on employment in sewing shops run by their family members or co-ethnics. Incidentally, Monder Ram *et al.* assume that second-generation Asians are more intent on pursuing professional careers than perpetuating the small business tradition of their parents.

Things turned out differently in Amsterdam, where the entrepreneurs and workers were predominantly male. According to Stephan Raes *et al.*, the specific history of illegal migration from Turkey to the Netherlands and specific features of the Dutch welfare state account for the limited role of Turkish women in Amsterdam. The city had a large reserve of undocumented immigrants from Turkey, predominantly relatively young men. This gender-specific aspect was echoed in the workforce at the Turkish sewing shops and in the population of Turkish entrepreneurs. In principle, Turkish entrepreneurs could recruit workers, male and female alike, from the ranks of the settled population. However, these legal immigrants were not willing to accept an unpleasant job at sewing shops. If they were unemployed, the Dutch welfare state provided them with relatively generous benefits, which mitigated the need to take up any job. This is another example of how regulation affects the mobilizing power of social networks and the division of labour in the garment industry.

Ethnic or familial networks can be instrumental in forging business connections, although the cases of Amsterdam and New York show that a strong reliance on these networks can also be detrimental. Developing stable relationships with main-stream retailers appears to be more rewarding. This supports the argument that economic transactions are embedded in social relations, albeit that these relations are not necessarily ethnic or familial. There is nevertheless strong evidence that ethnic or familial networks serve as an infrastructure to collect capital and recruit, train and discipline labour. The reliance of entrepreneurs on familial or ethnic ties rather than formal recruitment processes obviously affects the workplace regime in various ways. Most authors note that people who are well trusted, especially family members, perform key tasks such as bookkeeping, maintaining relations with jobbers, and planning production. This also holds for tasks that require special skills, such as cutting. Allocating these tasks to core network members, often men, allows the manager a certain degree of control over the production process, as these workers tend to be loyal. Tasks that are more general are done by employees with fewer skills who are less trusted. Entrepreneurs do prefer to recruit these workers from their networks as well, or at any rate from their own ethnic group, but in practice this is not always possible. Monder Ram *et al.* (Midlands) argue that the supply of cheap and flexible Asian labour for garment factories in the Midlands is depleting, since immigration regulations have been tightened and youngsters tend to prefer other jobs. Prodromos Panayiotopoulos and Marja Dreef (London) note that Greek Cypriot entrepreneurs in London encounter similar problems. Ivan Light and Victoria Ojeda (Los Angeles) discuss how Asian entre-preneurs, particularly Koreans, have faced similar problems but solved them by tapping Latino networks. In Los Angeles, a multi-tier system has also developed with Asian owners and managers in the better positions and Latino workers in the others. Asian entrepreneurs can continue to rely on non-ethnic networks as long as Latin American immigrants, legal and illegal, keep flocking to Southern Cali-fornia. Until recently, this mass influx secured a continuous supply of cheap and flexible workers. The extent to which this will continue to be the case remains to be seen.

Guillermo Grenier and Alex Stepick present an interesting case of a garment factory in Miami. Until recently, Cuban entrepreneurs and workers controlled the sector, but it became more difficult to keep the businesses afloat, and the supply of Cuban seamstresses was running dry. The garment factory in their chapter employed Cuban women who appeared to be well connected and organized. The previous owner had introduced a workplace regime that these women appreciated. They constituted more than just a number of individual workers. They were a group of organized workers who successfully opposed the non-Cuban management. This mobilization of political forces was possible because the women were strongly embedded in a wider social structure that they felt a great loyalty to. In contrast, a number of authors note the costs or even the perverse effects of social embeddedness. Prodromos Panayiotopoulos and Marja Dreef (London) discuss entrepreneurial partnerships and hold that pooling family labour is an important resource for new entrants; but it can also be a source of friction due to gossip, rumours, and malevolence among the families involved. They refer to cases of acrimonious break-ups between partners, often resulting in acrimonious break-ups between families.

The focus on embeddedness in social networks enhances our general understanding of immigrant entrepreneurship in the rag trade, but it is hard to trace local specificity. One interesting difference between the cities is related to the link between the immigration history of particular groups and the development of the garment industry. In Paris, London, New York and Los Angeles some of the more successful entrepreneurs among the older immigrant groups constituted a strong presence in the sector. They achieved upward social mobility but could no longer rely on co-ethnic and familial social networks, and needed to start recruiting from other groups. In some cases, such as Paris, New York, Los Angeles, Miami, and to some extent London, the entrepreneurs tapped the social networks of newer immigrants, leading to a sharp rise in the numbers of multi-ethnic workshops. But in Amsterdam and the Midlands this was harder to accomplish and the entrepreneurs faced serious survival problems. However, these problems were primarily generated by economic and regulatory matters.

## The Market

Economic restructuring has severely affected the garment industry ever since the Second World War. Like many other old manufacturing sectors, the garment industry rationalized production and relocated part of the production to sites outside the traditional economic nodes, particularly high unemployment areas in the interior and low-wage countries. This coincided with changing fashion cycles, fragmented consumer tastes and the breakdown of economies of scale. Until the 1960s the market was characterized by slow fashion changes and was quite predictable, but today the collections are constantly changed. Rapid fashion-cycle changes, small and fragmented demands and short lead-times do not mesh with the economies of scale associated with Fordist mass production and have created ample opportunities for nearby small garment factories. These producers supply small batches at short notice, which enables retailers to respond quickly to fashion changes or unexpected rises in the demand for particular garments. Together, these processes have expanded the local systems of subcontracting which involve a multitude of small contractors and homeworkers. In itself there is nothing innovative about putting out. As Green shows in her chapter on Paris, these systems with their characteristic chains of dependence were already around in the early days of the industrial era.

The international link is clearly very important, albeit in a specific local way. Contractors in the United States do not have to face competition from producers in North Africa, Turkey or Eastern Europe. They are, however, operating in a market with contractors in the Mexican *maquiladoras* and offshore contractors in Hong Kong and elsewhere in the Pacific Rim. Globalization – a convenient term to describe the internationalization of economic relations – is an overstatement, since in reality the scale of transactions is far less global. Economic transactions rarely cover the entire globe and are usually restricted to certain regions, countries or even districts, depending on the regional or local conditions. According to Ivan Light and Victoria Ojeda, the success of the Los Angeles garment industry is contingent on the availability of a cheap and flexible workforce, and on Hollywood's worldwide visibility. Without the cinematic visibility, which lends prestige to California Look clothing, the Los Angeles garment industry would never have developed as it did, and would have declined strongly with the passing of the North America Free Trade Agreement. Other cities obviously have no such appeal. In fact, the British Midlands area evokes images of dirty smokestacks in leaden skies rather than the glitter of tinsel town and the pleasures of sunny California.

The garment industry tends to be spatially concentrated. Most Amsterdam retailers operate from the World Fashion Center in the western part of the city. The Center, consisting of tall office buildings, confirms in brick the existence of a conglomerate garment industry in the city. It operates in much the same way as the garment districts of Los Angeles and New York, the boroughs of Tower Hamlets, Hackney, Islington, Haringey and Westminster (wholesalers) and the borough of Hackney (manufacturing) in London, and the Sentier neighbourhood in Paris. This conglomerate included designer houses, fashion institutes, fabric and accessory suppliers, manufacturers, contractors, distributors and marketing firms. There is an extensive web of information and exchange networks central to the industry that help lower transaction costs. The Manhattan fashion district between 6th and 9th Avenue from 35th to 41st Street has become a magnet for a variety of garment-related activities. Yu Zhou argues that this spatial proximity facilitates and encourages a particular division of labour, which gives the New York fashion industry flexibility and efficiency. She also notes, though, that numerous garment factories are moving from Manhattan to Brooklyn. It is not clear yet how this will affect the opportunity structure of the garment contractors.

The role of manufacturers and retailers is of key importance. Most authors note the powerful position of a few retailers. Ivan Light and Victoria Ojeda (Los Angeles) explicitly mention department stores like Macy's, the Gap, Nordstrom's, and K-Mart; Stephan Raes *et al.* (Amsterdam) mention Vendex/KBB, C&A and P&C;

and Prodromos Panayiotopoulos and Marja Dreef (London) mention Marks & Spencer and two other leading chain stores. The large retailers account for a substantial part of the total garment sales and, with the exception of the Gap which manufactures and produces its own clothing, the garment production as well. The fact that these large retailers order large quantities of garments from independent manufacturers and contractors enables them to build up considerable corporate power. Garments constitute a buyers' market where large retailers use their power to their advantage and play contractors off against each other.

Nancy Green (Paris), Stephan Raes *et al.* (Amsterdam) and Guillermo Grenier and Alex Stepick (Miami) demonstrate how large retailers and manufacturers have improved the management of the production and marketing process and how this has continuously affected the opportunity structure of small contractors. Zero stock control, made possible by modern technology, and computerized logistics have increasingly allowed retailers and manufacturers to improve their control over the production process, even if some parts of the production takes place off shore. Particularly in the case of Amsterdam, this undermined the market position of most of the Turkish contractors.

Large retailers do not always give orders directly to small contractors. They often work via intermediaries, partly in response to increased public awareness of illegal practices. Monder Ram *et al.* (Midlands) note that contractors have mixed feelings about the intermediaries. Of course they appreciate the orders, but they also feel they are used to 'top-up' orders only, and different factories are paid different rates for the same product. Besides, the intermediaries absorb a substantial part of the profits. This, to be sure, does not alter the fact that the cities have experienced a striking shift of corporate power to large retailers to the detriment of small contractors.

Garment factories are often described as small family businesses or firms critically dependent on the family labour input, but Nancy Green (Paris), Prodromos Panayiotopoulos and Marja Dreef (London), Yu Zhou (New York) and Ivan Light and Victoria Ojeda (Los Angeles) also observe large businesses with workers from a variety of immigrant groups. In essence, there is no typical immigrant garment factory. In some cities, particularly the ones with a long and uninterrupted history of immigrant involvement in the sector, a pronounced differentiation of immigrant businesses has evolved. A small and marginal garment contractor can become a large manufacturer operating as a micro multinational company and giving orders to newer small contractors. This process sometimes takes more than one generation, as in the case of Greek Cypriots in London or the Jewish entrepreneurs in Paris or New York City. In other cases, immigrants moved up more rapidly, as did the Asian entrepreneurs in Los Angeles. In other cases again, this process hardly occurred at all, because law enforcement agencies put a stop to further development or the market failed to provide sufficient scope for it, as in the cases of Amsterdam and the Midlands. A few dozen perceptive Turkish entrepreneurs nevertheless saw their chance and relocated their activities from Amsterdam to Turkey where they opened large factories.

As has been noted, sewing shops use relatively simple technology, rely on on-the-job training, do not require large capital outlays and are thus characterized by low entry barriers. This enhances the hyper competition between contractors, and the further development of vertical and horizontal subcontractual relations. In Amsterdam, London and the Midlands these relations sometimes extend to areas such as Cyprus, Turkey, Morocco or Eastern Europe.

Immigrant contractors only rarely if ever produce army uniforms or *haute couture*. Instead, they specialize in lower to medium quality, fashionable or medium-fashionable outerwear, in particular women's and junior outerwear. In some cases, especially in Los Angeles, they also specialize in sportswear. As Ivan Light and Victoria Ojeda note, Los Angeles sells the 'California Look', not just cheap cloth-ing. In Amsterdam, before the market conditions started deteriorating, garment contractors accepted orders in the less fashionable market segments or engaged in other activities such as wholesaling or import-export. Prodromos Panayiotopoulos and Marja Dreef (London) describe the product differentiation of Greek Cypriot entrepreneurs. Some of them develop new products or even a new brand, which results in a considerable price mark-up. A more widespread technique however is design pinching, using the latest fashion designs without paying for them. It is evident that these illegal practices are a source of friction, especially if contractors go as far as to pinch actual samples of the manufacturer's designs. Lastly, con-tractors engage in 'cabbage sales'. Cabbage is essentially an official or unofficial 'allowance' that the contractor squeezes out of the cloth and the design provided by the manufacturer. These small batches are then sold privately to small retailers or individual customers and constitute a source of extra income. Of course, cab-bage sales are only possible if the contractor can do the cutting, which is thus an important item in the negotiations with the manufacturer. Incidentally, this seems to be typical of London, since none of the other chapters refer to it. In most cases, cutting is part of the service supplied to jobbers.

## Regulation

Regulation influences the opportunities immigrant entrepreneurs have in various ways and come as complex packages of do's and don'ts, incentives and disincen-tives, and persuasions. Governmental and non-governmental regulation alike affect the opportunity structure at various levels.

At the supranational level, there are various forms of governance. In Europe, a more protectionist mood with regard to imports prevailed in the early 1980s, especially under the second Multi-Fibre Arrangement. However, this mood changed in the 1990s and steps were taken to liberalize the market. The European Union played a key role, granting additional import rights to specific non-member states. Mediterranean and Central and Eastern European non-members benefited from this change of policy and became major competitors of local garment contractors in Britain, France and the Netherlands. Likewise, the North American Free Trade Agreement encouraged the relocation of garment factories to Mexico, which harmed the garment industry in the United States, though local conditions in Los Angeles mitigated its negative effect. All these supranational arrangements influence the international division of labour and augment regional economies. Together they help shape the immigrant contractors' opportunity structure.

National and local governance generally influence the garment entrepreneurs' opportunities more directly. In each case a general trend can be observed towards market liberalization. On both sides of the Atlantic, first in the United States and Britain and later also throughout the European continent, governments have cleared the way for free enterprise. The reassessment of the rules and programmes governing the economy has resulted in deregulation – tax reduction and the abolition of business licensing requirements being but two examples – and in new programmes stimulating small entrepreneurship. These changes largely coincided with the revision of the welfare state and the role of the government in public life. Citizens have been given more responsibility for their own life and well-being. Notwithstanding the similarities, each country, and in the United States each state, dealt with this in a different way. The specificities are largely contingent on local political conditions. Regulation is rarely if ever self-evident or 'natural'; in a political environment it is always constructed. Various actors are involved in political struggles about regulation, each advocating certain political goals, engaging in different political coalitions, and accomplishing sometimes contradictory outcomes over time.

A closer review of the actual regulation in our seven cases reveals striking differences that can be reduced to three basic models of regulation. The models differ in terms of the formal rein given to small immigrant businesses, the implementation and enforcement of the regulation, and the immigrant entrepreneurs' position in the political arena. The first model typifies a situation of ignorance, the second a situation of active public support, and the third a strict application of non-permissive regulation. Of course, the local situation is much more complicated than this simple description of ideal typical situations suggests. After all, regulation is not static, it is not in the hands of a monolithic entity, and it certainly is not without contradictions. Still, I believe this typology can enhance our understanding of immigrant entrepreneurship in the garment sector.

*Ignorance*

The first model is illustrated by Los Angeles and characterized by a great deal of ignorance on the part of the regulatory agencies, despite the political fuss in the early and mid-1990s. Entrepreneurs are required by law to pay their employees at least the legal minimum wage, to refrain from giving out industrial homework, maintain clean and safe workplaces, and pay their taxes; but many employers fail to do so. In an effort to improve labour code enforcement, California passed the Montoya Act in 1982, requiring garment contractors to register their factories. Since then, registered firms have been subject to unannounced state inspections, but non-registration is still widespread and so are labour code violations. Although only legal residents are officially entitled to work, LA's garment industry would have a hard time doing without the numerous undocumented immigrants. This much is clear: a rather lax mood prevails as to the regulation in the Californian rag trade.

Some might argue that this is in keeping with the spirit in the land of free enterprise. This spirit is thought to inform a conception of economic citizenship where tasks and responsibilities are assigned to private individuals rather than the state, and governmental interference only serves to frustrate economic growth. This argument is evidently simplistic, if only because there *are* formal rules. Arguments of this kind nevertheless inform a cultural resistance to law enforcement. Ivan Light and Victoria Ojeda note the ubiquitous belief that industries that promote metropolitan growth should by no means be curbed, and that violations of the law should be tolerated. Moreover, violations are overlooked on the assumption that the industry engages in self-regulation. Next to this, jurisdictions are jumbled and several authorities share the responsibility for law enforcement, a situation that enhances an administrative culture of ignorance or even bribery. In fact, Light and Ojeda hold the corruption of the political system accountable for the blatant non-enforcement of laws. The garment industry, especially the larger companies, constitutes a political lobby that donates campaign funds to California politicians – something that is legal under American law. In return, elected neo-liberal politicians have reduced the law enforcement staffs to below the minimum required for effectiveness. In the light of this, one must well say LA's regulatory model is only ignorant when it comes to the interests of small contractors and workers, since it so clearly serves the interests of powerful garment manufacturers.

Negligence towards the interests of the weaker actors in the sector has provoked an unintended backlash. Growing numbers of legal and illegal immigrants who do poorly paid and unhealthy work and have no health insurance have turned to public emergency hospitals for free medical care, and this has imposed high costs upon the taxpayer. In effect, tax-supported hospitals subsidize the health care of the garment industry's immigrant workers. There is a similar situation in the educational system. Illegal immigrants send their children to public schools, thereby increasing the costs of the system. This became a public issue in 1994 when the Republicans tried to capitalize on a growing anti-immigrant backlash in the white electorate. Until then, leftist political attacks could not change the governance of the garment industry, but the right wing's resentment of illegal immigrants using public money reinforced the campaign for stricter regulation. This corroded the political tolerance of the widespread informal practices and pressured employers to pay the increased minimum wage and comply with the labour code and industrial health and safety legislation. The new law enforcement regime, effective as of 1996, detrimentally affected the competitiveness of the Los Angeles garment industry, even though it is still far from perfect. This suggests that a period of sheer ignorance has come to an end.

In this connection, Los Angeles, New York City and Miami have many features in common. Garment manufacturing could thrive as a result of the favourable immigration regime allowing for a continuous influx of new immigrants, and the ample tolerance of informal practices. What distinguishes New York, however, is the role of organized labour: New York is the best organized and unionized garment centre in the United States. The unions engage in collective bargaining with the industry to improve the working conditions and organize strikes, if necessary. Through the unions, garment workers exert some political clout. This influences the negotiating position of the employers and gives them less scope for blatant exploitation than in Los Angeles's outlaw economy. New York does not completely fit the model of ignorance. That being said, Yu Zhou reports that a substantial part of the immigrant garment sector does not fall under union control. Guillermo Grenier and Alex Stepick observe a similar situation in Miami, where the garment industry was traditionally unionized but where unionization was affected by economic restructuring. It is significant that the unions did not play any role whatsoever in the labour dispute described by Guillermo Grenier and Alex Stepick.

The New York garment industry, like the ones in Los Angeles and Miami, has been subjected to federal government efforts to regulate the sector. In the mid-1990s, the proliferation of sweatshops was the target of growing public criticism, particularly when more and more cases of abuse were disclosed and a popular talk show hostess publicly expressed her abhorrence of sweatshops when she was accused of having her own brand produced there. With public outrage mounting, United States President Bill Clinton set up a presidential task force in 1996 to work towards eliminating sweatshops. The White House Apparel Industry Partnership, consisting of companies, trade unions and human rights and religious groups, formulated a Workplace Code of Conduct. However, this voluntary partnership did not impose any new statutory penalties or launch any new enforcement efforts. In addition, key organizations such as UNITE, the AFL-CIO and a large union of department store workers rejected the code as a feeble effort to improve the sector.

Yu Zhou (New York) states that the anti-sweatshop campaign did manage to deal with a number of violators. However, non-union sewing shops continue to proliferate, especially in Brooklyn where many shops moved to escape these forms of regulation.

## Support

The second model of regulation is illustrated by London and characterized by strong and active state support for the SME sector in general and the rag trade in particular. Ever since Margaret Thatcher, the British government has strongly supported the small firm sector. A thriving small SME sector would help spread the capitalist ideology and way of life to the common people, and speed up the downfall of the loony left. Supporting small entrepreneurship was a characteristic Tory policy feature, but interestingly enough this has continued to be the case after Tony Blair's New Labour took office. This does not mean the government abstained from interfering before that. On the contrary, in the face of the industrial decline in the 1960s and 1970s the central government was actively involved in rationalizing the textile and garment industry in the Midlands and northern Britain. But as of the 1980s, the central government put more emphasis on developing the SME sector.

The central government's business support is channelled through soft loans, training schemes, inner-city employment-related initiatives, and tax cuts of various kinds. In addition, the government has abolished or relaxed various business regulations. Controlling activities regarding working conditions, taxes and social insurance has not been entirely discarded. According to Prodromos Panayiotopoulos and Marja Dreef, the state does not give high priority to controlling and regulating businesses and has underfunded the inspectorates. Furthermore, the United Kingdom, like France and the Netherlands but unlike the United States, pursues a policy of restricted immigration. However, unlike France and the Netherlands, immigration policy in Britain is generally implemented at the border, and only marginally throughout the country. Hunting undocumented aliens can easily amount to hunting 'foreign' or 'black' people, and that is forbidden under the 1976 Race Relations Act. Only after the mid-1990s, when illegality became a more politicized issue in Britain, did the central government intensify the checks and raids by immigration and tax officers.

These instances of regulation do not indicate that London and Los Angeles are that different. However, what distinguishes the two is the regulation implemented by the local government. In the early 1980s, local policy-makers considered garment businesses a useful vehicle for promoting objectives ranging from more jobs to racial equality. They engaged in these policies in their efforts to combat unemployment, protect their constituency from the economic crisis, counteract racist exclusion, and empower the immigrant minorities. The social deprivation immigrant minorities were suffering was felt to be largely caused by racism, and the central government was thought to be insufficiently receptive to this serious problem. In response to a series of riots in the early 1980s, in particular the Brixton riots in 1981, a government committee chaired by the Tory Lord Scarman recommended promoting entrepreneurship as an antidote to urban racial deprivation. Given the characteristics of the London economy, promoting small entrepreneurship in the rag trade was a logical choice. In these times of economic decline, the rag trade exhibited striking vitality, partly caused by a demand for higher-value fashion, style and quality and quicker responses.

The Greater London Council (GLC) and several London boroughs such as Haringey and Hackney have actively fostered small businesses in the garment industry, and it is no accident that all of them were Labour-controlled. Prodromos Panayiotopoulos and Marja Dreef emphasize that this policy was also a reflection of the realignment of local Labour Party politics, with minorities becoming more prominent, resulting in their increased political representation. The GLC and the boroughs formulated and implemented various measures aimed at collective services for the sector as a whole, but with special attention devoted to ethnic firms and co-operatives. The measures included decriminalizing homeworking and easing planning regulations on the use of buildings.

The controversial GLC was abolished in 1986, and the boroughs ceased their special interventions as well. In the mid-1990s, after a decade of non-intervention, attention was once again directed to the rag trade, this time in the context of urban regeneration politics. The boroughs of Hackney and Haringey reserved urban regeneration funds for entrepreneurs. In Hackney, a garment-manufacturing zone was developed to promote flexible specialization and reinforce links between chain stores and local garment factories. These interventions lacked the strong ideological underpinning typical of the interventions in the early 1980s.

This specific regulation history is obviously rooted in the specifics of local British politics. However, as Prodromos Panayiotopoulos and Marja Dreef explain, it is also sensitive to the differentiation of immigrant entrepreneurs. A number of Greek Cypriots and other immigrant minority entrepreneurs were upwardly mobile and achieved a place in the higher tiers of the industry. These emergent manufacturers were in a stronger economic position, more integrated in the local host society, better embedded in community organizations, and better placed to benefit from state support. The local Labour Party accepted them as ready-made partners and some of them actually became major beneficiaries of local government support. At the same time, some of the more successful entrepreneurs operated as political brokers. They served as community representatives and intermediated with policymakers. Their empowerment was a critical factor in reshaping the relations between the garment entrepreneurs and the regulatory agencies and informed the selectivity of the regulatory response, be it promotion or repression, soft or strong action.

Notwithstanding the Labour Party efforts, utopia never materialized, and the London rag trade retained its sweatshop image. Although some garment entrepreneurs moved up and gained more political power, most contractors stayed on the fringes of the urban economy. Many garment contractors still evade taxes, sell illegally, pinch designs and hire undocumented workers, and the exploitation – particularly of homeworkers – is still widespread. This being said, the interventions did save a number of jobs and create a couple of hundred other ones.

The situation in Birmingham and the neighbouring towns is rather different, which illustrates the role played by local contingencies. Entrepreneurs in the Midlands operate under the same national regulatory framework, but the local situation is more similar to the one in Los Angeles. Monder Ram *et al.* argue that local interventions have been of a more symbolic nature and have not really affected the position of garment firms. Moreover, the political link between upwardly mobile garment entrepreneurs and the leading political parties has not been well developed.

## Strict Law Enforcement

The third model of regulation is illustrated by Amsterdam after the *laissez-faire* period, and is characterized by strict law enforcement. The situation before the crackdown in 1994, or actually before 1989, can easily be typified as one of ignorance. Dynamics are everything in the game of regulation, this time resulting in a case with two sides to it. What makes the policy shift extra intriguing is that it goes in such a different direction than the regulation of the SME sector in general. In the Dutch welfare state, until recently people could not start a business just like that, but were required by law to have qualifications and permits and to register. In the 1980s, this system – an artefact of corporatist and Social-Democratic features – came to be considered too rigid and an impediment to full economic development. The government embarked on a fundamental reform of the system and, much to the satisfaction of the business community, deregularization became the buzzword. The aim was to liberalize the business sector wherever possible and keep regulation to a minimum. The system of rules, qualifications and permits was cut down to the bone. The first effects became apparent in the mid-1990s, when the economy experienced a record growth, partly thanks to an unprecedented rise in the number of small businesses. To be sure, the employment and welfare field have undergone reforms, but not to the same extent as the business sector.

In the 1980s, when the business regulation system was still elaborate, new immigrant garment entrepreneurs increasingly failed to comply with the rules. The state, curiously enough, did not take a firm line on these informal activities. Apart from a few individual officials at the Ministry of Social Affairs and Employment who were concerned with the Amsterdam rag trade, the government as a whole did not really bother. This underlines the importance of distinguishing between rules and their actual implementation or enforcement. The local authorities were aware of the situation, but chose to tolerate informal practices, which underlines the importance of distinguishing between various levels of regulation. They felt that immigrants had high unemployment rates and the government could not provide sufficient jobs. The authorities welcomed any business that could create jobs and in doing so contribute to the social integration of immigrants, and perhaps also to the revival of Amsterdam as an international garment manufacturing centre. They were prepared to put up with informal practices and assumed they were just a temporary problem. Stricter law enforcement would only serve to frustrate economic progress. The City of Amsterdam and the metropolitan police therefore prioritized hunting down criminals and illegal immigrants who were a nuisance to society rather than badgering diligent entrepreneurs.

This tolerant mood started to change at the national level around 1990. A new government took office in 1989 with welfare reform as one of its central policy objectives. However, the Labour Party feared social unrest, particularly among its grassroots supporters, and negotiated a political alternative: combating fraud, the improper use of welfare benefits and illegal residence would result in public spending cuts and lower the pressure for harsh welfare reforms. The Minister of Social Affairs and Employment considered the rag trade an obvious place to put this into practice. In anticipation of things to come, the sector was encouraged to engage in self-regulation and leading business associations introduced several schemes for this purpose, though to little avail. In 1994, a package of measures was introduced, one being the Law on Chain Liability. One of the direct consequences was the formation of an interdisciplinary hit-and-run team of law enforcers. The Clothing Intervention Team paid numerous visits to suspicious Turkish sewing shops and organized frequent raids, resulting in numerous people being charged with hiring undocumented immigrants, evading taxes and not paying social security premiums. This contributed to the downfall of immigrant contractors, who were already faced with increasing ruthless international competition.

The trade unions and the regular garment manufacturers association (FENECON) wholeheartedly welcomed the crackdown on the illegal sewing shops. After all, they had lobbied for strict law enforcement. The Amsterdam authorities, however, were initially unwilling to support the sector clean-up for the reasons mentioned above, and this caused friction with the central government. They eventually gave in and collaborated. Unlike the situation in London, where raids on undocumented immigrants led to social and political agitation in the local community, the events in Amsterdam did not cause much public outcry. The Turkish community did try to mobilize political forces, and a casual organization of Turkish garment entrepreneurs tried to promote the interests of the contractors, but they were insufficiently embedded in the local polity to make a difference.

The law enforcement campaign followed a relatively long period of ignorance, and came just when the SME sector was being deregulated. The vigour of the crackdown and the sheer unwillingness to compromise turned the campaign into something of a crusade. The Dutch authorities apparently felt they had to make amends for their failure to keep this sector on the right path. Oddly enough, just as the central government and the City of Amsterdam were cleaning up the sewing shop sector, the borough of Kralingen/Crooswijk in Rotterdam commissioned a market research bureau to assess the opportunities for Turkish sewing shops to be set up with local government support.

Every now and then cities engage in law enforcement campaigns, though usually not as vigorously as Amsterdam. Nancy Green (Paris) reports that the French government has cracked down on labour and capital practices in recent years, especially targeting 'creative accounting' and illegal labour. These regulatory changes are often triggered by specific events, and the rag trade seems to have no lack of them. In Amsterdam, the crash of a cargo plane on a residential district, killing a number of undocumented immigrants, helped the government gain popular support for its crackdown. In Los Angeles, the anti-sweatshop movement gained momentum in 1996 after a raid on a factory in El Monte where seventy-two Thai immigrants, mostly women, were working as industrial slaves in a guarded compound. Likewise, the American celebrity Kathie Lee Gifford, weeping on television in the same period, persuaded Bill Clinton to set up a presidential task force. The fact came out that some of her line of clothing was made in sweatshops in New York and Central America. Interestingly, or should I say sadly enough, the role of coincidences is not new in the rag trade. Prodromos Panayiotopoulos and Marja Dreef rake up the story of the United Kingdom's 1905 Aliens Act. Concerns about the social conditions of the London poor and the moral panic directed against Jewish immigrants informed the 'anti-sweating' campaign led by Liberal reformers, resulting in this Act.

## Long-term Outlook

Fluctuating styles, widespread subcontracting, homework, and the involvement of immigrants are part and parcel of the rag trade but, as Nancy Green demonstrates, this has been the case ever since it was mechanized and standardized in the late nineteenth century. This adds fresh fuel to the notion that the garment industry including the tier of immigrant contactors will continue to exist in advanced economies in one way or another. In the past, people felt that the SME sector was in jeopardy and assumed that garment manufacturing would relocate to low-wage countries. In practice, however, small businesses have demonstrated striking resilience.

Around the beginning of the millennium, Ivan Light and Victoria Ojeda observed that the Los Angeles garment industry was still thriving in the face of adverse trends in other local garment manufacturing sectors and the national garment industry. They were nevertheless fully aware of the processes that had already harmed the Los Angeles garment industry. They noted that manufacturing industries in Los Angeles had generally been in decline for over three decades, that the garment industry had witnessed an outflow of production jobs to Mexico following the North American Free Trade Agreement in 1993, and that the federal minimum wage had increased and immigration controls intensified following a public outrage. The resilience of the sector had its origins in two local specific factors, one being the powerful image of California Look clothing, the other its access to (illegal) immigrant labour.

Yu Zhou refers to intense international competition negatively affecting New York's garment industry. The market for clothing is losing its flexibility due to slow population growth, the ageing of the population, and so on. At the same time, deregulation and improved logistics have narrowed the time–space gap between domestic and offshore producers, and this decreased the competitiveness of the domestic ones. Moreover, a market power shift to large retailers and the reduction of the local manufacturing sector have occurred, pressuring New York garment producers to focus on the higher-value-added products. They now go for more styles, higher quality and better services, and it remains to be seen whether new immigrants can survive in such a harsh environment.

These two cases demonstrate that the continuation of garment manufacturing in advanced economies cannot be taken for granted – what with the general political and economic processes threatening the sector. Interestingly enough, they also underline that the perspective of small immigrant contractors is linked to local market characteristics, be it the cinematic appeal of the Californian Look or the Big Apple's accelerated life cycle of high-quality fashion products. The cases of the British Midlands and Amsterdam, however, demonstrate that survival is not a matter of course, and that in some cases local market characteristics only help to accelerate the fall of the contractor sector.

Local market features obviously matter, but so does regulation. For a long time, immigrant contractors survived by capitalizing on their social networks. In doing so, they generated the arrival of new immigrants, legal and illegal alike, willing to work long hours. In addition to their privileged access to cheap and flexible labour, they had a competitive edge by dodging the rules and evading taxes. They could go on like this as long as law enforcement agencies overlooked these informal practices. Paradoxically, now that deregulation has become *de rigueur*, the tolerance for these practices is decreasing. In each country, a political mood has grown where minimal regulation is regarded as a necessary condition for economic growth.

There is, however, also a growing public awareness that this sometimes leads to excesses and fuels anti-sweatshop and crackdown campaigns.

The deregulation of business regimes has not been accompanied by the deregulation of immigration regimes. On the contrary, in Europe and the United States immigration, especially of unskilled immigrants, is tighter now that illegality is a political issue. All the authors have reported a decrease in tolerance for undocumented immigrants and an increase in immigration controls, even though the controls are usually not as tough as in the extreme case of Amsterdam. Irrespective of legitimacy, strict immigration controls have a detrimental effect on a sector dependent on cheap and flexible labour, usually new unskilled immigrants. They also undermine the power of network mobilization, especially if the pool of cheap and flexible labour is depleting. This is particularly apparent in the Midlands and Amsterdam.

To what extent immigration control will continue is still unclear. In Europe and the United States, heated debates are taking places about relaxing the tight immigration rules. Prodromos Panayiotopoulos and Marja Dreef (London) and Stephan Raes *et al.* (Amsterdam) report that although immigration is a national or federal matter, local authorities sometimes take a position against immigration control because they want to consider the interests of the local community. This too may contribute to the local variations in an otherwise globalized industry.

## Note

1. This applies in particular to American researchers; European researchers seem to be more open to structural factors (see Barrett *et al.* 1996; Kloosterman *et al.* 1999; Ram *et al.* 2000; Rath 2000a).

# On the Authors

**Marja E.P. Dreef** is on the staff at the Institute for Migration and Ethnic Studies (IMES) at the University of Amsterdam, the Netherlands. She received her MA in Legal and Public Administration from the University of Brabant (Tilburg, the Netherlands), worked as Lecturer in Policy and Organizational Sciences at the Utrecht University, and conducted research in a multi-disciplinary project on the Amsterdam garment industry. Her focus is on public administration and immigration. She is currently preparing a Ph.D. thesis on the political and administrative developments pertaining to the garment industry in Amsterdam and London.

**Nancy L. Green** is Professor of History at the Ecole des Hautes Etudes en Sciences Sociales in Paris, France. She received her BA from the University of Wisconsin (Madison), her MA and Ph.D. from the University of Chicago, and her *thèse d'Etat* from the Université de Paris-7. She is the author of *The Pletzl of Paris: Jewish Immigrant Workers in the Belle Epoque* (Holmes and Meier, 1986), *Ready-to-wear and Ready-to-work: A Century of Industry and Immigrants in New York and Paris* (Duke University Press, 1997, winner of the Gilbert Chinard Prize of the Society for French Historical Studies), and numerous articles on migration history and comparative history.

**Guillermo J. Grenier** is Director of the Center for Labor Research and Studies and a member of the Sociology/Anthropology Department at Florida International University in Miami. He is the author of *Inhuman Relations: Quality Circles and Anti-Unionism in American Industry* (Temple University Press, 1988), *Employee Participation and Labor Law in the American Workplace* (with Ray Hogler, Greenwood, 1993), and *This Land is Our Land: Newcomers and Established Residents in Miami* (with Alex Stepick, forthcoming University of California Press), and co-editor of *Miami Now: Immigration, Ethnicity and Social Change* (University of Florida Press, 1992) and *Newcomers in the Workplace: Immigrants and the Restructuring of the US Economy* (Temple University Press, 1998). He has also published widely on ethnic relations, labour and Cuban-Americans in Miami. His current work focuses on the impact of immigration and ethnic diversity in the labour movement in Miami.

**Joy Husband** is involved in research into the clothing and textile industries at the University of Central England in Birmingham. She is currently examining the effects of globalization on regional and community-based clothing and textile enterprises, with a particular focus on informal working practices. She is the co-author of 'Design and Ethnicity: The Failure of West Midlands Clothing Enterprises to Enter the Design Market' (*Design Journal*, 2, 1999).

**Robert Jerrard** is Professor of Design Studies, Institute of Art and Design, University of Central England. His research interests include design theory, technology diffusion and work study. He is a council member of the Design Research Society and has published widely. Recent publications include *Managing New Product Innovation* (Taylor and Francis, 1999). He is the co-author of 'Design and Ethnicity: The Failure of the West Midlands Clothing Enterprises to Enter the Design Market' (*Design Journal*, 2, 1999).

**Adem Kumcu** received an MA in Sociology from Utrecht University and is currently a doctoral student at the Institute for Migration and Ethnic Studies (IMES). His subject is management strategies of Turkish contractors in Amsterdam. He is also the Chairman of the New European Business Foundation (NEB).

**Ivan H. Light** is Professor of Sociology at the University of California, Los Angeles. He is the author of five books on immigration including *Ethnic Enterprise in America* (University of California Press, 1972), *Immigrant Entrepreneurs* (with Edna Bonacich, University of California Press, 1991), and *Ethnic Economies* (with Steven Gold, Academic Press, 2000). In 2000 he received the Lifetime Career Achievement Award from the International Migration Section of the American Sociological Association.

**Victoria D. Ojeda** is a doctoral student at the School of Public Health, University of California, Los Angeles. Her work primarily focuses on women and immigrants and their access to health insurance coverage and health care. She is currently a Project Manager and Research Assistant at the UCLA Center for Health Policy Research. She previously worked for UCLA's Labor Occupational Safety and Health Program and the San Diego County Health Department, and was a Research Fellow at the Instituto Mexicano de Psiquiatria in Mexico City.

**Prodromos I. Panayiotopoulos** (aka Mike Pany) is a Lecturer in Development Studies at the School of Social Sciences and International Development at the University of Wales, Swansea. He received his Ph.D. from the Centre for Development Studies at Swansea. He has researched and published extensively on Cypriot entrepreneurs in the London garment industry and small enterprises in the Third World. His latest book is *World Development* (Pluto Press, 2001).

**Stephan Raes** received his MA and Ph.D. from the University of Amsterdam, worked as a Lecturer at the Department of Mediterranean and Middle Eastern Studies of the Catholic University of Nijmegen and as a doctoral student at the Institute for Migration and Ethnic Studies (IMES) and the International Relations Section in the Department of Political Science of the University of Amsterdam. He worked on a multi-disciplinary research project on the Amsterdam garment industry. He is the author of *Migrating Enterprise and Migrant Entrepreneurship: How Fashion and Migration Have Changed the Spatial Organization of Clothing Supply to Consumers in the Netherlands* (Het Spinhuis, 2000), and several other publications on the fashion trade. He is currently working at the Ministry of Economic Affairs in The Hague, the Netherlands.

**Monder Ram** is a Professor of Small Business at the Department of Corporate Strategy, and Co-director of the Small Business Research Group at De Montfort University, Leicester, United Kingdom. He is the author of *Managing to Survive: Working Lives in Small Firms* (Blackwell, 1994) and *Ethnic Minorities in Business* (with Trevor Jones, Small Business Research Trust, 1998).

**Jan Rath** is an Associate Professor and Co-director of the Institute for Migration and Ethnic Studies (IMES) at the University of Amsterdam, the Netherlands. An anthropologist, he is also active in political science, the sociology of law, economics and economic sociology. He co-founded an international network of experts on immigrant entrepreneurship (http://home.pscw.uva.nl/rath/imment.htm). He is the author of numerous articles, book chapters and reports on the sociology, politics and economics of post-migratory processes. He edited *Immigrant Businesses: The Economic, Political and Social Environment* (Macmillan, 2000), the 'Immigrant Entrepreneurship' issue of the *Journal of Ethnic and Migration Studies* (vol. 27, 2001, with Robert Kloosterman), and *Venturing Abroad: A Comparative Study of Immigrant Entrepreneurs in Advanced Economies* (with Robert Kloosterman, Berg, forthcoming).

**Flavia Reil** got an MA in Cultural Anthropology at the University of Amsterdam and worked at the Institute for Migration and Ethnic Studies (IMES) and at various research bureaux. She currently works as a policy official in the field of Diversity Management at the Amsterdam district De Baarsjes. She is the co-author of *En Meestal Zijn het Turken: Arbeid in de Amsterdamse Loonconfectie-industrie* on the quality of labour in Turkish sewing shops in Amsterdam (with Ton Korver, Het Spinhuis, 2001).

**Alex Stepick** is the Director of the Immigration & Ethnicity Institute and a Professor of Anthropology and Sociology at Florida International University in

Miami. He is a former winner of the Margaret Mead Award for his work with Haitian refugees. His book, *City on the Edge* (with Alejandro Portes, University of California Press, 1993), won the Robert Park Award for Best Book in Urban Sociology and the Anthony Leeds Award for Best Book in Urban Anthropology. He is also the author of *Pride Against Prejudice: Haitians in Miami* (Allyn and Bacon, 1998), and an editor of *Miami Now!* (with Guillermo Grenier, University of Florida Press, 1992) and *Newcomers in the Workplace* (with Louise Lamphere and Guillermo Grenier, Temple University Press, 1994).

**Yu Zhou** got an MA in Geography and Urban and Regional Planning from Beijing University and a Ph.D. in Geography from the University of Minnesota. She is currently an Assistant Professor of Geography at Vassar College in Poughkeepsie, New York, where she teaches Economic Geography, Population and Environment, East Asia, Global Diasporas and geographical research methods. She was also involved in the Urban Studies Program, International Studies and Asian Studies Program. Her research interests include ethnic economies in American cities, gender and immigration experiences, the transnational investments and transnational networks in the Pacific Rim, and high-tech enterprise development in China.

**Aslan Zorlu** got an MA in Economics at the University of Amsterdam and is currently a doctoral student at the Institute for Migration and Ethnic Studies (IMES) and the Tinbergen Institute, both at the University of Amsterdam. His subject is the performance of ethnic minorities on the labour market. He authored and co-authored a number of publications on the recruitment of labour by Turkish contractors in the Amsterdam garment industry.

# References

Abernathy, F.H., J.T. Dunlop, J.H. Hammond and D. Weil (1995), 'The Information-Integrated Channel: A Study of the US Apparel Industry in Transition', *Brookings Papers on Economic Activity, Microeconomics*, 175–246.

AEKTA (Clothing Industry Action Research Project) (1995–1996), *Annual Report*, Birmingham: AEKTA.

Ahmed, T. (1990), 'Asian Entrepreneurship in the Clothing Industry', *Hollings Apparel Industry Review*, 7: 3.

Albert, M. (1991), *Capitalisme Contre Capitalisme*, Paris: Éditions du Seuil.

Aldrich, H.E., J.C. Cater, T. Jones, and D. McEvoy (1981), 'Business Development and Self-segregation: Asian Enterprise in Three British Cities', in C. Peach, V. Robinson and S. Smith (eds), *Ethnic Segregation in Cities*, London: Croom Helm.

Aldrich, H.E., J. Cater, T. Jones and D. McEvoy (1982), 'From Periphery to Peripheral: The South Asian Petite Bourgeoisie in England', in I. Simpson and R. Simpson (eds), *Research in the Sociology of Work 2*, Greenwich, Conn.: JAI Press.

Aldrich, H.E., T. Jones and D. McEvoy (1984), 'Ethnic Advantage and Minority Business Development', in R. Ward and R. Jenkins (eds), *Ethnic Communities in Business: Strategies for Economic Survival*, Cambridge: Cambridge University Press.

Aldrich, H.E., R. Ward and R. Waldinger (1985), 'Minority Business Development in Industrial Societies', *European Studies Newsletter*, 14: 4–8.

Aldrich, H.E., J. Cater, T. Jones, D. McEvoy and P. Velleman (1986), 'Asian Residential Concentration and Business Development: An Analysis of Shopkeepers' Customers in Three Cities', *New Community*, 13: 52–64.

Alexandre, A. (1902), *Les Reines de l'Aiguille: Modistes et Couturières*, Paris: Théophile Belin.

Allen, J.P. and E. Turner (1997), *The Ethnic Guilt: Population Diversity in Southern California*, Northridge, Calif.: California State University.

Allilaire, J. (1947), *Les Industries de l'Habillement et du Travail des Étoffes*, Paris: Société d'éditions françaises et internationales.

Anderson, H. and J. Flatley (1997), *Contrasting London's Incomes: A Social and Spatial Analysis*, London: London Research Centre.

# References

Anson, R. (1997), 'EU Clothing Production May Have a Future: Editorial', *Textile Outlook International*, November: 3–5.

Anthias, F. (1992), *Ethnicity, Class, Gender and Migration: Greek Cypriots in Britain*, Aldershot: Avebury.

Apparel Industry Magazine (1999), *Sewn Products Expo*, Atlanta, Ga.: Apparel Industry Magazine.

Appelbaum, R.P. (1997), 'Using Religion's Suasion in Garment Industry', *Los Angeles Times*, 16 February, Section M: 1.

—— and G. Gereffi (1994), 'Power and Profits in the Apparel Commodity Chain', in E. Bonacich, L. Cheng, N. Chinchilla, N. Hamilton and P. Ong (eds), *Global Production: The Apparel Industry in the Pacific Rim*, Philadelphia, Pa.: Temple University Press.

Bailey, T.R. (1987), *Immigrant and Native Workers*, Boulder, Colo. and London: Westview Press.

—— and R. Waldinger (1991), 'Primary, Secondary, and Enclave Labor Markets: A Training Systems Approach', *American Sociological Review*, 56: 432–45.

Barlow, A. and J. Winterton (1996), 'Restructuring Production and Work Organisation', in I. Taplin and J. Winterton (eds), *Restructuring Within a Labour Intensive Industry*, Aldershot: Avebury.

Barnes, P. (1994), 'Profile of Marks and Spencer: A Growing International Presence', *Textile Outlook International*, September: 128–44.

Barrett, G., T. Jones and D. McEvoy (1996), 'Ethnic Minority Business: Theoretical Discourse in Britain and North America', *Urban Studies*, 33: 783–809.

Basu, D. (1991), 'Afro-Caribbean Businesses in Great Britain: Factors Affecting Business Success and Marginality', Unpublished Ph.D. thesis, Manchester University Business School.

Bates, T. (1997), *Race, Self-employment, and Upward Mobility: An Illusive American Dream*, Baltimore, Md.: Johns Hopkins University Press.

Bedford, R. (2000), 'Globalisation and the Transformation of Urban Societies in "New World" Cities on the Asia-Pacific Rim', in R. Bedford (ed.), *Perspectives on International Migration, Urban Social Transformation and the Research/ Policy Interface*, Hamilton: University of Waikato, Department of Geography, Migration Research Group and Population Studies Centre.

Bendix, R. (1956), *Work and Authority in Industry*, Berkeley, Calif.: University of California Press.

Benveniste, A. (1989), *Le Bosphore à la Roquette: La Communauté Judéo-espagnole à Paris, 1914–1940*, Paris: L'Harmattan.

Bermant, C. (1975), *London's East End: Point of Arrival*, New York: Macmillan.

Best, M. (1990), *The New Competition: Institutions of Industrial Restructuring*, Cambridge: Polity Press.

## References

Bhachu, P. (1997), 'Dangerous Designs: Asian Women and the New Landscapes of Fashion', in A. Oakley and J. Mitchell (eds), *Who's Afraid of Feminism? Seeing through the Backlash*, London: Hamish Hamilton.

Blankenburg, E. and F. Bruinsma (1994), *Dutch Legal Culture*, second revised and enlarged edition, Deventer/Boston, Mass.: Kluwer Law and Taxation Publishers.

Blaschke, J., J. Boissevain, H. Grotenbreg, I. Joseph, M. Morokvasic and R. Ward (1990), 'European Trends in Ethnic Business', in R. Waldinger, H. Aldrich, R. Ward and Associates (eds), *Ethnic Entrepreneurs: Immigrant Business in Industrial Societies*, Newbury Park, Calif.: Sage.

Block, F. (1990), *Postindustrial Possibilities: A Critique of Economic Discourse*, Berkeley, Calif.: University of California Press.

Bloeme, L. and R. van Geuns (1987), *Ongeregeld Ondernemen: Een Onderzoek naar Informele Bedrijvigheid*, Den Haag: Ministerie van Sociale Zaken en Werkgelegenheid.

Bögenhold, D. (2000), 'Ethnic Business in Society: On the Interface of Entrepreneurship, Self-Employment and Ethnic Minorities', Paper presented to the Euresco Conference on Self-Employment, Gender and Migration, San Feliu de Guixols, Spain, 28 October–2 November.

Bohning, W.R. (1972), *The Migration of Workers in the United Kingdom and the European Community*, Oxford: Oxford University Press.

Boissevain, J. (1981), *Small Entrepreneurs in Changing Europe: Towards a Research Agenda*, Work and Social Change 4, Maastricht: European Centre for Work and Society.

—— (1984), 'Small Entrepreneurs in Contemporary Europe', in R. Ward and R. Jenkins (eds), *Ethnic Communities in Business: Strategies for Economic Survival*, Cambridge: Cambridge University Press.

—— (1997), 'Small European Entrepreneurs', in M. Rutten and C. Upadhya (eds), *Small Business Entrepreneurs in Asia and Europe: Towards a Comparative Perspective*, New Delhi: Sage.

—— and H. Grotenbreg (1988), 'Culture, Structure and Ethnic Enterprise: The Surinamese of Amsterdam', in M. Cross and H. Entzinger (eds), *Lost Illusions: Caribbean Minorities in Britain and the Netherlands*, London: Routledge.

Bonacich, E. (1993a), 'Asian and Latino Immigrants in the Los Angeles Garment Industry: An Exploration of the Relationship Between Capitalism and Racial Oppression', in I. Light and P. Bhachu (eds), *Immigration and Entrepreneurship*, New Brunswick, N.J.: Transaction.

Bonacich, E. (1993b), 'The Other Side of Ethnic Entrepreneurship: A Dialogue with Waldinger, Aldrich, Ward and Associates', *International Migration Review*, 27: 685–92.

—— (1994), 'Asians in the Los Angeles Garment Industry', in P. Ong, E. Bonacich and L. Cheng (eds), *The New Asian Immigration in Los Angeles and Global Restructuring*, Philadelphia, Pa.: Temple University.

—— and R.P. Appelbaum (2000), *Behind the Label: Inequality in the Los Angeles Apparel Industry*, Berkeley, Calif.: University of California Press.

—— L. Cheng, N. Chinchilla, N. Hamilton and P. Ong (1994), *Global Production: The Apparel Industry in the Pacific Rim*, Philadelphia, Pa.: Temple University Press.

Bovenkerk, F., A. Eijken and W. Bovenkerk-Teerink (1983), *Italiaans IJs: De Opmerkelijke Historie van de Italiaanse IJsbereiders in Nederland*, Meppel/ Amsterdam: Boom.

Bovenkerk, F., R. Miles and G. Verbunt (1990), 'Racism, Migration and the State in Western Europe: A Case for Comparative Analysis', *International Sociology*, 5: 475–90.

Bowles, J. (2000), 'The Empire Has No Clothes: Raising Real Estate Prices and Declining City Support Threatens the Future of New York's Apparel Industry', Report by the Center for an Urban Future, February, Website address: http:// www.nycfuture.org/econdev/clothes.htm

Brandsma, R. (1970), *De Amsterdamse Confectie-industrie: Een Economisch-geografische Studie over Decentralisatiestruktuur*, Amsterdam: Universiteit van Amsterdam, Economisch-Geografisch Instituut.

Brettell, C.B. (1981), 'Is the Ethnic Community Inevitable? A Comparison of the Settlement Patterns of Portuguese Immigrants in Toronto and Paris', *The Journal of Ethnic Studies*, 9: 1–17.

Brizard, A. and C.-V. Marie (1993), *Travail Illegal et Suites Judiciaires*, Paris: Ministère de la Justice.

Broer, A. (ed.) (1977), *Herstructurering en Internationale Relokatie van de Nederlandse Textiel- en Konfektie-Industrie*, Utrechtse Geografische Studies 6, Utrecht: Geografisch Instituut Rijksuniversiteit Utrecht.

Buford, B. (1999), 'Sweat Is Good', *The New Yorker*, 75: 130–9.

Buiks, P. and G. van Tillo (1980), *Het Sociologisch Perspectief: Een Ontmoeting met de Sociologische Benaderingswijze*, Assen: Van Gorcum.

Burgers, J. (1996), 'No Polarization in Dutch Cities? Inequality in a Corporatist Country', *Urban Studies*, 33: 99–105.

Business Monitor (1992), *Report on the Census of Production 1990: Summary Volume*, London: Central Statistical Office, HMSO.

California Fashion Association (1999), *Fact Sheet – Los Angeles County*, Los Angeles, Calif.: California Fashion Association.

Camarota, S.A. (2000), *Reconsidering Immigrant Entrepreneurship: An Examination of Self-employment among Natives and Foreign-born*, Washington, DC: Center for Immigration Studies.

—— and J.R. Edwards Jr (2000), *Without Coverage: Immigration's Impact on the Size and Growth of the Population Lacking Health Insurance*, Washington, DC: Center for Immigration Studies (on line: www.cis.org 18 July 2000).

Castles, S. and G. Kosack (1973), *Immigrant Workers and Class Structure in Western Europe*, London: Oxford University Press.

Castles, S. and M.J. Miller (1993), *The Age of Migration: International Population Movements in the Modern World*, New York: Guilford Press.

CBS (Centraal Bureau voor de Statistiek/Central Bureau of Statistics (s.a.), *Samenvattend Overzicht van de Industrie*, The Hague: CBS.

Chevalier, L. (1950), *La Formation de la Population Parisienne au XIXe Siècle*, INED-Travaux et Documents 10, Paris: PUF.

Ching Louie, M. (1992), 'Immigrant Asian women in Bay Area Garment Sweatshops', *Amerasia Journal*, 18: 3–4.

City of Los Angeles (1993), *Hospitality and Garment Industries Survey*, Sacramento, Calif.: State of California Employment Development Department.

Cleeland, N. (1999), 'Garment Jobs: Hard, Bleak, and Vanishing', *Los Angeles Times*, 11 March, Section 1: 1.

Coffin, J. (1985), 'Woman's Place and Women's Work in the Paris Clothing Trades, 1830–1914', Dissertation, Yale University.

—— (1996), *The Politics of Women's Work: The Paris Garment Trades, 1750–1915*, Princeton, N.J.: Princeton University Press.

Collins, J., K. Gibson, C. Alcorso, S. Castles and D. Tait (1995), *A Shop Full of Dreams: Ethnic Small Business in Australia*, Sidney: Pluto Press Australia.

Coons, L. (1987), *Women Home Workers in the Parisian Garment Industry, 1860–1915*, New York: Garland Publishing.

Cornelius, W.A., Ph.L. Martin and J.F. Hollifield (1994), *Controlling Immigration: A Global Perspective*, Stanford, Calif.: Stanford University Press.

Costa-Lascoux, J. and Y.-S. Live (1995), *Paris-XIIIe: Lumières d'Asie*, Paris: Autrement.

Couder, L. (1986), 'Les Italiens dans la Région Parisienne dans les Années 1920', in P. Milza (ed.), *Les Italiens en France de 1914 à 1940*, Rome: Ecole Française de Rome.

Cross, M. and R. Waldinger (1992), 'Migrants, Minorities and the Ethnic Division of Labor', in S.S. Fainstein, I. Gordon and M. Harloe (eds), *Divided Cities: New York and London in the Contemporary World*, Oxford, UK and Cambridge, Mass.: Blackwell.

Das, S.K. and P. Panayiotopoulos (1996), 'Flexible Specialisation: New Paradigm for Industrialisation for Developing Countries?', *Economic and Political Weekly*, 28 December, 57–61.

Davenport, E. (1992), 'Changing Relationships in the Material World: UK Retailers' Sourcing Policies for Clothing Products', in D. Gillingwater and P. Totterdill (eds), *Prospects for Industrial Policy in the 1990s: The Case of the British Clothing Industry*, Aldershot: Gower.

—— P. Totterdill and J. Zeitlin (1986), 'Training for the Clothing Industry: A Strategy for Local Government', Unpublished report prepared for the Greater London Council.

Delorme, G. (1986), *Profession: Travailleur au Noir*, Paris: Ouest-France.

Deschamps, G. (1937), *La Crise dans les Industries du Vêtement et de la Mode à Paris pendant la Période de 1930 à 1937*, Paris: Librairie Technique et Économique.

Dicken, P. (1992), *Global Shift: The Internationalisation of Economic Activity*, 2nd edition, London: Paul Chapman Publishing.

Dickerson, M. (1999), 'LA trade cut from new cloth', *Los Angeles Times*, 21 July, Section 1: 1.

—— and N. Cleeland (2000), 'Employment in LA Garment Industry Trade Continues To Shrink', *Los Angeles Times*, 18 August, Section C: 1.

Dignan, D. (1981), 'Europe's Melting Pot: A Century of Large-scale Immigration into France', *Ethnic and Racial Studies*, 4: 137–52.

Dreef, M.E.P. (forthcoming), 'Politiek, Migranten en Informele Economie: Politieke en Bestuurlijke Ontwikkelingen met betrekking tot de Amsterdamse Naaiateliers 1980–1997', Ph.D. dissertation, University of Amsterdam.

Dubois, P. (1988), *L'Industrie de l'Habillement: L'Innovation Face à la Crise*, Paris: Documentation Française.

Elfring, T. (1999), *Oplevend Ondernemerschap*, Wageningen: Wageningen University/Stichting Wagenings Universiteits Fonds.

Engbersen, G., J. van der Leun, R. Staring and J. Kehla (1999), *De Ongekende Stad 2: Inbedding en Uitsluiting van Illegale Vreemdelingen*, Amsterdam: Boom.

Engelen, E. (2001), 'Breaking In and Breaking Out: A Weberian Approach to Entrepreneurial Opportunities', *Journal of Ethnic and Migration Studies*, 27: 203–40.

Epstein, R.A. (1994), 'The Moral and Practical Dilemmas of an Underground Economy', *Yale Law Journal*, 103: 2157–78.

Esping-Andersen, G. (1990), *The Three Worlds of Welfare Capitalism*, Cambridge: Polity Press.

Faraut, F. (1987), *Histoire de la Belle Jardinière*, Paris: Belin.

Farina, P., D. Cologna, A. Lanzani and L. Breveglieri (1997), *Cina a Milano: Famiglie, Ambienti e Lavori della Popolazione Cinese a Milano*, Milano: Associazione Interessi Metropolitani (AIM).

Favell, A. (1999), 'Integration Policy and Integration Research in Europe: A Review and Critique', in A. Aleinikoff and D. Klusmeyer (eds), *Citizenship: Comparisons and Perspectives*, Washington, DC: Brookings Institution.

## References

Fernández-Kelly, M.P. and A. Garcia (1989), 'Informalization at the Core: Hispanic Women, Home Work and the Advanced Capitalistic State', in A. Portes, M. Castells and L. Benton (eds), *The Informal Economy: Studies in Advanced and Less Developed Countries*, Baltimore, Md.: Johns Hopkins University Press.

Fernández-Kelly, M.P., M. Patricia and S. Sassen (1991), *A Collaborative Study of Hispanic Women in the Garment and Electronics Industries: Final Report presented to the Ford, Revson, and Tinker Foundations*, New York: Center for Latin American and Caribbean Studies, New York University.

Fishman, W. (1976), *East End Radicals 1875–1914*, London: Duckworth.

Flanigan, J. (1998), 'Immigrant Banks: A Model for Asia, a Boon to Us', *Los Angeles Times*, 14 January, D1, D15.

Flap, H., A. Kumcu and B. Bulder (2000), 'The Social Capital of Ethnic Entrepreneurs and their Business Success', in J. Rath (ed.), *Immigrant Businesses: The Economic, Political and Social Environment*, Houndmills, Basingstoke, and New York: Macmillan Press and St Martin's Press.

Freedberg, L. and S. Russell (1999), 'Immigrants' Fears Leave Children without Insurance', *San Francisco Chronicle*, 15 January.

Freeman, G.P. and N. Ögelman (2000), 'State Regulatory Regimes and Immigrants' Informal Economic Activity', in J. Rath (ed.), *Immigrant Businesses: The Economic, Political and Social Environment*, Houndmills, Basingstoke, and New York: Macmillan Press and St Martin's Press.

Friganovic, M., M. Morokvasic and I. Bauic (1972), *Iz Jugoslavije na Rad u Francusku*, Zagreb: Institut de Géographie de l'Université de Zagreb.

Fröbel, F., J. Heinrichs and O. Kreye (1980), *The New International Division of Labour: Structural Unemployment in Industrial Countries and Industrialisation in Developing Countries*, Cambridge: Cambridge University Press.

Froschauer, K. (2001), 'East Asian and European Entrepreneur Immigrants in British Columbia (Canada): Postmigration Conduct and Premigration Context', *Journal of Ethnic and Migration Studies*, 27: 225–40.

Gabaccia, D. (1998), *We Are What We Eat: Ethnic Food and the Making of Americans*, Cambridge, Mass.: Harvard University Press.

Gannagé, C. (1989–1990), 'Changing Dimensions of Control and Resistance: The Toronto Garment Industry', *Journal of Canadian Studies*, 24: 41–60.

Gans, H. (1981), 'Comment', *The Journal of Ethnic Studies*, 9: 45.

Garment Industry Development Corporation (GIDC) (1992), 'Keeping New York in Fashion: A Strategic Plan for the Future of the New York Fashion Apparel Industry', Research report.

—— (1995), *New York City Fashion Industry Statistics*, Research brochure.

Geddes, M. (1988), 'The Capitalist State and the Local Economy: "Restructuring for Labour" and Beyond', *Capital and Class*, 35: 85–120.

Gervereau, L., P. Milza and E. Témime (eds) (1998), *Histoire de l'Immigration en France au XXe Siècle*, Paris: Somogy Editions d'Art.

Geuns, R. van (1992), 'An Aspect of Informalisation of Women's Work in a High-tech Age: Turkish Sweatshops in the Netherlands', in S. Mitter (ed.), *Computer-Aided Manufacturing and Women's Employment: The Clothing Industry in Four EC Countries*, London/Berlin: Springer-Verlag.

—— and L. van Diepen (1994), *Illegale Arbeid in de Confectie*, Amsterdam: Regioplan.

Gough, J. (1986), 'Industrial Policy and Socialist Strategy: Restructuring and the Unity of the Working Class', *Capital and Class*, 29: 58–81.

Graham, D. and N. Spence (1995), 'Contemporary Deindustrialisation and Tertiarisation in the London Economy', *Urban Studies*, 32: 885–911.

Granovetter, M. (1983), 'The Strength of Weak Ties: A Network Theory Revisited', *Sociological Theory*, 1: 201–33.

—— (1992), 'Economic Action and Social Structures: The Problem of Embeddedness', in M. Granovetter and R. Swedberg (eds), *The Sociology of Economic Life*, Boulder, Colo.: Westview Press.

Greater London Council (1985), *London Industrial Strategy*, London: Greater London Council.

Green, N.L. (1985), '"Filling the Void": Immigration to France before World War I', in D. Hoerder (ed.), *Labor Migration in the Atlantic Economies*, Westport, Conn.: Greenwood Press.

—— (1986a), 'Immigrant Labor in the Garment Industries of New York and Paris: Variations on a Structure', *Comparative Social Research*, 9: 231–43.

—— (1986b), *The Pletzl of Paris: Jewish Immigrant Workers in the Belle Epoque*, New York: Holmes and Meier.

—— (1997), *Ready-to-Wear and Ready-to-Work: A Century of Industry and Immigrants in Paris and New York*, Durham: Duke University Press.

—— *et al.* (1987), 'Les Quartiers Parisiens de l'Industrie de l'Habillement et les Relations Pluri-ethniques', Report, Ministère de la Culture.

—— *et al.* (1988), 'Les Rapports Habitat/Travail dans l'Industrie de l'Habillement à Paris et dans Sa Banlieue', Report, Ministère de l'Equipement, du Logement, de l'Aménagement du Territoire et des Transports.

Green, R.E. (ed.) (1991), *Enterprise Zones: New Directions in Economic Development*, Newbury Park, Calif.: Sage.

Greenhouse, S. (1998a), 'Plan To Curtail Sweatshops Rejected by Union', *The New York Times*, 5 November.

—— (1998b), 'Two More Unions Reject Agreement for Curtailing Sweatshops', *The New York Times*, 6 November.

Grenier, G. (1992), 'The Cuban American Labor Movement in Dade County: An Emerging Immigrant Working Class', in G. Grenier and A. Stepick (eds),

*Miami Now! Immigration, Ethnicity and Social Change*, Gainesville, Fla.: University Press of Florida.

Grice, J. (1995), 'West Midlands Clothing Industry: Training Needs in Terms of Design and Markets', Research project, University of Central England, Birmingham.

Groenendael, A.J.M. van (1986), *Dilemma's van Regelgeving: De Regularisatie van Illegale Buitenlandse Werknemers 1975–1983*, Alphen a/d Rijn/Utrecht: Samsom H.D. Tjeenk Willink/NCB.

Groux, G., *et al.* (1989), 'L'Atelier, l'Habit et la Règle: l'Evolution Récente des Relations Professionnelles et des Stratégies Syndicales dans les PME de l'Habillement', Report, Ministère du Travail, de l'Emploi et de la Formation Professionnelle.

Guillon, M. and I. Taboada-Leonetti (1986), *Le Triangle de Choisy: Un Quartier Chinois à Paris*, Paris: L'Harmattan.

Hall, P. (1996) [1988], *Cities of Tomorrow: An Intellectual History of Urban Planning and Design in the Twentieth Century*, Updated edition, Oxford: Blackwell.

Halliday, S. (1991), 'How to Make the Most of Business Advisers', *Observer*, 3 November.

Hamilton, N. and N. Chinchilla (1995), *Central Americans in California: Transnational Communities, Economies and Cultures*, Center for Multiethnic and Transnational Studies, University of Southern California, Occasional Papers no. 1.

Hamnett, C. (1996), 'Why Sassen is Wrong: A Response to Burgers', *Urban Studies*, 33: 107–11.

Handsworth Technical College (1984a), *An Investigation into Technological and Management Education and Training Needs*, Birmingham: Handsworth Technical College.

—— (1984b), *The Clothing Industry in Birmingham*, Birmingham: Handsworth Technical College.

Hardill, I. and P. Wynarczyk (1996), 'Technology, Entrepreneurship and Company Performance in Textile and Clothing SMEs', *New Technology, Work & Employment*, 11: 107–17.

Harris, A. (1988), 'Hardship Hides Behind Doors of Homeworkers', *Observer*, 5 June.

Harris, N. (1995), *The New Untouchables: Immigration and the New World Worker*, London: Penguin.

Hassoun, J.-P. and Y.-P. Tan (1986), 'Les Chinois de Paris: Minorité Culturelle ou Constellation Ethnique', *Terrain*, 7: 34–44.

Hauser, H. and H. Hitier (eds) (1917), *Enquête sur la Production Française et la Concurrence Étrangère*, Vol. 2 of *Industries Textiles-Industries du Vêtement*, Paris: Association Nationale d'Expansion Économique.

## References

Hayden, C. (1992), 'A Case Study of the Clothing Industry in the West Midlands', in D. Gillingwater and P. Totterdill (eds), *Prospects for Industrial Policy in the 1990's: The Case of the British Clothing Industry*, Aldershot: Gower.

Heertje, H. (1977), 'Het Ateliermeisje van Amsterdam', in F. Bovenkerk and L. Brunt (eds), *De Rafelrand van Amsterdam: Jordaners, Pinda-Chinezen, Ateliermeisjes en Venters in de Jaren Dertig*, Amsterdam/Meppel: Boom.

Hendrie, K. (1993), '"Invisible Threads": From Homeworkers to the High Street. Investigating the Links in the Sub-contracting Chain', Unpublished MA thesis, University of Warwick.

Hess, D. (1990), 'Korean Garment Manufacturing in Los Angeles', Master's Thesis, Department of Geography, University of California at Los Angeles.

Hiebert, D. (1990), 'Discontinuity and the Emergence of Flexible Production: Garment Production in Toronto, 1901–1931', *Economic Geography*, 66: 229–53.

—— (1993), 'Jewish Immigrants and the Garment Industry of Toronto, 1901–1931: A Study of Ethnic and Class Relations', *Annals of the Association of American Geographers*, 83: 243–71.

—— (1999), 'Local Geographies of Labor Market Segmentation: Montréal, Toronto, and Vancouver, 1991', *Economic Geography*, 75: 339–69.

—— (2000), 'Economic Associations of Immigrant Self-Employment in Canada', Paper presented to the Second Conference of the International Thematic Network 'Working on the Fringes: Immigrant Businesses, Economic Integration and Informal Practices' on 'The Economic Embeddedness of Immigrant Enterprises', Maiersdorf House, Jerusalem, 17–20 June.

Hiltzik, M.A. (1995), 'Dependence on Employer Leaves Many Uncovered', *Los Angeles Times*, 30 October, Section A: 11.

Hirst, P. and J. Zeitlin (eds), (1989), *Reversing Industrial Decline? Industrial Structure and Policy in Britain and Her Competitors*, Berg: St Martin's Press.

Ho, E. and R. Bedford (1998), 'The Asian Crisis and Migrant Entrepreneurs in New Zealand: Some Reactions and Reflections', *New Zealand Population Review*, 24: 71–101.

Hoel, B. (1982), 'Contemporary Clothing Sweatshops: Asian Female Labour and Collective Organisation', in J. West (ed.), *Work, Women and the Labour Market*, London: Routledge and Kegan Paul.

Hoolt, J. and D. Scholten (1996), *Etnische Groepen in Amsterdam: Jaarbericht 1996*, Amsterdam: Amsterdam Municipal Council, Bureau for Strategic Minorities Policy.

Hovanessian, M. (1992), *Le Lien Communautaire: Trois Générations d'Arméniens*, Paris: Armand Colin.

Husbands, C.T. (1994), 'Crises of National Identity as the "New Moral Panics": Political Agenda Setting about Definitions of Nationhood', *New Community*, 20: 191–206.

Jackson, A. (1996), *Birmingham: An Industry Study for Birmingham City Council*, London: Annabel Jackson Associates.

Jansen, F.L. (1991), 'Kledinghandel in Transitie: Een Eeuw Detailverkoop te 's Hertogenbosch: Oorsprong en Ontwikkeling van het Familiebedrijf A.F. Jansen, 1889–1987', Ph.D. dissertation, Catholic University, Tilburg.

Johnson, C.H. (1975), 'Economic Change and Artisan Discontent: The Tailors' History, 1800–48', in R. Price (ed.), *Revolution and Reaction: 1848 and the 2nd French Republic*, London: Croom Helm.

Jones, G.S. (1976), *Outcast London: A Study in the Relationship between Classes in Victorian Society*, London: Peregrine.

Jones, T. (1981), 'Small Business Development and the Asian Community in Britain', *New Community*, 9: 467–77.

—— (1993), *Britain's Ethnic Minorities*, London: Policy Studies Institute.

—— and D. McEvoy (1992), 'Ressources Ethniques et Égalité des Chances: Les Entreprises Indo-pakistanaises en Grande-Bretagne et au Canada', *Revue Européenne des Migrations Internationales*, 8: 107–26.

—— J. Cater, P. De Silva and D. McEvoy (1989), 'Ethnic Business and Community Needs', Report to the Commission for Racial Equality, Liverpool Polytechnic.

—— D. McEvoy and G. Barrett (1992), *Small Business Initiative: Ethnic Minority Business Component*, Swindon: ESRC.

Josephides, S. (1987), 'Associations amongst the Greek Cypriot Population in Britain', in J. Rex, D. Jolly and W. Czarina (eds), *Immigrant Associations in Europe*, Aldershot: Gower.

—— (1988), 'Honour, Family, and Work: Greek Cypriot Women Before and After Migration', in S. Westwood and P. Bhachu (eds), *Enterprising Women: Ethnicity, Economy, and Gender*, London: Routledge.

Kabeer, N. (1994), 'The Structure of "Revealed" Preference: Race, Community and Female Labour Supply in the London Clothing Industry', *Development and Change*, 25: 307–31.

Kang, K.C. (1998a), 'Ex-workers' Suit Seeks Back Wages', *Los Angeles Times*, 5 August, Section B: 1.

—— (1998b), '41 Restaurants Violated Labor Laws', *Los Angeles Times*, 22 August, Section B: 1.

Kastoryano, R. (1986), *Etre Turc en France*, Paris: L'Harmattan.

Kershen, A. (1990), 'Huguenots, Jews and Bangladeshis in Spitalfields and the Spirit of Capitalism', in A. Kershen (ed.), *London: The Promised Land? The Migrant Experience in a Capital City*, Aldershot: Avebury.

Kessler, J. (1999), *Tying the Global to the Local: The LA Apparel Industry in Transition*, Los Angeles: Los Angeles Trade-Technical College.

KFAT (Knitwear, Footwear and Textiles and Apparel Union) (1999), *Knitwear, Footwear and Textile News*, Issue 31.

# References

Kim, R., K.K. Nakamura and G. Fong (1992), 'Asian Immigrant Women Garment Workers in Los Angeles', *Amerasia Journal*, 18: 69–82.

Kindleberger, Ch. (1967), *Europe's Post-War Growth: The Role of Labour Supply*, New York: Harvard University Press.

Kirzner, I.M. (1997), 'Entrepreneurial Discovery and the Competitive Market Process: An Austrian Approach', *Journal of Economic Literature*, 35: 60–85.

Klatzmann, J. (1957), *Le Travail à Domicile dans l'Industrie Parisienne du Vêtement*, Paris: Armand Colin.

Kloosterman, R. (2000), 'Immigrant Entrepreneurship and the Institutional Context: A Theoretical Exploration', in J. Rath (ed.), *Immigrant Businesses: The Economic, Political and Social Environment*, Houndmills, Basingstoke, and New York: Macmillan Press and St Martin's Press.

—— and J. van der Leun (1998), 'Een Dans om Dezelfde Stoelen? Stedelijke Kansenstructuur en Startende Immigrantenondernemers in Amsterdam en Rotterdam', in J. Rath and R. Kloosterman (eds), *Rijp & Groen: Het Zelfstandig Ondernemerschap van Immigranten in Nederland*, Amsterdam: Het Spinhuis.

—— and J. van der Leun (1999), 'Just for Starters: Commercial Gentrification by Immigrant Entrepreneurs in Amsterdam and Rotterdam Neighbourhoods', *Housing Studies*, 14: 659–77.

—— and J. Rath (2001), 'Immigrant Entrepreneurs in Advanced Economies: Mixed Embeddedness Further Explored', *Journal of Ethnic and Migration Studies*, 27, 189–202.

—— and J. Rath (eds) (forthcoming), *Venturing Abroad: A Comparative Study of Immigrant Entrepreneurs in Advanced Economies*, Oxford: Berg.

—— J. van der Leun and J. Rath (1997), *Over Grenzen: Immigranten en de Informele Economie*, Amsterdam: Het Spinhuis.

—— J. van der Leun and J. Rath (1998), 'Across the Border: Economic Opportunities, Social Capital and Informal Businesses Activities of Immigrants', *Journal of Ethnic and Migration Studies*, 24: 239–58.

—— J. van der Leun and J. Rath (1999), 'Mixed Embeddedness: (In)formal Economic Activities and Immigrant Business in the Netherlands', *International Journal of Urban and Regional Research*, 23: 253–67.

Kotkin, J. (1992), *Tribes: How Race, Religion, and Identity Determine Success in the New Global Economy*, New York: Random House.

Kumcu, A. (forthcoming), 'De Fil en Aiguille: Genèse et Déclin des Ateliers de Confections Turcs d'Amsterdam', Ph.D. dissertation, University of Amsterdam.

—— J. Lambooy and S. Safaklioglu (1998), 'De Financiering van Turkse Ondernemingen', in J. Rath and R. Kloosterman (eds), *Rijp & Groen: Het Zelfstandig Ondernemerschap van Immigranten in Nederland*, Amsterdam: Het Spinhuis.

Kwong, P. (1997), *Forbidden Workers*, New York: The New Press.

Ladbury, S. (1984), 'Choice, Change or No Alternative: Turkish Cypriots in Business in London', in R. Ward and R. Jenkins (eds), *Ethnic Communities in Business: Strategies for Economic Survival*, Cambridge: Cambridge University Press.

Lambrianidis, L. (1995), 'Flexibility in Production through Subcontracting: The Case of the Poultry Meat Industry in Greece', *Environment and Planning*, 27: 193–209.

Lamphere, L. (1987), *From Working Daughters to Working Mothers: Immigrant Women in a New England Industrial Community*, Ithaca, N.Y.: Cornell University Press.

Larsen, P. (1995), 'Hebben Nederlanders Dan Geen Cultuur? Een Beschouwing over Nederlands Onderzoek naar "Etnisch Ondernemerschap"', *Migranten-studies*, 11: 30–8.

Lazzarato, M., A. Negri and G. Santilli (1990), 'La Confection dans le Quartier du Sentier', Report, Ministère du Travail, de l'Emploi et de la Formation Professionnelle.

Lebon, A. (1977), *Immigration et 7e Plan, Analyse Économique*, Paris: Documen-tation Française.

Lee, D. (1994), 'Orange County Home Garment Work Targeted in Crackdown', *Los Angeles Times*, 30 September, Section D: 5.

—— (1996), 'Task Force in Tatters: State–Federal Tensions Hinder Garment Industry Crackdown', *Los Angeles Times*, 4 August, Section D: 1.

—— (1998), 'Fashion Forward: Southern California's Niche Role in the Garment Industry Has Helped Local Manufacturers Thrive Despite Job Losses Elsewhere and a Production Shift to Mexico', *Los Angeles Times*, 26 April, Section D: 1.

Lee, Dong-Ok (1992), 'Commodification of Ethnicity', *Urban Affairs Quarterly*, 28: 258–75.

Lee, Hye-Kyung (1993), 'Korean and Filipino Immigrant Women in the Los Angeles Labor Market', Ph.D. dissertation, University of California at Los Angeles.

Lee, J. (1999), 'Retail Niche Domination among African American, Jewish and Korean Entrepreneurs: Competition, Coethnic Advantage and Disadvantage', *American Behavioral Scientist*, 42: 1398–416.

Leeuw, K.P. de (1991), 'Kleding in Nederland 1813–1920: Van een Traditioneel Bepaald Kleedpatroon naar een Begin van Modern Kleedgedrag', Ph.D. dissertation, Catholic University, Tilburg.

Leigh, R. and D. North (1983), 'The Clothing Sector in the West Midlands', Preliminary report commissioned by the Economic Development Unit, West Midlands City Council, Birmingham.

Lequin, Y. (ed.) (1988), *La Mosaïque France: Histoire des Étrangers et de l'Immi-gration*, Paris: Larousse.

# References

Levy, S. (1997), *California Economic Growth 1996–97*, Palo Alto, Calif.: Center for Continuing Study of the California Economy.

Lewis, R. (1996), *Birmingham Clothing: An Action Plan for the Future*, Birmingham: Birmingham City Council, Economic Development Department.

Leydesdorff, S. (1987), *Wij Hebben als Mens Geleefd: Het Joodse Proletariaat van Amsterdam 1900–1940*, Amsterdam: Meulenhoff.

Li, P.S. (2000), 'Earning Disparities between Immigrants and Native-born Canadians', *Canadian Review of Sociology and Anthropology*, 37: 289–311.

Liebhold, P. and H.R. Rubenstein (1999), *Between a Rock and a Hard Place: A History of American Sweatshops, 1820–Present*, Los Angeles, Calif.: UCLA Asian American Studies Center and Simon Wiesenthal Center Museum of Tolerance.

Light, I. (1972), *Ethnic Enterprise in America: Business and Welfare among Chinese, Japanese, and Blacks*, Berkeley, Calif.: University of California Press.

—— (2000), 'Globalisation and Migration Networks', in J. Rath (ed.), *Immigrant Businesses: The Economic, Political and Social Environment*, Houndmills, Basingstoke, and New York: Macmillan Press and St Martin's Press.

—— and E. Bonacich (1988), *Immigrant Entrepreneurs: Koreans in Los Angeles, 1965–1982*, Berkeley and Los Angeles, Calif.: University of California.

—— and S.J. Gold (2000), *Ethnic Economies*, San Diego, Calif.: Academic Press.

—— and R.E. Isralowitz (eds) (1997), *Immigrant Entrepreneurs and Immigrant Absorption in the United States and Israel*, Aldershot: Ashgate.

—— and M. Pham (1998), 'Beyond Creditworthy: Microcredit and Informal Credit in the United States', *Journal of Developmental Entrepreneurship*, 3: 35–51.

—— and E. Roach (1996), 'Self-employment: Mobility Ladder or Economic Lifeboat?', in R. Waldinger and M. Bozorgmehr (eds), *Ethnic Los Angeles*, New York: Russell Sage Foundation.

—— and C. Rosenstein (1995), *Race, Ethnicity, and Entrepreneurship in Urban America*, New York: Aldine de Gruyter.

—— J.-K. Im and Z. Deng (1990), 'Korean Rotating Credit Associations in Los Angeles', *Amerasia*, 16: 35–54.

—— P. Bhachu and S. Karageorgis (1993), 'Migration Networks and Immigrant Entrepreneurship', in I. Light and P. Bhachu (eds), *Immigration and Entrepreneurship: Culture, Capital, and Ethnic Networks*, New Brunswick, N.J./London: Transaction Publishers.

—— R. Bernard and R. Kim (1999), 'Immigrant Incorporation in the Garment Industry of Los Angeles', *International Migration Review*, 33: 5–26.

Lindlaw, S. (1999), 'Davis to Decide on Cutting Prenatal Care for Illegal Immigrants', *Associated Press*, release dated 12 May.

Lloyd, C. (1996), 'Skill Shortages in the Clothing Industry: An Endemic Problem?', *Work, Employment and Society*, 10: 717–36.

Logan, J.R. and H.L. Molotch (1987), *Urban Fortunes*, Los Angeles, Calif.: University of California.

Loucky, J., M. Soldatenko, G. Scott and E. Bonacich (1994), 'Immigrant Enterprise and Labor in the Los Angeles Garment Industry', in E. Bonacich, L. Cheng, N. Chinchilla, N. Hamilton and P. Ong (eds), *Global Production: The Apparel Industry in the Pacific Rim*, Philadelphia, Pa.: Temple University.

Mackintosh, M. and H. Wainwright (1987), *A Taste of Power: The Politics of Local Economics*, London: Verso.

Ma Mung, E. (1991), 'Logiques du Travail Clandestin des Chinois', in S. Montagné-Villette (ed.), *Espaces et Travail Clandestins*, Paris: Masson.

Marger, M.N. (2000), 'The Use of Social and Human Capital Among Canadian Business Immigrants', Paper presented at the 8th Biennial Jerusalem Conference in Canadian Studies, Hebrew University of Jerusalem, 26 June.

Marshall, A. (1922) [1890], *Principles of Economics*, 8th edition, London: Macmillan.

Martin, Ph. (1994), 'The United States: Benign Neglect Toward Immigration', in W.A. Cornelius, Ph.L. Martin and J.F. Hollifield (eds), *Controlling Immigration: A Global Perspective*, Stanford, Calif.: Stanford University.

Marx, K. (1973) [1857–1858], *Grundrisse: Foundations of the Political Economy*, Harmondsworth: Penguin Books.

Massey, D. (1984), *Spatial Divisions of Labour: Social Structure and the Geography of Production*, London: Macmillan.

Matteoli, J., *et al.* (forthcoming), *La Persécution des Juifs de France: 1940–1944*, Paris: La Documentation Française.

Mauco, G. (1932), *Les Etrangers en France*, Paris: Armand Colin.

Mavrou, V. (1994), 'Patronage, Ethnicity, and the Secondary Economy: The Cypriot Clothing Industry in London', Unpublished Ph.D. thesis, London, City University.

Mawson, J. (1988), *The West Midlands Clothing and Textile Industry: A Sector Review*, Birmingham: West Midlands Enterprise Board.

McEvoy, D. and T. Jones (1993), 'Relative Economic Welcomes: South Asian Retailing in Britain and Canada', in H. Rudolph and M. Morokvasic (eds), *Bridging States and Markets: International Migration in the Early 1990s*, Berlin: Edition Sigma.

Meer, M. van der (1998), *Vaklieden en Werkzekerheid: Kansen en Rechten van Insiders en Outsiders op de Arbeidsmarkt in de Bouwnijverheid*, Amsterdam: Thela Thesis.

Metcalf, H., T. Modood and S. Virdee (1996), *Asian Self-employment: The Interaction of Culture and Economics in England*, London: Policy Studies Institute.

Miellet, R. (1993), *Honderd Jaar Grootwinkelbedrijf in Nederland*, Zwolle: Uitgeverij Catena.

## References

Miles, R. (1982), *Racism and Migrant Labour*, London: Routledge and Kegan Paul.

—— (1989), *Racism*, London: Routledge.

—— (1993), *Racism After 'Race Relations'*, London: Routledge.

—— and V. Satzewich (1990), 'Migration, Racism and "Postmodern" Capitalism', *Economy and Society*, 19: 334–58.

Miller, M.B. (1981), *The Bon Marché: Bourgeois Culture and the Department Store, 1869–1920*, Princeton, N.J.: Princeton University Press.

Min, P.G. and M. Bozorgmehr (2000), 'Immigrant Entrepreneurship and Business Patterns: A Comparison of Koreans and Iranians in Los Angeles', *International Migration Review*, 34: 707–38.

Mitter, S. (1986), 'Industrial Restructuring and Manufacturing Homework: Immigrant Women in the UK Clothing Industry', *Capital and Class*, 27: 37–80.

—— (ed.) (1992), *Computer-aided Manufacturing and Women's Employment: The Clothing Industry in Four EC Countries*, London/Berlin: Springer Verlag.

Model, S. (1985), 'Ethnic Bonds in the Work Place: Blacks, Italians, and Jews in New York City', Dissertation, University of Michigan.

Modood, T. (1997), 'Culture and Identity', in T. Modood, R. Berthoud, J. Lakey, J. Nazroo, P. Smith, S. Virdee and S. Beishon, *Ethnic Minorities in Britain: Diversity and Disadvantage*, London: Policy Studies Institute.

Montagné-Villette, S. (1986), *Bilan de la Lutte contre le Trafic de Main-d'oeuvre 1984–1985*, Paris: Documentation Française.

—— (1990), *Le Sentier, Un Espace Ambigu*, Paris: Masson.

Moore, D.D. (1981), *At Home in America*, New York: Columbia University Press.

Morin, E. (1989), *Vidal et les Siens*, Paris: Seuil.

Morokvasic, M. (1986), 'Le Recours aux Immigrés dans la Contection à Paris: Eléments de Comparaison avec la Ville Berlin-Ouest', Report, Ministère du Travail en de la Formation Professionnelle, Mission de liaison interministérielle pour la lute contre les trafics de main-d oeuvres.

—— (1987a), 'Le Recours aux Immigrés dans la Confection Parisienne: Eléments de Comparaison avec la Ville de Berlin Ouest', in *Luttes Contre les Trafics de la Main d'Ouvre 1985–86: Objectifs Prioritaires. Le Travail Clandestine*, Paris: Documentation Française.

—— (1987b), 'Immigrants in the Parisian Garment Industry', *Work, Employment and Society*, 1: 441–62.

—— (1988a), 'Garment Production in a Metropole of Fashion: Small Enterprise, Immigrants and Immigrant Entrepreneurs', *Economic and Industrial Democracy*, 9: 83–97.

—— (1988b), 'Minority and Immigrant Women in Self-employment and Business in France, Great Britain, Italy, Portugal, and the Federal Republic of Germany', V/1871/88-Engl, Paris: EEC.

—— (1988c), 'Le Comportement Économique des Immigrés dans le Secteur de la Confection', Paper presented at GRECO 13 Conference 'Mutations économiques et travailleurs immigrés dans des pays industriels', 28–30 January, Vaucresson.

—— (1991a), 'Die Kehrseite der Mode: Migranten als Flexibilisierungsquelle in der Pariser Bekleidungsproduktion. Ein Vergleich mit Berlin', *Prokla*, 83: 264–84.

—— (1991b), 'Roads to Independence: Self-employed Immigrants and Minority Women in Five European States', *International Migration*, 29: 407–20.

—— (1993), 'Immigrants in Garment Production in Paris and Berlin', in I. Light and P. Bhachu (eds), *Immigration and Entrepreneurship: Culture, Capital, and Ethnic Networks*, New Brunswick, N.J./London: Transaction Publishers.

—— and M. Miller (1998), 'Continuity and Change in Postwar French Legalization Policy', Unpublished paper prepared for conference on 'Europe: The New Melting Pot?' at University of Notre Dame, 22–24 March.

—— A. Phizacklea and H. Rudolph (1986), 'Small Firms and Minority Groups: Contradictory Trends in the French, German and British Clothing Industries', *International Sociology*, 1: 397–419.

—— R. Waldinger and A. Phizacklea (1990), 'Business on the Ragged Edge: Immigrant and Minority Business in the Garment Industries of Paris, London, and New York', in R. Waldinger, H. Aldrich, R. Ward and Associates, *Ethnic Entrepreneurs: Immigrant Business in Industrial Societies*, Newbury Park, Calif. and London: Sage.

Mullins, D. (1979), 'Asian Retailing in Croydon', *New Community*, 7: 403–5.

Murray, R. (1987), 'Ownership, Control and the Market', *New Left Review*, 164: 87–112.

Nazario, S. and D.P. Shutt (1995), 'Many in Middle Class Turn to County for Medical Help', *Los Angeles Times*, 30 October, Section 1: 1.

nDoen, M.L. (2000), *Migrants and Entrepreneurial Activities in Peripheral Indonesia: A Socio-Economic Model of Profit-seeking Behaviour*, Amsterdam: Tinbergen Institute Research Series.

Noiriel, G. (1988), *Le Creuset Français: Histoire de l'Immigration XIXe–XXe Siècles*, Paris: Seuil.

Oc, T. and S. Tiesdell (1999), 'Supporting Ethnic Minority Business: A Review of Business Support for Ethnic Minorities in City Challenge Areas', *Urban Studies*, 36: 1723–1946.

Ojeda, V. (1996), 'Mujeres y salud adelante', MA thesis, School of Public Health, University of California, Los Angeles.

Ong, P. and E. Blumenberg (1996), 'Income and Racial Inequality in Los Angeles', in A.J. Scott and E.W. Soja (eds), *The City: Los Angeles and Urban Theory at the End of the Twentieth Century*, Los Angeles, Calif.: University of California.

# References

Orfalea, G. (1999), 'A Kingdom of Rages', *Los Angeles Times Magazine*, 18 April: 14–15.

Orrenius, P. (1999), 'The Role of Income Shocks and Family Networks in Migration and Migrant Self-Selection: The Case of Return Migrants from Mexico, 1965–1994', Ph.D. dissertation, University of California, Los Angeles.

Oser, A.S. (1998), 'Rising Rents in Chinatown Displace Garment Matters', *The New York Times*, 21 October.

Ozturk, K. (1988), 'Les Turcs dans la Confection à Paris', *Hommes et Migrations*, 1116: 22–8.

Pairault, T. (1995), *L'Intégration Silencieuse*, Paris: L'Harmattan.

Palmer, H. (1990), 'Health and Safety', Report from one-day workshop on Women in Textiles and Clothing, Leeds: Local Action on Textiles and Clothing.

Panayiotopoulos, P. (1990), 'Cypriot Entrepreneurs in the North London Clothing Industry: A Colonial Legacy', in *Proceedings of the First International Symposium on Cypriot Migration: A Historical and Sociological Perspective*, Nicosia: Social Science Research Centre.

—— (1992a), 'Local Government Economic Initiatives. Planning, Choice and Politics: The London Experience', *Papers in International Development*, no. 7, Swansea: Centre for Development Studies.

—— (1992b), 'The Cypriot Clothing Industry', *The Cyprus Review*, 4: 77–123.

—— (1993), 'Cypriot Entrepreneurs in the Clothing Industry. North London and Cyprus: A Comparative Analysis', Ph.D. thesis, University of Wales, Swansea.

—— (1996a), 'Challenging Orthodoxies: Cypriot Entrepreneurs in the London Garment Industry', *New Community*, 22: 437–60.

—— (1996b), 'The State and Enterprise in the Cypriot Clothing Industry under Conditions of Globalisation', *Cyprus Journal of Economics*, 9: 5–29.

—— (2000), 'The Labour Regime under Conditions of Globalisation in the Cypriot Garment Industry, *Journal of Southern Europe and Balkan Studies*, 2: 75–88.

—— (2001) 'The Global Garment Industry: An Engendered Protectionism', in P. Panayiotopoulos and G. Capps (eds), *World Development*, London: Pluto Press.

Pennington, S. and B. Westover (1989), *A Hidden Workforce: Home Workers in England, 1850–1985*, London: Macmillan Education.

Penninx, R., J. Schoorl and C. van Praag (1993), *The Impact of International Migration on Receiving Countries: The Case of the Netherlands*, Amsterdam: Swets and Zeitlinger.

Perrot, M. (1978), 'De la Nourrice à l'Employée . . . Travaux de Femmes dans la France du XIXe Siècle', *Le Mouvement Social*, 105: 3–10.

Persky, J. and W. Wiewel (1994), 'The Growing Localness of the Global City', *Economic Geography*, 70: 129–43.

Pessar, P.R. (1994), 'Sweatshop Workers and Domestic Ideologies: Dominican Women in New York's Apparel Industry', *International Journal of Urban and Regional Research*, 18: 127–32.

Petras, E.M. (1992), 'The Shirt on Your Back: Immigrant Workers and the Reorganization of the Garment Industry', *Social Justice*, 19: 76–114.

Phizacklea, A. (1988), 'Entrepreneurship, Ethnicity and Gender', in S. Westwood and P. Bhachu (eds), *Enterprising Women*, London: Routledge.

—— (1990), *Unpacking the Fashion Industry*, London: Routledge and Kegan Paul.

Piore, M.J. and C.F. Sabel (1984), *The Second Industrial Divide: Possibilities of Prosperity*, New York: Basic Books.

Polanyi, K. (1957), *The Great Transformation*, Boston, Mass.: Beacon Press.

Portes, A. (1994), 'The Informal Economy and its Paradoxes', in N.J. Smelser and R. Swedberg (eds), *The Handbook of Economic Sociology*, Princeton, N.J. and New York: Princeton University Press and Russel Sage Foundation.

—— (ed.) (1995), *The Economic Sociology of Immigration: Essays on Networks, Ethnicity, and Entrepreneurship*, New York: Russell Sage Foundation.

—— and R.L. Bach (1985), *Latin Journey: Cuban and Mexican Immigrants in the United States*, Berkeley, Calif.: University of California Press.

—— and M. Castells (1989), 'World Underneath: The Origins, Dynamics and Effects of the Informal Economy', in A. Portes, M. Castells and L. Benton (eds), *The Informal Economy: Studies in Advanced and Less Developed Countries*, Baltimore, Md.: Johns Hopkins University Press.

—— and J. Sensenbrenner (1993), 'Embeddedness and Immigration: Notes on the Social Determinants of Economic Action', *American Journal of Sociology*, 98: 1320–50.

—— and A. Stepick (1993), *City on the Edge: The Transformation of Miami*, Los Angeles, Calif.: University of California Press.

Poutziouris, P. (1999), 'The Development of Ethnic Family Business Ventures: Lessons from the 'Breaking Out' Strategies of Anglo-Cypriots', Paper delivered to the conference on Cypriot Society into the New Millennium held at the University of Greenwich on 4–5 December.

Presser, J. (1965), *Ondergang: De Vervolging en Verdelging van het Nederlandse Jodendom, 1940–1945*, parts I and II, Den Haag: Staatsuitgeverij.

Preston, V. and W. Giles (1997), 'Ethnicity, Gender and Labour Markets in Canada: A Case Study of Immigrant Women in Canada', *Canadian Journal of Urban Research*, 6: 135–59.

Proper, C. (1997), 'New York: Defending the Union Contract', in A. Ross (ed.), *No Sweat*, New York: Verso.

Raes, S. (1995), 'Luchttransport van Textiel en Kleding', in M. Roscam Abbing (ed.), *Dan Liever de Lucht in: Toekomstperspectieven van Luchttransport voor Vier Nederlandse Sectoren*, Den Haag: Ministerie van Verkeer en Waterstaat.

—— (2000a), *Migrating Enterprise and Migrant Entrepreneurship: How Fashion and Migration have Changed the Spatial Organisation of Clothing Supply to Consumers in the Netherlands*, Amsterdam: Het Spinhuis.

—— (2000b), 'Regionalization in a Globalizing World: The Emergence of Clothing Sweatshops in the European Union', in J. Rath (ed.), *Immigrant Businesses: The Economic, Political and Social Environment*, Houndmills, Basingstoke, and New York: Macmillan Press and St Martin's Press.

Rainnie, A. (1989), *Industrial Relations in Small Firms: Small Isn't Beautiful*, London: Routledge.

—— (1991), 'Flexible Specialisation: New Times or Old Hat?', in P. Blyton and J. Morris (eds), *A Flexible Future? Prospects for Employment and Organisation*, Berlin: de Gruyter.

Ram, M. (1992), 'Coping with Racism: Asian Employers in the Inner City', *Work Employment and Society*, 6: 601–18.

—— (1993), 'Workplace Relations in Ethnic Minority Firms: Asians in the West Midlands Clothing Industry', *New Community*, 19: 567–80.

—— (1994), *Managing to Survive: Working Lives in Small Firms*, Oxford: Blackwell.

—— (1996), 'Unravelling the Hidden Clothing Industry: Managing the Ethnic Minority Garment Sector', in I.M. Taplin and J. Winterton (eds), *Restructuring Within a Labour Intensive Industry: The UK Clothing Industry in Transition*, Aldershot: Avebury.

—— (1998), 'Enterprise Support and Ethnic Minority Firms', *Journal of Ethnic and Migration Studies*, 24: 143–58.

—— and T. Jones (1998), *Ethnic Minorities in Business*, Milton Keynes: Small Business Research Trust.

—— B. Sanghera, T. Abbas, G. Barlow and T. Jones (2000), 'Ethnic Minority Business in Comparative Perspective: The Case of the Independent Restaurant Sector', *Journal of Ethnic and Migration Studies*, 26: 495–510.

Rath, J. (1999), 'The Informal Economy as Bastard Sphere of Social Integration: The Case of Amsterdam', in E. Eichenhofer (ed.), *Migration und Illegalität*, IMIS-Schriften Bd. 7, Osnabrück: Universitätsverlag Rasch.

—— (2000a), 'A Game of Ethnic Musical Chairs? Immigrant Businesses and the Formation and Succession of Niches in the Amsterdam Economy', in S. Body-Gendrot and M. Martiniello (eds), *Minorities in European Cities: The Dynamics of Social Integration and Social Exclusion at the Neighbourhood Level*, Houndmills, Basingstoke: Macmillan Press.

—— (ed.) (2000b), *Immigrant Businesses: The Economic, Political and Social Environment*, Houndmills, Basingstoke, and New York: Macmillan Press and St Martin's Press.

—— (2000c), 'Immigrant Businesses and their Embeddedness in the Economic, Politico-institutional and Social Environment', in J. Rath (ed.), *Immigrant Businesses: The Economic, Political and Social Environment*, Houndmills, Basingstoke, and New York: Macmillan Press and St Martin's Press.

—— (2000d), 'A Dutch Bargain: The Remarkable Absence of Immigrant Entrepreneurs in Construction', Paper prepared for the session on 'The Mixed Embeddedness of Immigrant Entrepreneurs', at the 12th International Conference of Europeanists, Chicago, 30 March–1 April.

—— (2001), 'Research on Immigrant Ethnic Minorities in The Netherlands: Avoiding the M-word', in P. Ratcliffe (ed.), *Sociology, the State and Social Change*, Houndmills, Basingstoke: Macmillan Press.

—— and R. Kloosterman (2000), 'Outsiders' Business: A Critical Review of Research on Immigrant Entrepreneurship', *International Migration Review*, 34: 657–81.

Raulin, A. (1988), 'Espaces Marchands et Concentrations Urbaines Minoritaires: La Petite Asie de Paris', *Cahiers Internationaux de Sociologie*, 85: 225–42.

Razin, E. (1988), 'Entrepreneurship among Foreign Immigrants in the Los Angeles and San Fransisco Metropolitan Area', *Urban Geography*, 9: 283–301.

—— (1993), 'Immigrant Entrepreneurs in Israel, Canada and California', in I. Light and P. Bhachu (eds), *Immigration and Entrepreneurship: Culture, Capital and Ethnic Network*, New Brunswick, N.J./London: Transaction Publishers.

—— (1999), *Immigrant Entrepreneurs and the Urban Milieu: Evidence from the US, Canada and Israel*, Working Paper 99–01, Vancouver: Vancouver Centre of Excellence, Research on Immigration and Integration in the Metropolis.

—— and A. Langlois (1992), 'Location and Entrepreneurship among New Immigrants in Israel and Canada', *Geography Research Forum*, 12: 16–36.

—— and A. Langlois (1996), 'Metropolitan Characteristics and Entrepreneurship among Immigrants and Ethnic Groups in Canada', *International Migration Review*, 30: 703–27.

—— and I. Light (1988a), 'Ethnic Entrepreneurs in America's Largest Metropolitan Areas', *Urban Affairs Review*, 33: 332–60.

—— and I. Light (1988b), 'The Income Consequences of Entrepreneurial Concentrations', *Urban Geography*, 19: 554–76.

—— and D. Scheinberg (2001), 'Immigrant Entrepreneurs from the former USSR in Israel: Not the Traditional Enclave Economy', *Journal of Ethnic and Migration Studies*, 27: 259–76.

Recensement Général (1966), *Recensement Général de la Population de 1962*, no. 75: *Seine*, Paris: Imprimerie Nationale.

Reeves, F. and R. Ward (1984), 'West Indian Business in Britain', in R. Ward and R. Jenkins (eds), *Ethnic Communities in Business*, Cambridge: Cambridge University Press.

Reil, F. and T. Korver (2001), *En Meestal Zijn het Turken: Arbeid in de Amsterdamse Loonconfectie-industrie*, Amsterdam: Het Spinhuis.

Rekers, A.M. (1993), 'A Tale of Two Cities: A Comparison of Turkish Enterprises in Amsterdam and Rotterdam', in D. Crommentuyn-Ondaatje (ed.), *Nethur School Proceedings 1992*, Utrecht: Nethur.

—— (1998), 'Migrantenondernemerschap Anders Bekeken: Locatie, Spreiding en Oriëntatie van Turkse Ondernemers in Amsterdam en Rotterdam', in J. Rath and R. Kloosterman (eds), *Rijp & Groen: Het Zelfstandig Ondernemerschap van Immigranten in Nederland*, Amsterdam: Het Spinhuis.

Résultats Statistiques (1925), *Résultats Statistiques du Recensement Général de la Population (1921)*, Vol. II, Paris: Imprimerie Nationale.

—— (1929), *Résultats Statistiques du Recensement Général de la Population (1926)*, Vol. III, Paris: Imprimerie Nationale.

—— (1935), *Résultats Statistiques du Recensement Général de la Population (1931)*, Vol. II, Paris: Imprimerie Nationale.

—— (1941), *Résultats Statistiques du Recensement Général de la Population (1936)*, Vol. II, Paris: Imprimerie Nationale.

—— (1951), *Résultats Statistiques du Recensement Général de la Population (1946)*, Vol. V, tableaux pour le département de la Seine, Paris: Imprimerie Nationale.

Rex, J. and S. Josephides (1987), 'Asian and Greek Cypriot Associations and Identity', in J. Rex, D. Jolly and C. Wilpert (eds), *Immigrant Associations in Europe*, Aldershot: Gower.

Rex, J. and S. Tomlinson (1979), *Colonial Immigrants in a British City: A Class Analysis*, London: Routledge and Kegan Paul.

Risen, J. (1981), 'Sweatshops Pervasive in Miami', *Miami Herald*, 18 May.

Roberts, B. (1994), 'Informal Economy and Family Strategies', *International Journal of Urban and Regional Research*, 18: 6–23.

Robinson, V. and I. Flintoff (1982), 'Asian Retailing in Coventry', *New Community*, 10: 251–8.

Roblin, M. (1952), *Les Juifs de Paris*, Paris: A. et J. Picard.

Roche, D. (1989), *La Culture des Apparences: Une Histoire du Vêtement XVIIe–XVIIIe Siècle*, Paris: Fayard.

Rogerson, C.M. (1999), 'Johannesburg's Clothing Industry: The Role of African Immigrant Entrepreneurs', Report for BEES.

—— (2000), 'Successful SMEs in South Africa: The Case of Clothing Producers in the Witwatersrand', *Development Southern Africa*, 17: 687–716.

Sabel, C. and J. Zeitlin (1985), 'Historical Alternatives to Mass Production: Politics, Markets and Technology in Nineteenth-century Industrialisation', *Past and Present*, 108: 133–76.

Sanders, J. and V. Nee (1987), 'The Limits of Ethnic Solidarity in the Enclave Economy', *American Sociological Review*, 52: 745–73.

Sarmiento, S.T. (1996), 'Who Subsidizes Whom? Latina/o Immigrants in the Los Angeles Garment Industry', *Humboldt Journal of Social Relations*, 22: 37–42.

Sassen, S. (1988), *The Mobility of Labour and Capital*, Cambridge: Cambridge University Press.

References

—— (1989), 'New Trends in the Sociospatial Organization of the New York City Economy', *Urban Affairs Annual Review*, 34: 69–113.

—— (1991), *The Global City: New York, London, Tokyo*, Princeton, N.J.: Princeton University Press.

Saxenian, A. (1999), *Silicon Valley's New Immigrant Entrepreneurs*, San Francisco, Calif.: Public Policy Institute of California.

Schama, S. (1987), *The Embarrassment of Riches: An Interpretation of Dutch Culture in the Goldon Age*, New York: Knopf.

Scheffer, M.R. (1992), *Trading Places: Fashion, Retailers and the Changing Geography of Clothing Production*, Nederlandse Geografische Studies 150, Utrecht: Koninklijk Nederlands Aardrijkskundig Genootschap (KNAG).

Schirmacher, K. (1908), *La Spécialisation du Travail: Par Nationalités, à Paris*, Paris: Arthur Rousseau.

Schlauffler, H.H., S. McMenamin, H. Zawacki and J. Mordavsky (2000), *The State of Health Insurance in California, 1999*, Los Angeles: Center for Health Policy Research of the University of California.

Schmiechen, J. (1984), *Sweated Industries and Sweated Labor: The London Clothing Trades, 1860–1914*, London: Croom Helm.

Schrover, M. (2001), 'Immigrant Business and Niche Formation in a Historical Perspective: The Netherlands in the Nineteenth Century', *Journal of Ethnic and Migration Studies*, 27: 295–312.

Schumpeter, J.A. (1980) [1934], *The Theory of Economic Development*, Oxford: Oxford University Press.

Scott, A.J. (1988), *The New Industrial Space: Flexible Production Organization and Regional Development in North America and Western Europe*, London: Pion.

—— (1993), *Technopolis: High-Technology Industry and Regional Development in Southern California*, Berkeley, Calif.: University of California Press.

—— (1996), 'The Manufacturing Economy: Ethnic and Gender Divisions of Labor', in R. Waldinger and M. Bozorgmehr (eds), *Ethnic Los Angeles*, New York: Russell Sage.

Scott, J.W. (1984), 'Men and Women in the Parisian Garment Trades: Discussions of Family and Work in the 1830s and 1840s', in P. Thane, G. Crossick and R. Floud (eds), *The Power of the Past: Essays for Eric Hobsbawm*, Cambridge and Paris: Cambridge University Press and Maison des Sciences de l'Homme.

Shachar, A. (1994), 'Randstad Holland: A "World City"', *Urban Studies*, 31: 381–400.

Shaikh, A. (1995), *Industrial Restructuring, Informalisation and Casual Labour in the 'East End' Clothing Industry*, Working Paper no. 69, Development Planning Unit, University College London.

Shane, S. and S. Venkataraman (2000), 'The Promise of Entrepreneurship as a Field of Research', *Academy of Management Review*, 25: 217–26.

## References

Silverstein, S. and D. Lee (1996), 'Sweatshop Task Force Makes Biggest Sweep Ever', *Los Angeles Times*, 23 August, Section D: 1.

Silverstein, S. and G. White (1996), 'Hazards Found in Nearly 75% of Garment Shops', *Los Angeles Times*, 8 May, Section 1: 1.

Simmons, C. and C. Kalantaridis (1994), 'Flexible Specialisation in the Southern European Periphery: The Growth of Garment Manufacturing in Peonia County, Greece', *Comparative Study of Society and History*, 36: 649–75.

Simmons, C. and C. Kalantaridis (1995), 'Labour Regimes and the Domestic Domain: Manufacturing Garments in Greece', *Work, Employment and Society*, 9: 125–56.

Simon, Ph. (1931), *Monographie d'une Industrie de Luxe, la Haute Couture*, Paris: Presses Universitaires de France.

Skelton, G. (1999), 'Prop. 187 Decision Puts Governor to No-win Test', *Los Angeles Times*, 29 March.

Soja, E.W. (1996), 'Los Angeles, 1965–1992', in A.J. Scott and E.W. Soja (eds), *The City: Los Angeles and Urban Theory at the End of the Twentieth Century*, Los Angeles, Calif.: University of California.

Sowell, T. (1981), *Ethnic America: A History*, New York: Basic Books.

Speiser (1910), *Kalendar*, Paris: n.p.

Srinivasan, S. (1995), *The South Asian Petty Bourgeoisie in Britain: An Oxford Case Study*, Aldershot: Avebury, Ashgate.

State of California, Department of Finance, Financial and Economic Research Unit (1992), *California Statistical Abstract*, Sacramento, Calif.: State Printing Office.

Stepick, A. (1989), 'Miami's Two Informal Sectors', in A. Portes, M. Castells and L. Benton (eds), *The Informal Economy: Studies in Advanced and Less Developed Countries*, Baltimore, Md.: Johns Hopkins University Press.

—— (1990), 'Community Growth versus Simply Surviving: The Informal Sectors of Cubans and Haitians in Miami', in M.E. Smith (ed.), *Perspectives on the Informal Economy*, Washington, DC: University Press of America.

Steward, M. and L. Hunter (1964), *The Needle is Threaded: The History of an Industry*, London: Heinemann.

Swedberg, R. (1994), 'Markets as Social Structures', in N.J. Smelser and R. Swedberg (eds), *The Handbook of Economic Sociology*, Princeton, N.J. and New York: Princeton University Press and Russell Sage Foundation.

—— (1998), *Max Weber and the Idea of Economic Sociology*, Princeton, N.J.: Princeton University Press.

Tan, Y.P. (1984), 'Restaurants et Ateliers: Le Travail des Sino-khmers à Paris', *ASEMI*, 15: 277–91.

Tap, L.J. (1983), 'Het Turkse Bedrijfsleven in Amsterdam', MA dissertation, University of Groningen.

Taplin, I.M. (1996), 'Rethinking Flexibility: The Case of the Apparel Industry', *Review of Social Economy*, 54: 191–219.

—— and J. Winterton (1991), 'Restructuring and Flexibility in the British and American Clothing Industries', Paper presented to the 10th Annual Labour Process Conference, Aston University, Birmingham, UK.

—— and J. Winterton (1996), *Restructuring Within a Labour Intensive Industry*, Aldershot: Avebury.

Ter Minassian, A. (1988), 'Les Arméniens de France', *Les Temps Modernes*, 43: 207.

Totterdill P. and J. Zeitlin (1989), 'Markets, Technology and Local Intervention', in P. Hirst and J. Zeitlin (eds), *Reversing Industrial Decline: Industrial Structure and Industrial Policy in Britain and her Competitors*, Berg: St Martin's Press.

Tripier, M. (1987), 'L'Immigration dans la Classe Ouvrière en France', Thèse d'état, Université de Nantes.

—— (1990), *L'Immigration dans la Classe Ouvrière Française*, Paris: CIEMI L'Harmattan.

Tseng, Yen-Fen (1997), 'Ethnic Resources as Forms of Social Capital', *Taiwanese Sociological Review*, 1: 169–205.

UK Department of Employment (1976), *Immigrants in the Labour Market, Unit of Manpower Studies Project Report*, London: HMSO.

UK Department of Employment/Training Commission (1988), *Assistance to Small Firms*, London: National Audit Office, HMSO.

UK National Statistics (1996), *Manufacturing Data for 1993*, London: The Stationery Office.

—— (1998), *Labour Market Trends*, June, London: HMSO.

US Bureau of the Census (1963), *Census of the Population, 1960*, Vol. 1, *Characteristics of the Population*, part 11, 'Florida', Washington, DC: Government Printing Office.

—— (1973), *1970 Census of the Population, General Social and Economic Characteristics, Florida*, Final report, Washington, DC: Government Printing Office.

—— (1983), *1980 Census of Population, General Population Characteristics, Florida*, Washington, DC: Government Printing Office.

—— (1998), *State and Metropolitan Area Data Book 1997–1998*, Washington, DC: US Government Printing Office, Table B–8.

US Department of Commerce, Bureau of the Census (1992), *Census of Population and Housing, 1990. Public Use Microdata Sample: 5-Percent Sample*, Washington, DC: US Department of Commerce, Bureau for Political and Social Research.

—— (1993), *Census of Population and Housing, 1990. Public Use Microdata Sample: 5-Percent Sample*, 2nd release, Washington, DC: US Department of Commerce, Bureau for Political and Social Research.

## References

US Department of Labor (1998), *FY 1998 Garment Enforcement Report*, Washington, DC.

—— (2000), 'Dynamic Change in the Garment Industry: How Firms and Workers Can Survive and Thrive', Website address: http://www.dol.gov/dol/esa/public/forum/report.htm

US General Accounting Office (USGAO) (1989), *'Sweatshops' in New York City: A Local Example of a Nationwide Problem*, Washington, DC: GAO.

—— (1994), *Garment Industry: Efforts to Address the Prevalence and Conditions of Sweatshops*, HEHS–95–29, Washington, DC: GAO.

Uzzi, B. (1996), 'The Sources and Consequences of Embeddedness for the Economic Performance of Organizations: The Network Effect', *American Sociological Review*, 61: 674–98.

Valk, R. (1961), 'Hou Je Echt Nog van Mij, Rockin' Billy', Go to http://www.giga.nl/walter/gnsa/

Vernez, G. and K.E. McCarthy (1996), *The Costs of Immigration to Taxpayers*, Santa Monica, Calif.: RAND Corporation.

Villaraigosa, A.R. (1999), 'End the Politics of Vitriol and Division over Immigration', *Los Angeles Times*, 18 April, Section M: 5.

Vincent-Ricard, F. (1983), *Raison et Passion: Langages de Société, La Mode 1940–1990*, Paris: Textile/Art/Language.

Vries, B.W. de (1989), *From Pedlars to Textile Barons: The Economic Development of a Jewish Minority Group in the Netherlands*, Verhandelingen der Koninklijke Nederlandse Akademie van Wetenschappen, Afdeling Letterkunde, Nieuwe Reeks 141, Amsterdam: North-Holland.

Vuddamalay, V. (1993), 'Les Mécanismes de Structuration du Mouvement Migratoire Mauricien en France', Dissertation, Ecole des Hautes Etudes en Sciences Sociales.

Waldinger, R.D. (1986), *Through the Eye of the Needle: Immigrants and Enterprise in New York's Garment Trades*, New York: New York University Press.

—— (1993), 'The Two Sides of Ethnic Entrepreneurship: Reply to Bonacich', *International Migration Review*, 27: 692–701.

—— (1996a), 'From Ellis Island to LAX: Immigrant Prospects in the American City', *International Migration Review*, 30: 1078–86.

—— (1996b), *Still the Promised City? African-Americans and New Immigrants in Postindustrial New York*, Cambridge, Mass.: Harvard University Press.

—— and M. Bozorgmehr (1996), *Ethnic Los Angeles*, New York: Russell Sage Foundation.

—— and M. Lapp (1993), 'Back to the Sweatshop or Ahead to the Informal Sector?', *International Journal of Urban and Regional Research*, 17: 6–29.

—— H. Aldrich and R. Ward (1985), 'Trend Report: Ethnic Business and Occupational Mobility in Advanced Societies', *Sociology*, 19: 586–97.

*References*

—— H. Aldrich, R. Ward and Associates (1990), *Ethnic Entrepreneurs: Immigrant Business in Industrial Societies*, Newbury Park, Calif.: Sage.

Walton-Roberts, M. and D. Hiebert (1997), 'Immigration, Entrepreneurship, and the Family: Indo-Canadian Enterprise in the Construction Industry of Vancouver', *Canadian Journal of Regional Science*, 20: 119–40.

Ward, R. (1987), 'Ethnic Entrepreneurs in Britain and Europe', in R. Goffee and R. Scase (eds), *Entrepreneurship in Europe: The Social Processes*, New York: Croom Helm.

—— (1988), 'Caribbean Business Enterprise in Britain', in M. Cross and H. Entzinger (eds), *Lost Illusions: Caribbean Minorities in Britain and the Netherlands*, London: Routledge.

—— (1991), 'Economic Development and Ethnic Business', in J. Curran and R. Blackburn (eds), *Paths of Enterprise: The Future of Small Business*, London: Routledge.

Weber, M. (1947), *The Theory of Social and Economic Organizations*, Fairlawn, N.J.: Oxford University Press.

—— (1968), *Economy and Society: An Outline of Interpretative Sociology*, Berkeley, Calif.: University of California Press.

WERAS (1998), *Employment Law*, Birmingham: West Midlands Low Pay Unit.

Werbner, P. (1980), 'From Rags to Riches: Manchester Pakistanis in the Textile Trade', *New Community*, 8: 84–95.

—— (1984), 'Business on Trust: Pakistani Entrepreneurship in the Manchester Garment Trade', in R. Ward and R. Jenkins (eds), *Ethnic Communities in Business: Strategies for Economic Survival*, Cambridge: Cambridge University Press.

—— (2000), 'What Colour "Success"? Distorting Value in Studies of Ethnic Entrepreneurship', in H. Vermeulen and J. Perlmann (eds), *Immigrants, Schooling and Social Mobility: Does Culture Make a Difference?*, Houndmills, Basingstoke, and New York: Macmillan Press and St Martin's Press.

Western, B. and K. Beckett (1999), 'How Unregulated is the US Labor Market? The Penal System as a Labor Market Institution', *American Journal of Sociology*, 104: 1030–60.

White, P., H. Winchester and M. Guillon (1987), 'South East Asian Refugees in Paris', *Ethnic and Racial Relations*, 10: 48–61.

Whitley, R. (1999), *Divergent Capitalism: The Social Structuring and Change of Business Systems*, Oxford: Oxford University Press.

WMLPU (West Midlands Low Pay Unit) (1991), *The Clothes Showdown: The Future of the West Midlands Clothing Industry*, Birmingham: WMLPU.

—— (1993), *Ethnicity and Gender in the West Midlands Labour Force*, Birmingham: WMLPU.

—— (1997–1998), *People, Employment & Earnings in the West Midlands*, Birmingham: WMLPU.

Wolff, G. (1995), *California Community College Fashion Consortia 1995 Economic Report*, Los Angeles: Los Angeles Trade-Technical College.

Wolff, R. and J. Rath (2000), *Centen Tellen: Een Inventariserende en Verkennende Studie naar de Financiering van Immigrantenondernemingen*, Amsterdam: Het Spinhuis.

Wolff-Gerzon, A. (1949), *Au Bonheur des Dames: Uit het Nederlandse Kledingbedrijf van de Laatste Honderd Jaar*, Amsterdam: Uitgeverij De Spieghel.

Wong, B. (1987), 'The Role of Ethnicity in Enclave Enterprises: A Study of the Chinese Garment Factories in New York City', *Human Organization*, 46: 120–30.

—— (1998), *Ethnicity and Entrepreneurship: The New Chinese Immigrants in the San Francisco Bay Area*, Boston, Mass.: Allyn and Bacon.

Wong, L. (1998), *The Los Angeles Apparel Industry: Wage and Occupational Survey 1998 Report*, Los Angeles: Community Development Trade-Technical Center.

Yoo, J.K. (1998), *Korean Immigrant Entrepreneurs: Networks and Ethnic Resources*, New York and London: Garland Publishing.

Yoon, I.Y. (1997), *On My Own: Korean Businesses and Race Relations in America*, Chicago, Ill.: University of Chicago Press.

Zeitlin, J. (1992a), 'Industrial Districts and Local Economic Regeneration', in F. Pyke and W. Sengenberger (eds), *Industrial Districts and Local Economic Regeneration*, Geneva: International Institute for Labour Studies.

—— (1992b), 'Reconfiguration of the Market and the Use of Computerised Technology', in S. Mitter (ed.), *Computer-aided Manufacturing and Women's Employment: The Clothing Industry in Four EC Countries*, London: Springer-Verlag.

Zeldenrust, I. and J. van Eijk (1992), *Op Zoek naar Schone Kleren: Strategieën voor de Verbetering van de Arbeidssituatie in de Confectie-Industrie*, Amsterdam: Stichting Onderzoek Multinationale Ondernemingen (SOMO).

Zhou, M. (1992), *Chinatown: The Socioeconomic Potential of an Urban Enclave*, Philadelphia, Pa.: Temple University Press.

Zincone, G. (ed.) (2000), *Primo Rapporto Sull'Integrazione degli Immigrati in Italia*, Comissione per le Politiche di Integrazione degli Immigratie, Bologna: Società editrice il Mulino.

Zola, E. (1901), *Au Bonheur des Dames*, Paris: Eugene Fasquelle.

Zorlu, A. (1997), 'Determinants of the Miraculous Survival of the Amsterdam Clothing Sector: Immigrant Labour Does Not Know Borders', MA dissertation, University of Amsterdam, Faculty of Economics.

—— (1998), 'Goedkope Arbeid als Wondermiddel? Hoe Immigrantenondernemers in de Amsterdamse Confectie-industrie Hun Personeel Rekruteren', in J. Rath and R. Kloosterman (eds), *Rijp & Groen: Het Zelfstandig Ondernemerschap van Immigranten in Nederland*, Amsterdam: Het Spinhuis.

——— and F. Reil (1997), 'De Amsterdamse Confectie-industrie', *Economische Statistische Berichten*, 8 October.

# Index

## Index

# Index